"Bullies in Power" is written from the heart with a down-to-earth style intended to move the reader along a path of life as experienced by a family dealing with the challenges of poverty and racially-motivated abusive authorities. This book conveys a powerful message that love, hope and determination provide the tools necessary to overcome life's challenges.

"Not what I expected at all. When I began reading the manuscript I found it mesmerizing and had to read it all before putting it down." Ken Salter, BSW, RSW.

"Bullies in Power captivated me emotionally and spiritually. I couldn't help but admire the love and courage shared by this family" Bernie Rothenburger, editor.

There are many ways to tell a story but "Bullies in Power" reflects honesty at its most primitive level. There is no mistaking what the writer means. The facts are beyond contesting and so clearly presented that the reader feels the emotional content of the events described. It's as though the reader is living the experience.

BULLIES IN POWER©

[Handwritten inscription: Darryl my friend. I know you will enjoy this book. All the Best! All My Relations. Paul M. Lagace]

Sergeant (Ret'd) Paul M. Lagace, CD., B.A.

authorHOUSE™

1663 Liberty Drive, Suite 200
Bloomington, Indiana 47403
(800) 839-8640
www.AuthorHouse.com

This book is a work of non-fiction. Unless otherwise noted, the author and the publisher make no explicit guarantees as to the accuracy of the information contained in this book.

© 2005 Sergeant (Ret'd) Paul M. Lagace, CD., B.A.. All Rights Reserved.

No part of this book may be reproduced, stored in a retrieval system, or transmitted by any means without the written permission of the author.

First published by AuthorHouse 07/12/05

ISBN: 1-4208-5756-8 (sc)

Printed in the United States of America
Bloomington, Indiana

This book is printed on acid-free paper.

DEDICATION

My darling Amy, I have often envied your patience and tolerance as we walked our challenging path. Your quiet demeanour calmed many of those outside storms that accompanied me from work. My most wishful dreams of a soul mate could not compare to the enchanting reality of your gaze.

CONTENTS

DEDICATION   v

ACKNOWLEDGEMENT   ix

FOREWORD   xi

INTRODUCTION   xiii

LIFE AND POVERTY IN RURAL NEW BRUNSWICK   1

MILITARY LIFE: THE EARLY YEARS   21

TRANSITION TO THE AIR FORCE   52

AMY: THE RESIDENTIAL SCHOOL EXPERIENCE   71

CONSPIRACY AMONG HYPOCRITES   78

THE OLD BOYS' NETWORK IN ACTION   116

THE CHALLENGE: TURNING THE TIDES   140

DECEPTIVE PROCESS BECOMES OBVIOUS   158

THE NEW BOYS' NETWORK IN ACTION   186

CONCLUSION   211

APPENDIX I: STEPS TO CHALLENGING BUREAUCRATIC
INJUSTICE   223

APPENDIX II: IN RECOGNITION OF THOSE TO COMMEND   239

APPENDIX III: IN RECOGNITION OF THOSE TO BLAME   243

REFERENCES   251

ACKNOWLEDGEMENT

It's expected that parents are the first teachers of their children. My son Ken's little reminders that life is meant to be experienced with joy has taught me that parents can also learn from children.

Hope is the lifeblood of dreams. Iris Rich-McQuay had faith in my potential to learn when I first met her at the Kamloops office of The Open Learning Institute in late 1981. Her faith fed my hope and the dream is now reality.

"Every incident has a history that needs to be examined objectively if the pattern of events forming the background is to be understood. To focus on the end result only narrows your field of vision and dilutes your credibility." Major James Lucas, 1985

Many thanks to my good friend Keith Gagné who helped me acknowledge the anger that filled the initial draft of this book.

In December 1998, I was hired to work with the AIDS Society of Kamloops. Once again I found myself in a position that involved advocating for people in need. I want to express my sincere gratitude to all members of the Board of Directors and staff (past and present). Without your support and the bonds of friendship we formed, this book would most likely have remained on the shelf.

Last but not least, my friend and retired school principal, Bernie Rothenburger applied a meticulous approach to the editorial task of addressing as many of my grammatical and spelling mistakes as possible. Bernie, you've helped to make this book a pleasure to read.

FOREWORD

When I set out to write this book it was intended to be a means of letting go of anger and avoid building resentment. After being released from captivity, Terry Waite (1993) stated: ***"Writing a book is a way of containing the experience."*** Having contained the experience, it seems appropriate to share the knowledge with others. I don't know who first said: ***"Learn from the mistakes of others, you'll never live long enough to make them all yourself"*** but it's been repeated enough by people I've known that I choose to apply it.

If you expect a long dissertation of dry bureaucratic language in this book, you may be disappointed. Although I grew up speaking French in rural New Brunswick and failed most of my English language courses in school, my introduction to military life in Cornwallis, Nova Scotia at twenty years of age provided a crash course in English. Writing this book wasn't difficult after I listened to my loving spouse, Amy, who said: ***"Write like you talk!"*** I suspect she may have wanted me to shut up and give her ears a rest. However, I chose to take her advice as a loving hint that I could write as well as I could talk.

Love is a very powerful emotion that can motivate almost anyone to overcome seemingly impossible obstacles. The story you are about to read takes you into the realms of life in rural poverty and adaptation to military life. Make no mistake about it: abusive authorities are not limited to poor or military environments. In fact,

I suspect many readers will find an uncanny similarity of their own circumstances to those described in this book. It is my firm belief that where there's love, there's a way to meet challenges.

I ask that you read this book with an open mind and remind yourself often that the characters are not fictitious. I have not changed any names because that would only perpetuate the façade that abusive authorities have worn as a cloak. It's not about guilt or innocence either. It's about life and the bonds of love that gives us courage to stand in truth. It's been said that a picture is worth a thousand words. The pictures in this book are meant to give the reader a flavour for the life we lived. Despite all the turmoil, there was always love in every moment we shared.

Right or wrong, the circumstances described in this book reflect the realities that many would prefer remain hidden in the silence of oppression. This book is not about the wisdom found in books. It's about wisdom of the heart and how you can motivate positive change in the world around you.

INTRODUCTION

Telling the story of Amy, Ken and I, will give a glimpse of the true nature of bureaucratic authority and how it can really be a tool of abuse in the hands of narrow-minded officials. What makes the process impossible to correct is that authorities are given the full protection of our legal system and political channels while they exercise abusive control over subordinates. The process cultivates institutionalization among many victims. You don't have to be in a penitentiary or mental facility to be institutionalized. It can be a state of mind long before it becomes a physical condition.

Although I focus on the military, there are many different kinds of institutions that foster dependency through the demands of authorities. The real survivor in this story is a quiet native woman who faced military bigotry with the silent acceptance that so many native people have been programmed to do through residential school training. It was only recently that Amy shared some of the memories of her childhood spent in residential school. What she describes in this book can be compared to the visible part of an iceberg. The extent of the harm caused, to generations of residential school students, remains under the cover of government denial and restricted media representation. It's a sad irony that residential schools adopted military strategies in overseeing the transition of native peoples into Canadian society. Ironic because military discipline would reappear

xiii

many years later, with new measures aimed at removing the last remnants of Amy's native heritage.

The messenger is cloaked, but the abusive means of imposing the message remain very obvious. Perhaps many, who have yet to share their painful memories, will make their voices heard and proudly rebuild a crushed culture. It is my personal hope that military members of all ranks and government employees at all levels will actively confront injustice before it develops into the travesty reflected in our situation.

A brief description of our background allows the reader to associate environmental influences during childhood with institutionalization in adulthood. A low self-esteem and drained self-confidence characterize institutionalization. I will begin by identifying the pattern of events that formed the naivety which predisposed Amy and me to becoming victims of bigotry from military authorities. I will also describe the events that motivated change.

It's important to note that those who make the rules assure themselves escape clauses in the use of those rules. That's why most military regulations are interpreted through the rank structure, rather than through correct meaning. If you challenge abusive authorities, you will attract a great deal of criticism from those expecting blind obedience. Unfortunately, bullies prey on those least likely to offer challenge. Such is the true nature of our military authorities. I was expected to obey orders even if it meant supporting bigotry against my spouse. The Canadian Human Rights Commission offered a ray of hope that would soon be veiled by clouds of political and military influence. The line had been drawn and we refused to cross. The results of our decision will become apparent as you read on.

LIFE AND POVERTY
IN RURAL NEW BRUNSWICK

Poverty! That's what I remember. I heard a joke once that describes the poverty in our house. "We were so poor the flies brought box lunches when they came in". We thought it was a common way of life until we were old enough to realize that there are two classes of people in the world: those who have nothing, and those who find it funny. While children can be cruel, it's important to emphasize that selfish attitudes are often as hereditary as wealth.

Life in rural New Brunswick is characterized by conservative social values and a lack of economic diversity. There is a reciprocal influence between economic limits and social values. The difficulties of the Great Depression brought people together. That spirit of support among neighbours seemed woven into the social fabric and remains a persistent feature of life in the Maritimes. It's also the fabric that characterizes Métis passion and determination with a "cause".

Our paternal grand father had passed away in 1945 and left the farm to his eldest son, Uncle Leo. We knew little about grandpa, as his death was seldom discussed in our house. It appears alcohol had contributed to a serious illness that took his life at only 59 years of age. The secrets of his life were as well preserved as was the exact cause of his death. It wasn't until I spoke to Uncle Samuel Beaulieu about our family tree that grandpa's character was revealed.

They had been friends as children and Uncle Sam became a family member by his marriage to grandpa's sister. Uncle Sam shared memories of their friendship with colourful descriptions of many good times as well as some of the more difficult times. He also described a darker side of grandpa's nature that once threatened their friendship. Grandpa had been a strict man whose anger dominated his actions. Tears filled Uncle Sam's eyes and his voice trembled as he described an incident that took place at grandpa's farm. It was late in the day and grandpa was taking one of his horses to the barn. The horse mistakenly stepped on grandpa's foot. In a fit of rage, grandpa tied the horse to a post just outside the barn. He then picked up a logging peavey and beat the horse to death.

Uncle Sam had been the only family member who would speak of grandpa. There remains an aura of mystery with grandpa's life. It seems those who knew him were reluctant to say things that might honestly describe the man. Perhaps their reluctance is based on the belief that one should not speak ill of the dead. Uncle Sam's account of grandpa's character and lifestyle left no doubt about the origin of the blind rage that often plagued my behaviour.

Father was brought up in an abusive and critical environment, where children were made to feel the pressures of economic limits as though they were somehow to blame. It was a time when large families were considered an important measure of religious status in the community. Twelve to fifteen children was not an uncommon family size. The church played a key role in social attitudes, as Sunday sermons called attention to the numerous sins of daily life. While some families listened to the moral of the story, others made use of church warnings to justify their excessive demands on family members. If something bad happened to you, it was because God found it necessary to punish a bad behaviour. This superstitious influence led to very negative results. Self-blame became almost instinctual. There were few activities that did not fall under the self-criticism of one's pessimistic outlook on life.

Life was made difficult by economic conditions that often fell on the shoulders of children. The church confused matters through its glorification of poverty as a means of fulfilling religious obligations. On the one hand, children were described by the church as blessings from God, while on the other hand they were treated by parents as the curse that fostered poverty. The ravings of religious fanatics sought to impress the spiritual benefits of poverty. It's my belief the only benefit to being poor is that you can't lose what you don't have. It's also difficult to define poverty in positive terms when its practical nature leaves you in misery.

As I look back at my childhood in an attempt to make sense of confusing events, it's clear the dysfunctional atmosphere in our father's own childhood had simply continued through a blending of genetic and social heredity. The abrasive nature of our paternal side of the family became a serious social impediment to our development. Positive feelings of love, friendship, encouragement, and genuine caring for one another were covered with a veil of criticism. But behind that wall of criticism our father desperately lacked self-esteem and the courage to change.

Parental expectations appeared impossible to satisfy and, no matter how great the effort, the standards were always out of reach. When efforts are not acknowledged or fail to gain encouraging support, the natural reaction is to do only the necessary. Continuous criticism during childhood produces an adult with poor confidence and a lack of self-esteem. That was our father. To compensate for inadequacies, father found fault in all that we did. The cycle of pessimism, so prevalent in previous generations, was perpetuated through father's unrealistic expectations.

Our mother's side of the family had a much different history. While our maternal grand-father was known as a very jealous man who enjoyed a few beers, he was also responsible for the fondest memories of my childhood. His barn and farmyard was our Sunday afternoon playground. The large wooden swing in the front yard was a focus of our attention as soon as our truck pulled into the driveway. There was always something new to explore. Uncle Gilbert gave us a ride in a converted horse buggy one Sunday, and I'll never forget how that had upset grandpa. He seemed more scared of what could have happened if we had lost control while going down the long hill behind the house. Needless to say, that was our last ride in the buggy.

It was odd to us that grandpa expressed his feelings in a loving way, even when it was disapproval. There was calm in his voice that took away fear and allowed common sense to develop. There was no criticism, only advice. I remember taking his razor and trying to shave one day. He took the time to explain that I had to be patient and wait for my beard to appear. When I asked how long, he laughed and said it would be at least until my next birthday. I couldn't wait to be eight.

Grand father sold his farm in the mid-1960s in order to finance their move to the United States in search of an improved standard of living. We missed those play times after my grandparents moved to New York.

Grandpa Emery Levesque

The most common feature on both sides of the family was poverty. In all other respects, however, mother and father grew up under very different conditions. Mother was the eldest and given the most responsibility. Grand father was a source of encouragement for his eight children. They were poor and lacked many necessities, but the blame was never passed on to the children. Everyone helped out and efforts were supported. Mother's caring approach to our needs was founded in traditional beliefs that mothers are responsible for the nurturing in the family. These traditional values kept her from interfering with father's critical approach in dealing with us.

Mother's lack of experience in family management is not difficult to understand. She was married at 15 and gave birth to my brother Jean-Baptiste less than seven months later. Father was 24 years of age, but his emotional maturity was governed by selfish motives and attitudes. While I believe mother loved father, it's not clear that father really knew how to express love.

The first years of marriage were difficult, as mother lived by the traditional values that enslaved her to father's expectations. It appears that father no longer shaved himself. This was a task that mother had assumed, along with his daily bath and manicure. When children began to crowd our small house, mother had no time to perform those traditional services and father reluctantly assumed the task of maintaining his personal hygiene.

It's been said that opposites attract and our parents were certainly opposites. Mother never seemed to find enough time during the day to do what she felt had to be done. Father, on the other hand, sat in the house waiting for job offers to come waltzing in the door. He had many dreams of big money jobs, but never took the time to search for work.

Our first house was located on a corner lot given to us by Uncle Leo. The front yard was small and there was no backyard since our uncle Roland occupied the lot next to us. It was a small house with no running water. There was a well outside, by the porch, and the outhouse was at the far corner of the yard, near Uncle Leo's fence. The cows often stretched their heads through the fence to get long grass they could reach in our yard. Father didn't own a lawnmower, but he complained about the cows.

One day mother gave me a bucket of potato peels and carrot tops to throw over the fence for the cows. The bucket slipped out of my hands and fell on the other side of the fence. When I touched the fence I was stuck. Uncle Leo had hooked a battery to the fence in order to keep the cows from pushing their heads through it. My brother didn't know what to do as I screamed and felt as though my feet were sinking in the ground. Mother came out of the house and pushed me away from the fence. Father couldn't think of anything to say other than how stupid and clumsy I was.

My older brother had a two-year head start on me in dealing with criticism. As the second in a family that would eventually grow to twelve, I often felt unable to follow in my brother's footsteps. Father seldom worked in those days so he took us fishing and hunting. Jean-Baptiste tried to catch fish, but spent more time trying to bait his hook. Perhaps if father had taken the time to explain how, we might have been more successful. We were expected to know without being taught.

When my brother started school, I couldn't wait for my turn. He brought his first report card and mother was proud of his 99 percent average. Father destroyed the moment with a simple question. "Why didn't you get 100 percent?" I saw the pride in my brother's face turn to shame and guilt. Somehow that missing 1 percent was more important than the accomplished 99. His disappointment was obvious and mother's eyes turned sad. It was a scene that would repeat itself many times as we tried, in vain, to accomplish that illusive perfect score of 100. I have a feeling that if we had achieved perfection, father would have found a way to criticize it.

The school was an old two-room building in the middle of a small empty playground. My first day was marked with fear of the unknown. The teacher appeared very strict and I looked to my brother for protection. He, of course, made a beeline through the backdoor and ran toward the outhouse. The teacher took my hand and led me to my desk. The girl sitting behind me was a second cousin. Anne-Marie and I quickly became friends. She lived up the hill from our house. I waited for her in the morning and we walked to school together. I suppose that might be considered my first relationship. It wasn't destined to be long and would end during grade two, when we moved. Although Anne-Marie was special to me at that time, the years would change us. Seven years would pass before we'd meet again. Her new friends wouldn't include a boy from poverty row. But, I don't want to get ahead of myself.

I had just started school in the fall of 1959. Potato picking season was fast approaching. That dreaded time of year when we worked in potato fields with our parents. Being small was a serious disadvantage, as father expected adult performance from us. My brother and I shared a row so that we could carry the basket together. To an adult the 40-pound basket was relatively easy to carry and empty into a barrel. But, for Jean-Baptiste and I, we had a difficult time dragging the basket, much less lifting it to empty it into the barrel. Nevertheless, at 7 and 5 years of age, we were both expected to work as fast as adults. When we got tired, which happened often, father thought nothing of exercising his authority in verbal and physical ways. Many days were spent in fear of getting kicked or slapped for not working fast enough.

There was never enough money to buy food, even less for clothing. Friends and relatives gave mother second hand clothes that she would mend for us. On Saturday nights, we would visit uncle Pete. We couldn't afford a television, so it was customary to visit relatives who had one. Somehow arguments always seemed to erupt. It was apparent that father's attitude and behaviour were abrasive.

Our sister Line (pronounced Lynn in French) and brother Allain also became targets of father's frustrations. Anne was just a baby and mother was pregnant with Brigitte at the end of my first year of school. Father had been shamed into getting a job. There was no happiness in our house and arguments often focused on the lack of food and money.

Brigitte's birth is difficult to remember, perhaps because her life was so short. She was barely a month old when she passed away. Today the cause of her death is known as Sudden Infant Death Syndrome (SIDS). However, in 1959, self-blame and religious beliefs dominated mother's grief. Bills accumulated, resulting in pressures that father would take out on us in the form of beatings for the most trivial misbehaviour. Mother tried to pacify father's abusive nature, but it was a futile effort.

The beatings didn't hurt as much physically as they did emotionally. The reasons were unpredictable. We never knew what we did wrong. I recall visiting relatives one Saturday and we were told to play outside. A sudden urge to use the washroom made it necessary to go into the house. I had barely made it in the doorway when father appeared and grabbed my arm in that familiar way. There was no time to explain anything as I felt the sharp pain of his boot in my lower back. Father was told he was no longer welcomed at their house. The beating continued when we got home. I felt responsible, not only for causing my father to lose his temper, but also for spoiling everyone's good time. There were many similar incidents for which we were made to feel responsible for father's ill-tempered behaviour.

While out for a drive to town early one Saturday evening, in the late fall of 1959, we met a neighbour who informed us our house had caught fire. The pickup's speedometer hit the outer edge during the rush home. Fire fighters had put out the fire. Damage was limited to the basement entrance and the back wall of the house. While the cause of the fire was not known, it appeared to have started in a woodpile in the basement. As the fire fighters were leaving, they briefly explained the situation and asked father to attend their office later for more details. While he was out we went to bed. A short while later mother rushed into our room with a look of panic on her face. She told us to hurry out of bed and run outside. There was no time to dress and the smoke was getting thick. Our dog, Browny, was barking at the door. We ran out.

As we reached the end of the gravel driveway, the loud snaps and creaking of wood called our attention. Looking back we could see the roof caving in and the windows burst out. Mother held our hands and cried as we walked toward Mrs. Bertha Beaulieu's house. She was a good friend of the family, even if father disliked her honest address of his poor efforts in looking for work. All that was left of our house was a rocking chair that had been thrown out when the fire was initially discovered. I can still smell the burnt material of our mattresses and clothes.

Although father had sworn off alcohol for almost ten years, he found it necessary to get drunk. I guess it was a heavy burden to carry since it had only been a few months since our sister Brigitte had passed away. The fire caused financial disaster. No furniture, no clothes, no food, and most importantly, no insurance. Mother's belief in God may have been stronger than her fear of the future, because she remained reasonably calm. Perhaps the grief over our sister's death numbed mother's feelings. It seemed like bad luck had taken residence with our family. Taking temporary refuge in an old abandoned house across from uncle Leo's, we soon received assistance from the Red Cross and assorted donations from relatives and friends. We spent the winter at that old house.

Father started building a new house on a lot given to us in exchange for our previous lot. We finally settled in our new home during the spring of 1960. While the exterior of the house was ready, there remained a great deal of work to do inside. Walls were incomplete and bed sheets were used as dividers between bedrooms.

BULLIES IN POWER

Mother had taken up sewing for people who needed various clothing items. She used her natural talent and people looked to her for assistance in sewing everything from hemlines to drapes. Gardening played an important role in daily activities. We had a large garden and every year I was called upon to turn the ground in preparation for spring planting. Mother always relied on me to do this task and I suppose it would have been a disappointment to me if she hadn't asked me. Having witnessed how tired she became after long days at her sewing machine or pulling weeds in the garden, I felt she needed help. Her encouraging words still ring in my ears. "Paul, you're the only one who can turn the ground properly," she'd say. From about 8 years of age, I noticed the sacrifices mother made for us. I guess if my mind had been receptive to father's needs, I might have noticed the problems he was experiencing.

Shortly after moving to our new house, our brother David was born. As with all of us, mother gave birth at home. The doctor came to our house early in the evening. Jean-Baptiste and I heard noise and we knew another brother or sister would be with us by morning.

Father had been working for a while and he seemed happier after David was born. The drinking was gradually getting worse and he would come home from work on Friday nights with candy for us. We looked forward to his arrival on those nights. But the good times were short lived as he would go to work Saturday mornings with a hangover and come home at noon with a bad temper. We knew better than to stay in the house.

Throughout my early years at school I tried to achieve the best reports possible. Every report card seemed to bring bad news as the average went down from 98 percent in grade one to 89 percent in grade five. It was a very depressing walk home after receiving my fifth grade report card. I had been afraid of this all year and I knew my marks would make father angry. The reward for my year of effort was a beating. To add to my punishment I went to bed without supper. There was little comfort in knowing that Jean-Baptiste and Line also received the same treatment. I don't remember much about the report card, but I do remember swallowing a great deal of anger that night. I suddenly knew what Jean-Baptiste felt after he failed his grade four. Year after year, he had gone through this feeling. We

9

thought about running away. But where do you run when you feel the whole world is against you? When you can't seem to do anything right at home, the prospects of success elsewhere are dimmed.

Father's criticism left us feeling different from other "normal" children. We assumed the difference was our fault. The thought of asking other children if they were punished for their grades never entered our minds. It was a personal burden that got heavier with time. When you're made to feel different long enough, you begin to act different. Soon our lack of self-esteem and poor confidence became visible to other children. At a time when making friends at school is important, we were isolated because we didn't fit in. I would later discover the reality of our heritage.

Other children were allowed to grow their hair and have friends visit. Our hairstyle was dictated by father's expectations. We looked like prisoners of war just released from concentration camps. Of course in father's mind we had to conform to his way of maintaining appearances. "Only hippies have long hair, and I won't raise you to be hippies," he'd say. Consequently, my brothers and I were the only boys at school with shaved heads. Father also held a deep fear that our native background would be discovered. The word Métis was never spoken in our house even if the practices and heritage were obvious in our daily lives.

1966 Dad takes a picture of the Family

Our appearance was often the centre of attention at school. My older brother's first day in grade seven was marked by name-calling and ridicule. He came home crying. Father's response was to call Jean-Baptiste a wimp and coward because he didn't fight back.

Three weeks later, I was being pushed in the bus so I punched the culprit in the face. While it put an end to the pushing, the principal used the strap on me and sent me home with a note. Having witnessed father's reaction to my brother's situation, I thought my actions were appropriate. The beating I received from father left me confused about how to react under difficult circumstances. If I didn't fight back and came home crying, I would be called names and sometimes beaten. When I fought back, the results at home were equally negative. So I learned to run. Bullies had to run if they wanted to fight me. Running became a way of life in more ways than one.

The provincial health nurse who came to our home one summer morning found it difficult to understand how 10 kids could fit comfortably in a 3-bedroom bungalow. It seemed simple enough to us. Our parents shared their bedroom with our baby brother, leaving the other 5 boys to share the second bedroom while the four girls shared the third. Although our bedrooms were somewhat small, the one large bed and adjoining cot left us enough room to enjoy the company of our family dog in the corner. The nurse decided it was time to remodel. We all received individual bunk beds which would replace the two large beds. This seemed like a great idea until the nurse emphasized the need for bedroom doors which would keep our dog out. It seemed that every time we opened our new door to tease the girls, dad would be there to exercise the authority of his voice and hand. We soon adjusted.

There was a basement in our house, but that was used not only to store the winter's supply of firewood but to serve as a punishment cell for those who chose not to listen to mother's directives.

Our father enjoyed hunting and fishing. It was dad's dual purpose recreation. He would enjoy a few dozen beers while maintaining the impression that he could provide food for our dinner table. Of course the boys were expected to participate.

My resistance to this traditional habit started at an early age. I suppose if I had been able to catch a fish or gun down some poor animal, dad might have been less critical. It seemed I could never do anything right in his view. Fishing and hunting remain a distasteful activity because of the many critical episodes that followed unproductive efforts on our father's expeditions. These adverse memories contributed to self-doubt about potential for success in other areas of my life. It's perhaps the most influential

Sergeant (Ret'd) Paul M. Lagace, CD., B.A.

factor motivating my efforts to be the best or the worst, but never average. Standards were always at extremes. On the few occasions in which my accomplishments have been notable, I felt there was still something missing.

I was a loner at school because I felt there was something wrong with me. After all, why would father be so critical if I didn't somehow deserve it? By the time I reached grade seven, my poor self-esteem had left me with the impression that being laughed at was better than getting no attention at all. Consequently, I often acted out in ways that called attention to my pretense of being stupid. Trouble soon followed these attention-getting devices, as teachers didn't care to have the class continuously disturbed by my efforts to be a clown. I had no friends with whom to confide my feelings.

I was about 12 years old when it became apparent that we lacked the basic needs. It was early fall and we were picking potatoes, as we always did at that time of year. The work was hard and the pay was low, but it was our only way of earning a few dollars for winter clothes. Even the youngest attended in potato fields. Besides, we couldn't afford day-care even if it had been available.

I can remember the frosty mornings when we left the house before the sun came up, only to arrive in the field and find the farmer had already been digging up rows for an hour or so. The smell of freshly dug potatoes, mixed with the dust, left an impression of misery that would never wash away. It felt like the sun's warmth would never reach our end of the field. The days started early and finished late. The desperation of the farmer, to get his crop out of the ground, dictated how late we worked after dark. Harvest season was only three weeks long, but this seemingly endless process involved backaches and sore joints, often made worse by the cold ground.

One of the most painful memories of my childhood took place at lunchtime on a particularly hot day in the potato fields. The sandwiches were thin that day and I noticed our mother continued to work. After we each took a sandwich, I suddenly realized mother was crying silently as she hunched over her picking basket. The fact that there had not been enough for mother wasn't the only reason she cried. She had a discouraged look on her face that said everything about our condition. Hunger was replaced by anger and

12

that sandwich seemed to remain caught in my throat. It's a memory that shadowed my perception of social class throughout my teens and into adulthood. Authorities would become the targets of frustration and blamed for our condition. It was somehow acceptable to blame those who ridiculed our state of poverty because they knew nothing about it.

As a teenager, working for wages was a necessity not a choice. Picking potatoes was an initiation to becoming a farm worker. After harvest season, it was sorting and shipping work in the potato sheds that kept many employed. The most difficult job in the sheds was shovelling potatoes into the conveyor feeding box. It paid the least but was the most physically demanding.

I was thirteen when I took my first job in the sheds. The first day at shovelling took its toll on my back and wrists. After two days, my wrists were swollen and weakened to the point where I had to use my knee to assist in pushing the shovel over the edge of the conveyor box. By noon on the third day the boss explained that I wasn't physically able to do the job. At twenty-five cents an hour, I had earned seven dollars. I went home frustrated and disappointed at having been unable to break into the work force. Mother understood how I felt. She explained that I needed an education in order to avoid a lifetime in the sheds. She rubbed my wrists with rubbing alcohol to help reduce the swelling. I went back to school.

Summer jobs were scarce, but sometimes after spring planting, farmers hired kids to walk the fields behind a tractor and pick large rocks from the rows in order to prevent farm tools from being damaged. The pay wasn't much at ten to fifteen cents an hour, but it was better than sitting at home doing nothing. Later in the summer we took jobs in the hay fields. The pay was about the same as for picking rocks, but we sometimes enjoyed tumbling around in the farmer's barn.

It didn't matter where we worked or how much pay we received, we always gave it to mother. Everyone worked at supporting the household. While mother appreciated and encouraged our efforts, father's response was less supportive. He always managed to dilute our efforts and contributions with critical remarks. "I put the roof over your heads and the food in your mouths," he'd say. There were

Sergeant (Ret'd) Paul M. Lagace, CD., B.A.

times when I felt like telling him where he could put his roof. As for food, we were always hungry and mother seemed to be the only one buying it out of the money she earned at sewing.

Poverty is a heartless condition. The less fortunate always seem to receive the critical scrutiny of those who can afford to maintain the image of being well off. I remember Mother went to the Army Surplus one winter to buy winter shoes and pants for us. It was the only place where the prices met our limited budget. She was able to buy three pairs of shoes and five pairs of dark green wool pants. The shoes were somewhat large but the pants were mended to fit. I was happy to wear these new items to school. The attention received was not as I expected. The cruel jokes and ridicule left the impression that poverty was a terrible punishment for some unknown sin in one's past. I drew comfort in the warmth that my pants offered during the long walks to school on cold winter mornings. I avoided the bus in fear of ridicule.

My brother's failure in grade nine convinced him to run away from home. Fear motivated his drastic measure of escape. He hitched a ride to New York, where he located Grand father. Mother's worry soon changed to anger at Father for his abusive attitude and behaviour. While she wouldn't allow herself to confront him in our presence, I heard the argument later that night. It was the first time I heard Father cry. After three days of worrying, Mother received a call from Grand father which brought a sigh of relief. Jean-Baptiste had broken Mother's silence and the rules of the house were modified. Father's control deteriorated slowly until the fear he once imposed through abuse was no longer tolerated. Mother assumed control.

Mother did the best she could to provide food and clothing, but her efforts were limited to work she could perform at home. Sewing brought about twenty dollars a week and she couldn't let Father know because he didn't approve of her working. His pride also prevented any form of social assistance. Here we were going hungry and Father was worried about appearances. It seemed he changed vehicles every two or three years, but we had to pass our clothes and shoes to the next in line until they could no longer be mended.

Our father's limited and sporadic work pattern failed to provide for the many needs of a large family. Jean-Baptiste had grown up since running away. He was tired of going hungry and thought of a way to change the situation. He and I came up with a plan to sell bootlegged liquor from the basement. Although against the law, bootlegging presented an opportunity. We passed the word around to farm workers and soon had steady clients coming around in the evening after work. They used the basement entrance to avoid running into Dad.

He was unaware of our enterprise for about three months. Then one night a less experienced client made the mistake of going in the front door instead of the basement. He asked for a couple of beers to go. We heard the footsteps upstairs and knew it was too late. My brother dropped everything and ran up the stairs. Dad almost went through the roof. A heated argument followed which almost erupted into a fist fight. Mother stepped in and cooled things off. We finally convinced him to allow us to continue until he got back on his feet. Besides, it was necessary if we were to continue school.

Most people would argue we had the choice of seeking social assistance. But that was not a choice in our father's prideful repertoire of economic solutions. We had no idea that he would quit his job when he saw the kind of money we were making. What began as a supplementary source of income soon turned to full time work for Father. It was also an opportunity to have a few beers from the profits.

People gathered in our kitchen and living room for weekend parties. The old stereo played country music in the familiar style often found in bars. Weekend parties gradually increased in length to include most weeknights as well. Sales went up but profits were shared with Father's drinking as he progressed to being drunk on a daily basis. There was no question of turning back time or quitting the business. The family's financial needs were being met by the profits of this uncomfortable business.

The expected difficulties of grade nine manifested themselves like a self-fulfilling prophecy. Unlike today's school system, passing grades were based on performance as there was no learning assistance. A lack of effort naturally led to failure and I was guilty. Consequently, I spent three years in grade nine. I had gone from being the class clown to unpredictably violent. The change may be attributed to the physical and emotional turmoil of puberty. But the nature of my immaturity certainly reflects an attempt to conceal feelings of profound insecurity.

I sought refuge in trying to play the guitar. Like most teenagers, I listened to music which reflected the particular emotions or feelings that appeared prevalent in my life at the time. Hank Williams was my idol. His songs reflected the feelings of loneliness and isolation that I experienced at home and at school. Listening to records and singing along seemed to provide a measure of relaxation. Attempts at learning to play the guitar were unsuccessful for a few years. The depressive moods that dominated my life may have also been responsible for a lack of patience in practice.

Determination would blend with guidance in grade eleven music class. I soon gained confidence in my ability to learn, as playing chords allowed me to sing the songs that I had listened to for years. Playing my guitar and singing encouraged our business and, as word got around, sales went up.

There was a small wooded area behind our house. Whenever the parties got too loud, or the company was not to my liking, I would go off into the woods and fantasize about living under different conditions. Unfortunately, the fantasies only lasted while I was in the shelter of my little forest world. Reality at home occupied most of my time.

After a few years of bootlegging, my father decided to go back to work. One of our cousins had talked to him about an opening at the local potato processing plant. We took care of the business but seriously thought of giving it up. Somehow selling bootlegged liquor didn't appeal to my hopes for career development. The friends we had made kept visiting and brought their own beer when we didn't have any in stock. Parties became weekend events again.

While celebrating his nineteenth birthday, my brother Jean-Baptiste and a few of his friends decided to visit one of the more reputable bootleggers of our area. She was a widow whose only means of support was the familiar business which allowed her to avoid social assistance. Jean-Baptiste would become close friends with her and, upon graduating from high school that year, they began a relationship that would last over ten years.

The summer of 1972 was marked by an unfortunate accident that took our sister's life. Jean-Baptiste had taken Anne, Allain and David to a friend's farm to pick raspberries. Jean-Baptiste was driving the old tractor. The mudguard on which Anne was sitting suddenly gave way and she fell under the wheel. I remember sitting at the table, reviewing a few songs in preparation for the upcoming weekend, when a taxi stopped in the driveway. Jean-Baptiste came in the house and went to our mother. He kept saying it was an accident as he sobbed in Mother's arms. That summer day remains etched in my mind as if it happened yesterday. Anne is remembered for her jovial personality and exuberant enjoyment of life.

Graduation in June, 1973, left me very apprehensive about getting a job. There was no fear of work, but the question of where to work and what to do would go unanswered for some time. School had not prepared me for making decisions about life and my high school marks didn't offer much opportunity to pursue post-secondary education. I could pick potatoes, work the fields and sheds, perhaps get temporary work at the local processing plant, or maybe carry on with bootlegging. Many of my friends had progressed to a life of seasonal employment with unemployment insurance as a main source of income during the off season. I wanted to avoid the trap of seasonal employment prospects but lacked confidence to explore job markets elsewhere.

In early July, a job came up at the lumber mill where Jean-Baptiste had been working. It involved running a band saw during night shift for minimum wage. It was also the first year in which Mother decided to venture off to Southern Ontario for tomato and cucumber harvest season. We agreed that I would remain at home while the rest of the family travelled to Chatham. Father wasn't keen on the idea and offered some resistance in the form of complaints about working for nothing. However, Mother saw the summer employment as an avenue to finally quit bootlegging. Our family doctor confirmed that Mother was pregnant. Pregnancy and her determined approach to needed change convinced Father that he was fighting a losing battle. They returned in early September with enough money to pay the bills and, for the first time in years, bought new school clothes for my brothers and sisters. The work had been hard, but the rewards included temporary relief from "the business".

The job at the mill dried up and I was looking for work once again. After a few days as a shelf person in a local supermarket, I took advantage of an opportunity to visit distant relatives in Springfield, Massachusetts. Encouraging comments about my singing abilities left the impression that the music business might hold the secrets of my future. With my guitar and a small bag of clothes I took my first step away from the sheltered security of the family home.

The uncertainty of this new experience was frightening and exciting all at once. Upon arriving at my new home, I sat quietly at the dinner table with an unfamiliar lump in my throat. Junior, as he was known to us, recognized the symptoms. The anxiety of being too far from home to run back had suddenly stolen my appetite and left a terrible feeling of emptiness in the pit of my stomach. We sat in Junior's living room and he explained why I found it difficult to eat and how it would go away after a few days of feeling the newfound freedom.

My first performance at a local bar brought supportive cheers from patrons. They liked my style and enjoyed the choice of songs. Junior took me to various bars where I played and enjoyed the company of other musicians. My inexperience with the music world left me unaware of union rules. After a couple of months, I found out anybody can sing, but only a few can make money at it. The dream ended a month later. Without the appropriate documents, my stay in the United States was limited. In December, 1973, I returned to Grand Falls with no money and no job prospects in the music business. The visit with Junior and his family had given me a new outlook on life. I was no longer afraid to travel.

Christmas holidays were spent entertaining our usual crowd of clients as bootlegging had once again provided a familiar avenue to make financial ends meet. By New Years Day, 1974, father's drinking had left him incapacitated and unemployed. Mother's pregnancy was approaching full term and the business was plagued by police raids. It seemed like the more effort we made, the less progress we achieved.

BULLIES IN POWER

When our sister Carole was born, she was diagnosed with Down's Syndrome. Once again religious misconceptions led mother to believe Carole's condition was somehow attributed to a punishment from God. Isn't it ironic that God would choose to add genetic punishment to our already difficult situation? Looking back at our bootlegging days, I can see why Mother felt God had it in for us. It seems like nothing turned out right.

The town of Grand Falls is small and not much of an attraction, but I spent most of my time walking up and down the boulevard. In April, 1974, while on one of my walks, I noticed military recruiters were located in the local Legion Hall. With no particular intention of joining the Canadian Forces, I walked in and inquired about military lifestyles. That recruiter should have been a salesman. With glamorous descriptions of life in the military, it sounded very appealing. Visions of driving across fields in a tank, or flying around in a helicopter invited further discussion. After taking the initial battery of tests, I soon found myself undergoing an enrolment medical.

I went home and told Mother about my intentions. She felt happy that I was doing something about my life, but she was also concerned that life in the military might present a difficult challenge. Difficult or not, life in the military offered a more favourable alternative than the prospects of poverty.

Father was unusually quiet for a few days. Then one evening he asked if I was joining the military because of his drinking. It was a sensitive side of Father's character that I had never seen. He seemed saddened by my decision. This was his attempt at supporting my decision in the only way he knew how. It was his way of saying that if his drinking had pushed me away, he was sorry. I accepted his silent apology and emphasized my need to establish a career.

It suddenly dawned on me that Father simply didn't know how to express positive feelings. He was proud of my decision, but felt he had to relate my choice to his drinking behaviour. Regardless how abusive he had been, it was clear he silently wished me well.

Mother was silent as she drove me to the bus depot. She was sad about my leaving, but didn't want to make it more difficult than it already was. It was early in the morning and I was still tired from a restless sleep. I could tell her heart was heavy as she wished me luck and reminded me that the door was always open if I chose to return home. She managed to hold back her tears until I was in my seat and looking out the bus window. As the bus pulled away, she stood on the sidewalk and waved. There was no turning back and I knew it.

MILITARY LIFE:
THE EARLY YEARS

It was a sunny afternoon and the humid breeze blended with perspiration, causing my shirt to cling uncomfortably to my back. The Greyhound bus arrived early, which allowed about an hour to look around. Saint John, New Brunswick, is a quiet port city with many old buildings that mark its historical background. I probably would have taken more time to walk around, but the heat drew my attention to a restaurant sign advertising ice cream sodas. Air conditioning was a welcomed relief. I relaxed while gazing at sea gulls feeding from a sidewalk garbage can. Soon it was time to board the ferry.

The trip across the Bay of Fundy was my first experience on the ocean. The rough ride certainly confirmed that I would not have been suitable for the navy. I looked over the side of the ship in hope of catching a glimpse of sharks. My impression of ocean travel had been formed from movies in which sharks always seemed to play a role. This naive expectation left me disappointed as we docked at Digby, Nova Scotia.

Canadian Forces Base Cornwallis is located about twenty minutes from Digby and the taxi ride took me through some of the greenest farm areas I had ever seen. The salty ocean breeze had a unique smell which blended with the scent of dandelions to leave the air thick to breathe.

As we approached the front gate of the base, the driver pointed to the guardroom and told me to ask the military police where to report. He appeared experienced at seeing recruits who, like me, had a lost look on their face as they stepped out of his car to walk into an unfamiliar place. He smiled and wished me luck. The butterflies in my stomach became increasingly active as I approached the door to the guardroom.

My assignment to Eighth Platoon sent me to a barrack block by the beach, across from the wood hobby shop. As I walked in the front door, a corporal sitting at a large desk was directing recruits to their bed spaces. Not being familiar with military procedures, I stood without saying a word. He looked at me with an impatient stare and asked my name. My experience at speaking English was very limited and I didn't know how to address this fellow. So I blurted out my name, trying to hide the heavy accent of my French-Canadian background. He pointed out that he was a corporal and that I was to address him as such. We would later discover that he was a recruit who had been in the militia and decided to wear his uniform on the way in. Even the other recruits, who had arrived earlier in the week, didn't know he was just another recruit like us. It appears, shortly after arriving that morning, he had appointed himself to direct other recruits to their bed spaces. This was a mistake he would later regret.

One of the staff suddenly appeared in the door and all I heard was the single word, "ROOM". It was a word that carried a specific meaning and the dead silence told me it was best if I too remained quiet and stood still.

The staff member approached the corporal in uniform and screamed, "What are you doing in a uniform you ugly little man? Stand at attention when I'm talking to you! You do know what that means don't you? Who do you think you're impressing here?"

I think he must have been heard all the way to Digby. He looked around and told us to stand quietly by our beds. With a clipboard and pen he walked up to each of us and checked off our names from a list. We were also assigned to one of four squads. I was in squad two with about 30 other recruits. He then advised us of the meal hours and where the mess hall was located. As he was heading toward the back door, he turned and addressed the militia "corporal" with a stern warning. "Don't ever wear that uniform again while on training here."

It was almost supper time and some of the men already knew the way to the mess hall. Those who had arrived earlier in the week also knew their way around the base and pointed out the social centre. I felt somewhat out of place because I knew nothing about the military and even less about the base. There were a total of sixteen platoons going through recruit training at that time. Three of these platoons were formed entirely of female recruits. Each platoon was at a different stage of training. Members of other platoons were quick to let us know the areas that were out of bounds to all recruits.

We were told it would cost $100.00 per footstep for any recruit caught walking on the beach. The female barracks were also out of bounds to male personnel, but we would soon hear of those famous "panty raids". The mess hall was the most popular place to find out the latest rumours. The line of recruits, waiting in turn for their meal, gave me time to look around at how the process worked. I had never seen so much food. Those who complained about mess hall food had never grown up hungry. I had no complaints.

Whether it was nervous tension or just the new surroundings, I couldn't sleep for most of the night. Reveille, we were told, was at 0530. It was June 8, 1974. It was day 'one' in recruit training for me and 129 other recruits with my platoon. Getting up early wasn't a problem. It was the yelling and screaming that threw me off. The showers, bathroom sinks, and laundry machines were all working at once. I didn't know what to do and certainly couldn't find anyone who would stay still long enough to explain it to me. Besides, with my English being so poor, I doubt the message would have been understood anyway.

A morning shower was unknown to me. Our house had a bathtub and we used it once or twice a week. Family traditions, based on economic limitations, were no longer applicable. Consequently, hygienic practices would be modified to meet the standards of a military lifestyle. I would learn these important lessons over the next twelve weeks.

I returned from breakfast in time to hastily make my bed and fall in for roll call outside the barracks. Staff members briefly introduced themselves and began to instruct us on the day's activities along with their expectations. It was our last day in civilian clothing. We would wear uniforms everywhere, including the few occasions on which we were allowed off base.

The first task of the day involved visiting the supply building for an issue of uniforms and all necessary kit. The organization was astounding to me. In less than an hour the entire platoon marched in the entrance door and was reformed in three ranks outside, with each of us carrying a barrack box and duffle bag full of uniforms and assorted kit. We would march everywhere.

The staff had already begun their training methods as they yelled, "arms up shoulder high, dig those heels in, get it together!" The marching was always accompanied by a staff calling the step every once in a while. When he said "left, right, left," it was expected that the appropriate foot landed in time with the call. Within a few hours, all 130 of us heard and felt our cadence. Arms swung shoulder high, heads and eyes faced the front, and shoulders were pulled back to keep the body straight. There's nothing like marching drill to bring a group together. A sense of unity had already begun to form the expected bond so necessary to a military unit. While at home we were made to feel different from everyone else, in the military the emphasis is on making everyone alike.

Arriving at the barracks, we were given five minutes to get out of civilian clothing and into work dress uniforms. The introduction of authorities was followed by the platoon commander's address. He started by pointing out that only 1 of every 3 recruits would make it through basic training. It was difficult to understand much of his speech as he spoke too fast for my limited ability in English. I really wanted to belong and the fear of not making it served to strengthen my determination. I had chosen to attend basic training at Cornwallis because I wanted to learn to speak English. The thought of going to Saint Jean, Quebec, didn't appeal to me.

During the first few weeks I would be teased about being a "frog", but after ignoring the jokes for a while the teasing stopped and I was accepted. There were four other French-speaking recruits

BULLIES IN POWER

in our platoon, but they chose to transfer to Saint Jean after the third week of training. I guess they couldn't deal with the focus of language jokes.

Our squad's staff member was a tall infantry Master Corporal named Gordon Longpre. At over six feet and 225 pounds, he certainly impressed most of us. We were blessed with his wearing metal clickers under the toes and heels of his shoes. This allowed us to hear him coming toward the barracks from about 200 yards. He would thunder in the door and down the middle of our dormitory with a pace stick under his arm. We were expected to stand at attention beside our beds during morning inspection. He never walked, he marched everywhere. The brim of his forge cap shaded his eyes, preventing us from knowing which direction he was looking.

The ground rules were set during the first morning inspection. He possessed the ability, and size, to place remarkable emphasis on the rules. While he was strict, his manner said something of fairness as well. After that first morning inspection, we were told to correct all defects in our kit and be ready for the next morning.

Most of us had never experienced the fury displayed by Master Corporal Longpre on the second morning. He went from one bed space to the next and roared out criticisms to each occupant with increasing ferocity. As he approached my bed space, I felt shivers going through me as my knees weakened. I remember thinking, "I left home for this!"

Standing at attention meant you had to look straight ahead. To move even your eyes in any direction could earn you extra duties and drill. So I waited. Suddenly he marched across the room to a recruit who had simply cleared his throat. From about an inch in front of his face Master Corporal Longpre screamed "Why?" I guess the answer didn't come fast enough because his next command was for the recruit to get down and do 30 push-ups. When that was over he stared at the recruit for a few moments and went back to the task of inspecting bed spaces and lockers.

As he left the bed space next to mine, I felt myself stiffen up and I could hear my heartbeat. I think he could too. Having been used to the name Paul, it was hard to adjust to being addressed by my last name. When he called my name from behind me it took a few seconds to gain enough energy to respond. It was too late. "Are you deaf?" he screamed over my shoulder. One black sock had rolled out of position in my locker and I think a pile of horse manure would have been less offensive to him. That second inspection generated interest in cooperation among all squad members so that everyone might avoid mistakes. Most mistakes would be considered trivial to civilians, but to the staff there was no tolerance of any mistakes.

Life during basic training was also marked with humorous moments. Like one morning, after a particularly successful inspection, we were proud of our turnout. While standing outside in three ranks, waiting for our staff to march us to first class, an unmistakable scream came from our second floor window. Suddenly a barrack box came flying out along with its contents. MCpl Longpre's head appeared out the window and, with a sarcastic tone, he pointed out, "Someone forgot to lock that barrack box and it flew out. I couldn't reach it in time."

The first two weeks were spent confined to barracks after which passes were made available on an earned system. Good results on morning inspections could earn recruits a pass to attend the social centre on base. Of course a pass to the Green and Gold Club, where one might enjoy a beer, was not granted until the end of the fourth week of training. Off base passes were also controlled and could only be accessed after six weeks of training. Of course these rewards were made available on the basis of good performance. A pass could easily be revoked for the trivial mistake of any squad member. Therefore, everyone was expected to cooperate in gaining access to good behaviour passes.

While there were difficult times during the first few weeks, we also learned some positive lessons. The training was aimed at developing a sound knowledge of military objectives. We practised drill and team sports to enhance group unity; studied first aid to develop individual skills in dealing with medical emergencies; performed weapons training to become familiar with some of the tools of military defence; and followed a physical fitness program designed to prepare recruits for the physical demands of military tasking. Pride in the uniform was accomplished through long hours of spit polishing shoes and boots, as well as meticulous care for all items of our personal kit. Weekly parades fostered a spirit of competition among the different platoons. The hope of winning the Commandant's Pennant went with every platoon on parade. Our platoon never made it, but it wasn't because we didn't try.

Friendships were established early in training on the basis of common bonds between recruits. Ken Macgillivray and I seemed to fit the mould of what might be termed "buddies". We came from different backgrounds, but both liked boxing. He also enjoyed listening to my guitar once in a while. In times of stress we often turned to one another for support. It was a shared feeling that we would pull each other through rough spots. Morning inspections were Ken's most serious concern. He always felt his kit would be criticized, so I often relieved some of his apprehension by looking over his locker prior to inspection.

My greatest concern was focused on improving communication skills. The credit for my learning English goes to Ken for patient hours spent teaching me some of the pronunciation and grammar of the language. Ken also introduced me to Singapore Slings on our first Saturday evening pass off base. Our seventh week inspection had gone very well and we gained the first of only two passes during basic training. We took a taxi to a bar in Digby where we would enjoy the relaxing effect of a few drinks. With limited experience in any form of night life, I discovered the wonders of getting drunk. It was a means of escape. Eventually, it would also threaten my health and military career.

Our return to barracks required us to stop at the guardroom, where we would be subjected to a personal inspection by the military police on duty. Of course being drunk in uniform was not acceptable. On our way from the taxi, Ken told me to keep my mouth shut because I was drunk. I stood at attention as soon as we marched in. Ken requested the return of our passes. After a careful look at both of us, the duty MP returned my pass but told Ken he would have to come back the next morning since he was drunk. I felt guilty because Ken received extra work and drill the next weekend. It seemed unfair, since I was more intoxicated than he had been.

A practical aspect of our training involved spending the ninth week in the field. Granville training area provided an initiation to life in the great outdoors. Nothing compares to the excitement of sleeping in the rain, while mosquitoes take advantage of any exposed skin to extract whatever blood isn't already frozen.

Building shelters and eating ration packs soon became second nature. The camping trips of my youth had always involved catching our meals or going hungry. It was a novelty to open a new ration pack and discover a variety of food items such as canned beans, peanut butter, crackers, cheese and juice. I looked forward to mealtimes.

After four seemingly short days in the field, we spent an evening cleaning rifles and preparing for the next day's hike back to base. We had gone through the obstacle course a few times, but this time it would include a preliminary eight-mile hike and a run up heartbreak hill in full combat gear with rifles. This final field task was aimed at testing individual physical endurance as well as our team effort. It was expected that if a squad member suffered an injury or became unable to continue, the rest of the squad would carry him. We were motivated by the fear of not being able to keep up.

While the march followed a gravel road for the first seven miles or so, the last mile of the course involved going through some of the roughest terrain imaginable. At the end was a series of obstacles. The rope bridge and loosely tied pontoons were made more difficult by a cloud of smoke so thick you could taste the sweet aroma it left in the air. After jumping over a series of 8-foot walls, we climbed a rope net that hung over a cross beam about 20 feet high.

There was no question of taking your time along the course, as staff members provided familiar words of encouragement. After crawling through a metal tunnel, the small nightmare building became visible. It was the final obstacle but perhaps the most difficult. Inside this small building was a maze of walls which called for flexible manoeuvring in order to avoid getting stuck. The nightmare, however, involved having to deal with the tear gas in the building.

Granville Week, as it was known, marked the last difficult hurdle of basic training. The next two weeks were spent preparing for Graduation Parade. The demands of recruit training took its toll on our platoon as the final parade saw 47 graduates of the initial 130 recruits. It's most rewarding to finally realize a goal. Completing military basic training was a dream come true for me. It seemed like an eternity since that first night in barracks.

Father glowed with pride and mother cried with joy at this accomplishment. They had travelled from home to be with me on that special day. It seemed a lifetime had gone by since that long bus ride. We spent the afternoon together. Mother's concern about my transfer to Calgary seemed to vanish when I explained how exciting it would be to live out west. We had a quiet supper at a small restaurant in Digby. As we parted early that evening, Father choked back the tears that threatened his composure and he wished me luck. Mother made me promise to visit at Christmas as she tried in vain to control her emotions.

The successful completion of basic training confirmed a move away from home. Only twelve weeks had passed and I felt almost invincible. I was confident about this accomplishment and looked forward to life as an Armoured Corps Crewman. The salty smell of the ocean blended with the scent of freshly cut grass to create a particularly unique memory of life at Canadian Armed Forces Base Cornwallis.

The thought of leaving Cornwallis brought feelings of excitement and anxiety all at once. While I looked forward to Calgary, the flight across the country evoked apprehension and fear. I had never been near an aircraft much less flown on one.

There were seven of us destined for the Armoured Regiment in Calgary. Our flight took us from Greenwood to Trenton, where we spent the night in transit barracks. It was our first opportunity to wear civilian clothes and venture off base

At Cornwallis, Nova Scotia August 1974

without a pass. This newfound freedom to visit without the drawbacks of a curfew left us at a loss of what to do. Not knowing anyone, we travelled together to the downtown area. People must have thought we were from some other country because we stuck together like a misplaced group of aliens.

Trenton is not a large city, but it was certainly larger than the confines of the base in Cornwallis. Restaurant food tasted much better with the spice of freedom that followed twelve weeks of restriction to a uniformed environment. After a relatively ordinary spaghetti dinner, the seven of us walked around for a while and returned to base. The evening ritual of preparing our uniforms for the next day was an engrained routine.

The early morning fog lifted and our service flight took us to Winnipeg for a two-hour stopover before going on to Edmonton. There was little time to visit in Winnipeg, so we killed time in the terminal coffee shop. Our recruit haircuts and highly shined shoes left no doubt that we were fresh out of Cornwallis. A military transport bus awaited our arrival at Edmonton. It was early evening and our duffle bags seemed heavier, perhaps a sign of jet lag effects. The bus ride to Calgary involved about three hours of restless sleep in uncomfortable seats. After life in Cornwallis, the big city appeared overwhelming.

Sarcee Barracks is the home of the Lord Strathcona Horse (Royal Canadian) Armoured Regiment. As the bus turned off the main street, on the left a Sherman tank facing the entrance stood as a monument of an unforgotten era. As we approached the front gate, a tracked vehicle became visible through the hedge of small trees along the roadway. It was a strange piece of machinery that looked like a large truck with wheels on the front and tracks in the back. It too represented regimental history.

After being waved through the front gate, the bus turned right and headed toward a group of buildings. The roadway took us around the parade square until we reached our new home. Building A-13 had been designated the new regimental training quarters and also housed a few single members of "A" Squadron.

Building A-13 at Sarcee Barracks Calgary

The large pillars at the top of the steps stood like guard posts for the three sets of large wooden doors marking the front entrance. The duty corporal greeted us outside with a clipboard in hand, ready to check our names with the room assignment roster. There would be four to each room and we were expected to select our own bed space. It was almost two in the morning when we finally settled into bed. Morning wasn't far away.

Mark Turton and Jeff Martel had been up for a short while, but Tony Lee and I were still sleeping when Jeff yelled "ROOM". Reacting in an almost subconscious way, we were standing at attention beside our beds before we realized it. A surprised Master Corporal stood in the doorway and stared at us for a few moments.

"Relax", he said.

"My name is Master Corporal Eric Penny and I'm here to let you know where everything is located around the base."

I noticed Tony's clock had stopped at 8:37. That meant we were late. With worry written all over our faces, Eric reassured us to relax since we had arrived late the night before. Still half asleep, we sat in our underwear and listened to instructions from someone who seemed less interested in discipline and more in getting his point across. This fellow treated us like soldiers, not recruits. Our expectations were pleasantly relieved by this more relaxed atmosphere. A sigh of relief followed his departure, as we scrambled to get dressed and report to the Regimental Orderly Room.

Eddie Hiscock, Dave Jennings and Andy Lawson had been assigned a room across the hall. Jeff wasted no time in letting them know the score. Once we were all ready, we marched to the orderly room. With arms shoulder high, we dug our heels in and maintained our cadence.

The Regimental Sergeant Major explained that much of the knowledge acquired in Cornwallis would provide a framework for Regimental training. However, now we belonged to a unit with colours and history. A more specific pride would develop as our identity became shaped by traditions of the Armoured Corps. We weren't simply Armed Forces members, we were now members of the Armoured Corps; more specifically, we were Strathconas.

The motto: "Once a Strathcona, always a Strathcona" can best be understood by those who wear the regimental hat badge. Such privilege is reserved for those determined enough to go through almost eight months of crewman training. It would involve learning to operate radios, vehicles, and various weapons systems. The test of our knowledge would take place in Wainwright training area.

The dusty dry August heat made it difficult to sleep for the first few weeks. Driving tanks certainly seemed more glamorous than working in potato fields. Much to our dismay, the only tanks we would see were two stationary Centurions held for reference in the hangars. The Lord Strathcona Horse Regiment had a very impressive battle history. But history is all that seemed left of the Regimental status. The initial trades training phase was not scheduled to begin until early October, after all expected recruits arrived. This meant we would gain experience working in the hangars with the more experienced crewmen. As many were on leave, our first task involved painting tracked vehicles in three camouflaged colours.

It would take about two weeks to paint the Squadron's vehicles. While the task sounds somewhat monotonous, Eric took time to create interest in it by showing us how to operate each type of vehicle. It was hot in those black coveralls. Consequently, afternoons were often spent inside the hangars assisting maintenance crews.

Throughout my adolescence I had avoided assisting in changing the oil in Father's car or truck because it meant getting my hands dirty. After a few days working on these vehicles, the dirt and oil didn't bother me.

It took very little time to get familiar with the base and its facilities. Evenings were spent at the Junior Ranks Mess, where the enjoyment of a few drinks often led to late nights. It was a common practice that required no encouragement to adopt. Weekends allowed time to visit the city's downtown. After taking the wrong bus a few times, I soon became familiar with the transit system schedule. I had only been in Calgary for about two weeks when the urge to buy a pair of cowboy boots and a Stetson hat was satisfied. Since a private's pay didn't allow for many expenditures window shopping was an important activity. The cost of a smoking habit was compounded by an increasing devotion to drinking in the Mess.

Our occupational training was scheduled to begin in early October, but this was difficult to confirm as ours was the first course in years to be held in regiment. More graduates of basic training came in every week. New recruits filled the rooms on our wing by the end of September. Finally, training began and life seemed to acquire a more meaningful purpose as we found out about the realities of life in the armoured corps. Relaxed discipline came to an end on the first day of crewman training. The troop sergeant's morning inspection sent eight of us on extra duties for neglected haircuts. Overall, the inspection was a disaster.

Familiar restrictions were imposed in order to bring about improvements. Sergeant Major Bill Ovens made his formal appearance on the first Friday's inspection. He wasted no time in letting us know the expected level of performance. Needless to say it would be a few weeks before our inspections met his approval. In the meantime, we remained confined to barracks.

The glamour presented in advertisements, of tanks thundering over rough terrain with guns blazing, didn't mention anything about the long hours of theoretical studies in radio procedures, field driving regulations, characteristics of armoured weaponry, and field tactics. Consequently, evenings were spent in preparation for written tests and exams. Study groups soon formed in order to assist weaker students.

Jeff Martel and Tony Lee were particularly well organized and knew how to study. They provided Mark Turton and me the necessary guidance to get through a number of exams. By this time my skills in English had improved. Jeff often teased about my being a "frog". As roommates, the bonds that had been loosely formed during basic training became more solid. While we had our differences, most problems were settled without serious conflict. A unique spirit of friendship formed between us. We partied together and soon developed a protective circle that marks a very important feature of life as a crewman. The staff emphasized the need to maintain this necessary component to teamwork. "Work together; team work is what this job is all about."

Practical training began with radio procedures. By the end of November it was time to work at driver training. This was the moment we had waited for. To actually get in the driver's seat of a Lynx or Armoured Personnel Carrier (APC), provided reward for the long hours of classroom studies. Most of us had no experience in driving standard vehicles. The troop sergeant's task often led him to use very descriptive language when discussing our performance. During this first phase of training, our weekends were occupied with additional studies. As Christmas approached, most written exams were completed by mid-December.

Sergeant Major Ovens encouraged everyone to take advantage of the opportunity to visit family during the holidays. Unfortunately, the trip would cost more than my pay could support at the time. Memories of my father's loans to finance companies, where friendly relations turned out to be very costly, were still fresh in my mind. Having promised Mother a visit at Christmas, I took my first bank loan to pay the airfare home. The thought of owing money brought on mixed feelings of apprehension and pride at having taken a new step towards independence.

The flight to New Brunswick involved stops in Toronto and Montreal. Fear of flying still caused some stress, but after a few drinks I was able to relax and enjoy the ride. Leaving Calgary's blue skies to be greeted by a snow storm in Fredericton certainly dampened my holiday spirit. The few months away from home seemed like years to my brothers and sisters, as they crowded our little house to welcome me home. A steady stream of relatives and friends dropped by to see for themselves what military life had done for me. There were parties to attend and not a quiet moment for the first few days. Once the novelty wore off and friends became preoccupied with their own families, it was a relief to have time to describe Calgary to my family.

While mother felt more at ease with my decision to make a career in the military, Father confessed he felt his drinking had driven me away. It appears he had quit drinking shortly after my departure from Cornwallis. For years it seemed we were burdens to him, and yet we never knew that he felt so dependent on us for emotional support. These previously hidden feelings were quietly discussed a few days before my scheduled return to Calgary. Somehow the intended message got across and father took a positive outlook on my chosen path. For the first time, there was agreement between father and me. It remains a most memorable Christmas. The taste of life in Calgary had severed any ties to rural lifestyles at home. Our landing approach brought the glow of Calgary's lights. This was home now.

Calgary can be quite cold in January as we soon found out in the Sarcee training area during practical testing of our driving skills. A very light coat of snow covered the frozen ground. Heavy parkas, mukluks, thick leather and wool mittens, and our wool caps provided some comfort from the cold. However, the experience of checking the oil levels at minus 50 degrees can be challenging when one has to remove mittens in order to replace the dipstick. With about one instructor for every five students, a great deal of time was spent waiting around for each turn. Although an old shack provided some shelter during bad weather, it lacked a stove to keep us warm during the wait.

We all enjoyed the experience of driving tracked vehicles over rough terrain. As each student returned to the shack, those awaiting their turn would listen to the details of the trip. Of course the stories told of increasingly dangerous manoeuvres as the day progressed. We all knew some of the guys were particularly good at telling stories, but comparing adventures was a part of the day's experiences.

There was one story that blossomed into an embarrassing account of a particular trip. While on driver training with a Lynx, a tracked reconnaissance vehicle, I chose to go over a rock pile in order to see if it would knock down the lone dead tree that stood in the middle. I didn't realize how fast we were travelling until it was too late. The Lynx cleared the rock pile and the tree, but the instructor gave me the impression I had destroyed the only tree in Alberta. I don't know what made him angrier, the downed tree or the fact that my taking a run at it caused us to land pretty hard on the other side. Needless to say the story got around without my having time to modify the details. For awhile, rumours of my "flight" made my experience a topic of jokes. It was a story I preferred to forget.

Being a part of the group meant we did things together. That included spending time in the mess. I liked that part of belonging. As a matter of fact, my efforts were notably greater than that of my peers. In particular, I enjoyed drinking. Come to think of it, there were no other activities, unless they led to drinking afterwards. Naturally my peer group was formed of those who, like me, enjoyed getting drunk. It was traditionally accepted that a good soldier could drink, fight, go to jail and be ready for work the next morning. I was determined to belong. But, unlike my peers, I often went too far in my efforts to gain recognition. Arguments became common after a few drinks. It was a pattern that would steadily grow worse with time.

By mid-April we were prepared for the two-week field exercise that would take us to Wainwright for practical application of many months of training. Gun camp involved using live ammunition against static and moving targets. Additionally, battle runs would allow us to fire guns at targets as we moved through the range. It was exciting and well worth the time spent in classrooms. Sleeping in tents for those two weeks was our first field experience since Granville Week in Cornwallis. It was also our initiation to the annual Waincon Exercise scheduled for May and June.

While some of us returned to Calgary for a few days following gun camp, others remained in the field to prepare for the upcoming six-week training exercise. Waincon would be the final phase of our

LdSH (RC) 'A' Squadron 'B' Crew

BRow WO Turner, MCpls Carter, McGowan, Maxon, and Capt Bell
MRow Troopers Lagace, Kasawan and Lever
FRow Troopers Hill, Hrynyk, Braun, and MCpl Dorion

crewman training. Most of us didn't really know what to expect on the exercise. We knew how to drive vehicles and operate radios, but we were unprepared for the routines of field operations.

Main camp involved a virtual tent city. All the services available on base had been set up under field conditions. The mess hall provided hot meals three times a day and we also had a mess tent with wet bar. Even church services were made available at a central location every Sunday morning. The padre circulated among the men regularly to discuss any concerns. It was during this field exercise that the crewman lifestyle became obvious.

Crewmen developed special bonds of togetherness that came alive under field conditions. As students we were assigned to work with experienced crew commanders so that each manoeuvre was explained in terms of overall objectives. By the end of Waincon 75, we knew what was expected and how to perform under field conditions. The drawbacks, of being bled by very large mosquitoes while on observation posts and the headaches that followed those late evenings in the bar tent, also provided an initiation into regimental lifestyle. Alcohol consumption was a common practice enjoyed by everyone. It became apparent that I enjoyed it more than most.

Returning to Calgary in June, we prepared for graduation parade which would finally allow us to wear the Armoured Corps black beret and the Strathcona hat badge. Everyone, including the instructors, looked forward to our graduation. It had been a long course. The bonds formed during crewman training remain important and unique memories among the first A Squadron graduates of 1975.

Shortly after our graduation, block leave provided a much deserved period of relaxation. The need to share the news of my successful completion of crewman trades training led to my taking another trip home for a month. Visiting the family required a stop in Southern Ontario's vegetable farms where they had been working the fields for almost a month. Mother tried in vain to give a good impression of the work. But I knew it was need, not pleasure that had driven them to these difficult conditions. Father was not drinking and that seemed encouraging. I could tell he hated picking tomatoes, but he said very little about it.

Memories of working in potato fields made me uncomfortable as I accompanied them for a few days in tomato fields. David and Pierre were visibly happy as they laughed and joked with me at every opportunity. Cecile and Helene seemed less energetic, perhaps because of the added responsibilities of helping Mother prepare meals. The shack they occupied was in desperate need of windows and doors, not to mention a proper floor. It was a two-room place with makeshift walls that consisted of blankets hung over a rope tied between the outer walls. An odour of misery permeated the walls of the shack.

Carole's Down's Syndrome condition was apparent as she sat motionless for hours. Cecile took care of her during the day so that mother could work without interruption. Jacques spent most of his time learning about vegetable farming. He enjoyed operating the machinery and took every opportunity to assist farm owners with loading and shipping. After a few days, I felt an overwhelming urge to visit the rest of the family in Grand Falls. It was a need to escape the emotional turmoil, of seeing the desperate work conditions that seemed to doom my family to an undeserved fate.

Jean-Baptiste met me at the train station in Edmundston. My hangover was obvious, but a few jokes seemed to conceal the obvious results of overindulgence. The last thing on my mind was lunch; however, the opportunity to have a few drinks made our stop at a restaurant more appealing. After washing down a small piece of fish with two bottles of wine I was ready to go. Jean-Baptiste didn't seem too disturbed by my drinking until a few days into my visit. It was an uncomfortable topic that drew evasive reactions. The atmosphere grew sombre as days and nights were spent drinking with visiting friends. The visit ended with my return to Southern Ontario, where I spent two days helping in the fields.

It's not clear if it was picking tomatoes in the hot humid weather or the after effects of a hangover that led to my buying a bottle of whiskey the day before returning to Calgary. Father sat at the table with me that evening and drank coke while I rationalized drinking whiskey. He quietly listened to my excuses. Mother was tired but she sat up with us. I fell asleep in the chair shortly after finishing the bottle. The early morning sun appeared through the open doorway and woke me up. Once again, mother drove me to the bus depot. The visit had not been pleasant for them, or for me.

Germany had always been discussed in terms of the First and Second World Wars. The thought of going to Europe so early in my career never crossed my mind. When I arrived at my room, there was a note on the door. It appears the Sergeant Major had an urgent matter to discuss with me. Two days later I was on a flight bound for Lahr, Germany. As an umpire staff driver I would witness the blending of various military units on NATO land manoeuvres.

Germany is a beautiful country, but I saw little of it as most of my spare time was spent in the Centennial Club. Sightseeing tours involved the initial planning phase at the club. I seldom made it to the actual visiting phase. The social atmosphere at the club met my every expectation. There was music, alcohol, and plenty of opportunities to argue. I blended well. I gained the reputation for getting drunk and passing out during

Trooper Lagace as Umpire Staff Driver Germany 1975

arguments. There was always a large crowd and the drinks were cheap. Getting drunk was almost mandatory to fit in. I certainly didn't want to be different. The return trip remains a lost memory.

It was late November and already the winter was settling in as daytime temperatures seldom went above freezing. I made plans to stay in Calgary over the Christmas holidays. Besides, my drinking left very little for savings. So I really couldn't afford to travel anyway. Rumours began to float around the barracks that some of us would be assigned to United Nations duties in the Middle East. By mid-February, a number of us were preparing for a projected six-month tour in Egypt.

During a routine medical exam the doctor convinced me to quit smoking in order to have my request for U.N. duties approved. What the heck, cigarettes were going up again and I could use the extra money anyway. So I went from being a three-pack-a-day smoker to non-smoker overnight. It took about three weeks to get over the withdrawals, but my assignment to Egypt came through.

Stepping off the aircraft in Cairo, I felt like I had walked into an oven. There seemed to be as much sand in the air as there was on the ground. An air conditioned bus ride to Ismailia was a relief, until we arrived at our new home. New arrivals in the Middle East were called pinkies because the heat gave newcomers a pink glow for about a week. Once settled into my bed space, I went around and met all the guys on the floor. The introductions included a drink at the mess. I certainly didn't want to appear unsociable, so I indulged. Because of the heat, work hours were from 7am to 2pm daily. Off hours were spent relaxing in the mess or working out at the gymnasium. Physical exercise was not a high priority for me. I did manage to do a little running and some weight training.

Everyone gathered at the pool side three nights a week to watch movies. It was the only place where the side of a building could be used as a projection screen while providing enough room for everyone to sit. Surprisingly, temperatures dropped rapidly after the sun went down. It was common practice to bring a warm coat or blanket to keep warm during the movies.

Working in the materials platoon compound didn't involve much physical labour. I was assigned to distribute kitchen equipment and office supplies. All materials were stored in two large tents. A small desk, just inside the office supplies tent, provided adequate space to do the paperwork. A breeze moved the sand around but did very little to cool the air. By noon the heat inside the tent was almost unbearable. Air conditioners were not widely used because of limited power sources.

Although military police were on site, guard duties in the materials compound were a part of the job for those of us who worked there. I recall my introduction to this overnight extra duty. It was made clear that material losses due to theft would result in a charge of neglect against the individual on guard. In other words, the guard on duty had to protect the materials from theft. A large wooden club was the guard's tool and it was to be used against any intruder. The unwritten message from authorities was simple: beat any intruders and throw them back over the fence as a warning to others.

Shortly after arriving in Ismailia I was introduced to the Canadian Forces Radio Station Director who invited me to volunteer in my spare time. While there was plenty of spare time, it was the air conditioning that influenced my decision to become a Disk Jockey. The staff were all volunteers from different sections and it was an opportunity to make new friends.

Because of my habit of getting into arguments, it wasn't long before my drinking attracted the attention of authorities. Saint Jean-Baptiste Day marks a particularly vivid example of a problem in full bloom. Diane, one of the Disk Jockeys, invited me to attend a gathering of French-Canadians who planned to celebrate this important holiday. I had never heard of Saint Jean-Baptiste Day before, but it involved my favourite activity so I wasn't about to ask questions.

There was a little song that everyone sang as each group member was directed to drink a full glass of rum without pausing. I could hardly wait for my turn. A lapse of memory remains between that first drink and my encounter with the military police a few hours later. It appears I was trying to get over the razor wire fence in order to go for a swim across the sweet water canal. The next thing that flashed in my eyes was the sun coming through the crack in my jail cell door. I was handcuffed to the end of the bed.

There wasn't enough light to see the floor and fear of spiders, scorpions and vipers began to work on my imagination. After pulling the bed off the wall, I went towards the door. A voice on the other side told me to back away from the door. It was a relief to see another Canadian when the door opened. My mind was blank, but it was a familiar feeling. My commanding officer provided an outline of my activities as he read the police report. I took his advice and avoided the mess for a few days.

Canada Day celebrations involved a ration of two Canadian beers for each of us. I decided to try beer instead of rum or whiskey. It worked. I didn't get drunk as fast and my behaviour had time to mellow out in the process. I rationalized the consumption of alcohol with the argument that the water was bad.

The month of July was hot and dry. To break the monotony three of us decided to visit the Pyramids around Cairo. The trip would take about a day. Of course a little celebration the night before made the drive through the desert a most miserable experience. After a few beers the headache went away but the sun burned my arms and neck as I sat in the back seat of an open jeep.

Trooper Lagace in Cairo Egypt, 1976

While visiting one of the pyramids, we were offered a ride on a camel. I couldn't see any pleasure in riding anything that spit and slobbered. Perhaps the camel's behaviour may have

BULLIES IN POWER

evoked memories of my own behaviour on those mornings, when I too spit and slobbered in the big white telephone. Regardless of the motive, I couldn't ride a horse and I wasn't about to get my first riding experience on a camel. It was a good trip, but I looked forward to arriving in Ismailia where a few beers would wash some of the sand from my throat.

Discussions during high school history classes had focused on the most desirable aspects of a visit to the Pyramids. Although I saw the pyramids, there was another side to the glamour of history that didn't include learning about the pain of a hangover in 130 degree heat.

While most of the time we worked regular hours, there were occasions calling for extra effort. A shipment of pre-fabricated buildings began arriving by truckload in mid-August. It was a round-the-clock task that would involve unloading 110 trucks over a six-day period. Bruce Webster and I worked almost continuously, as we were the only two forklift operators in materials platoon at the time. To compensate us for the overtime hours the Commanding Officer gave us four days off. I took advantage of the time off to go on an organized tour of the Holy Lands. The eight-day trip would take us across Israel, from Haifa to Elat.

The air conditioned bus provided a very comfortable ride to Tel Aviv for our first overnight stop. Hotel accommodations had been pre-arranged for two people per room. Bob McSween and I would share rooms during the trip. He and I had a lot in common. We both enjoyed Canadian Club whiskey. Bob was an experienced sergeant in the Corps of Engineers and he knew the ropes on such trips. After a few days visiting the sites in northern Israel, we travelled along the Jordan River towards Jerusalem. It was a memorable experience to actually see the places so often discussed in school and at church.

The highlight of the tour was Jerusalem. The city represents the birth place of Christianity, but many different religions are practised within the city's walls. Bob and I decided to try and take a picture of Isaac's rock in the Dome of the Rock shrine. I noticed everyone who entered this place took their shoes off and prayed on the steps before going in. Having had a few drinks, it appeared easy enough to just walk in and take a picture. What harm could it do? Bob thought he'd wait for me outside. Well, the flash of my camera drew attention

43

from a variety of offended worshippers. Attempts to grab my camera were unsuccessful and my diplomatic experience was a little rough around the edges.

Fearing an international incident, the police quickly came to rescue me from worshippers determined to relieve my body of its intoxicated head. Once safely outside, we thought it best to locate the rest of the group and keep a low profile. It seemed like a good idea to seek out less hazardous sights to represent in my photo collection. Green fields and developed farmlands characterized Israel's countryside, a marked difference from Egypt, where there were no green fields and signs of poverty plagued the streets. After visiting Elat, we headed back to Ismailia.

With only a month left on my tour of duty in the Middle East, time seemed to drag on. My scheduled return to Calgary was delayed for a week as a result of an ear problem that prevented aircraft travel. On October 6, 1976, I left Ismailia bound for Cairo airport to catch the flight to Lahr, Germany. A few days later I felt the cold of Calgary's fall weather. It would take some time to adjust to the change in temperatures.

The first night in Calgary we received word that a young boy was reported lost and volunteers were needed for the search. After about three hours, the boy was located and we returned to barracks. Of course a celebration was rationalized. Besides, the cold warranted a few drinks to warm up the bloodstream. The party went on until morning.

My return from the Middle East had freed any restraints from drinking. I was losing friends and even the old drinking buddies seemed reluctant to associate with me. An aura of unpredictability seemed to accompany me whenever I attended the mess. By late 1976, my alcohol problem posed a threat at work. Supervisors strongly suggested I stop drinking.

Having saved over a thousand dollars while in the Middle East, it was possible to buy a car. Not wanting to deal with the troubles of owning a used vehicle, I bought a new 1976 Charger. The freedom of driving meant less time in the mess. But the novelty soon wore off as the choice between gas for the car, or a bottle for me, left the car empty between pay days. At Christmas, I called mother and gave

BULLIES IN POWER

her a list of excuses why I couldn't visit for the holidays. There was disappointment in her voice. After talking to everyone at the house, I felt alone. So I got drunk for a few days.

In early 1977, after a drunken escapade, there was no alternative but to seek a way of dealing with my problem. I made my first attempt at controlled drinking. The effort lasted less than a week. The party that followed resulted in a weekend blackout. Another violent episode in the barracks convinced me to quit drinking. A childhood fear of drinking like my father had become reality. Not only did I drink like him, I had become more arrogant.

The threat of career reprisals left very few options. Our new Sergeant Major made it clear that alcohol-related problems would not be tolerated and offenders would be subject to disciplinary action. While attendance at the Basic Alcohol Rehabilitation clinic was offensive to my pride, the thought of spending time in jail was even less appealing. Ironically, the violent episode that led to questions about my drinking also confirmed the need to seek help in dealing with an addiction to alcohol. I could no longer enjoy the luxury of maintaining companionships in the bar.

At 23 years of age, it was difficult to accept that I could no longer drink alcohol. Physically, I was a mess. Time spent in the mess had done very little to maintain physical conditioning. My 37-inch waist did not enhance the athletic appearance of very thin legs and pathetically skinny arms attached to a 38-inch chest. After attending a few self-help group meetings, it was suggested that my lifestyle needed to change. I would have to replace the time previously spent in the mess with other activities, including a physical exercise program. The medical officer emphasized the importance of developing healthy living habits. So, I stayed out of the mess and bought a weight training set. Although drinking was no longer a problem, the extremist attitudes that had motivated alcohol abuse would persist. A focus on physical fitness led to obsessive training methods involving up to 4 hours of gym work every night.

While at the gym one day, I met a swimming instructor who convinced me to enrol in a Bronze Medallion program at the base swimming pool. During basic training I had failed to meet the swimming standard because of a paralysing fear of deep water. It was a challenge to actually dive into water above my head.

I turned my attention to physical activities and attending self-help group meetings. Having devoted a great deal of time to drinking, it was necessary to fill these empty hours. Within a few weeks of quitting drinking, my schedule of activities included running, weight training, swimming, and at least one meeting every night. While it might be argued that my time was well spent, there was no enjoyment in it. Working out became as much an addiction as alcohol had been.

It was at a meeting that I met a lady who would help change my whole outlook on life. Lois held my attention from the first time I saw her. Her brown eyes seemed to smile when she spoke. At first, fear of rejection kept me from approaching her. One night, after a meeting, I accepted an invitation to go for coffee with other group members. She was sitting across from me and spoke so openly about feelings that I never expected anyone else to understand.

Unlike others, my experience with women was very limited. As a matter of fact, I had never been able to work up enough courage to ask girls out during my high school years. Feeling different had left me with an overwhelming inferiority complex. Who would have anything to do with me, I thought? That negative self-perception accompanied me throughout my years of drinking. It would take some time before I could accept a sense of equality with women. Lois helped me deal with my fear of rejection and gave me a realistic perception of women. We became very close friends over the next few months.

The test of my sobriety came in the field, where outside contact was most limited. Going to Waincon Exercise and staying sober for six weeks helped to develop my sense of humour. I also met others who chose not to drink. We soon formed our own self-help group and met as often as possible. A change of attitudes slowly took effect as I felt more comfortable with a new circle of friends. We shared something in common.

Returning to Calgary after Waincon 77, I took leave to visit the family. This visit would be a sober one. Driving from Calgary to Toronto in two days reflects how anxious I was to get there. I had heard that Ken Macgillivray lived in Whitby, so I stopped in to say hello. Ken had been out of the military for a while. It appears his drinking had caused a few problems. He greeted me at the door with a bottle and a smile. His condition saddened me. We went out for a coffee but he spiked his with whiskey. After turning down his offer for a drink about a dozen times, he stopped offering. There were so many things I wanted to tell him, but he would not have understood in his condition. We visited his wife, Debbie, at the hospital. Problems with her pregnancy were compounded by Ken's drinking. She spoke of Ken's problem gradually getting worse. I offered him the same advice that had been offered to me. I left Whitby feeling guilty about not being able to help Ken. Little did I know that years later he would call on me for help to get sober. The friendship developed during basic training has remained an important link between us.

Arriving in Grand-Falls late the following day took everyone by surprise. There was a quiet atmosphere surrounding this visit. Mother and Father understood my reasons for not drinking and ensured visiting friends didn't offer. Perhaps the fear of accepting offers to drink also motivated me to contact a local self-help group. A relative, who had quit drinking for a few years, picked me up for a few meetings during the visit. It was comforting to know that I wasn't alone. I invited Father to attend meetings with me but he simply felt uncomfortable.

After three weeks of enjoying a sober visit, it was time to return to Calgary. The drive back would take at least four days. So Mother decided to cook an old fashioned family dinner the night before my departure. Our whole family was there along with a few close friends. For the first time in years, I played my guitar without the use of a drink to loosen me up. It remains one of the few happy memories of life at home.

Driving back to Calgary gave me some time to think about the experience. A feeling of relief came over me now that my family knew about my sobriety. I was also anxious to get back to my friends, Lois in particular. The summer of 1977 marked a giant step in emotional growth. I suppose my experience is not unique. However, it felt as though I was the only 23 year-old going through the emotional turmoil of puberty. I began to re-evaluate the goals of my career. Sober for about six months, the reality of not fitting in the Armoured Corps slowly crept in. It was as though something needed adjustment in my life. With most of my friends still drinking, it was increasingly difficult to fit in. Perhaps it was time to change jobs. Friends suggested that I give myself at least a year of sobriety before making any serious decisions about my life.

Physical exercise became an obsession. Attitudes that had served to justify abusing alcohol were now motivating an extremist approach to my fitness program. A daily 12-mile run after work was followed by about two hours of weight training in my room. There was no time for supper, so I often ate out after meetings.

Lois and Rosalyn in Calgary 1977

For years, my physical appearance had been the basis of self-criticism. Father had left the impression that my appearance, like everything else about me, was something to be ashamed of. If you dared to feel good about yourself, Father always found a way to reduce the feeling to shame and guilt.

While I was having coffee with Lois one evening, she commented about the change in me. Looking in the mirror I still saw a skinny and unattractive kid. At 204 pounds, the weight training presented a different image to others. It was February 1978. One year had gone by since my last drink. Physically, the change appeared for the best. However, my attitudes remained abrasive and often unpredictable.

A discussion with the Base Personnel Selection Officer in early 1978 confirmed a change of trades was possible. My position at Headquarters Squadron Stores was boring and monotonous. The prospect of going on Waincon Exercise as a storesman was even more distasteful. Knowing this would be my last field exercise as an Armoured Corps Crewman, I decided to enjoy the trip. Being

BULLIES IN POWER

somewhat eccentric, I thought it seemed like a good idea to take my bed and mattress. No one would know because I was the only storesman with the Squadron, which meant I would use a tent all to myself. Of course a bed and mattress would not be complete without the accompanying pillows, sheets and blankets. When Warrant Officer Pete Hagan told me to load the vehicles in preparation for the exercise, I simply slipped in my upgraded bedding equipment. It wasn't expected to attract attention, but it did when Warrant Hagan happened to inspect my tent after about four weeks in the field.

"Jumping, diabolical sweet Jesus," he said, "do you realize even the Colonel of the Regiment doesn't have this kind of comfort?"

All I could think of saying was, "Well sir, I could have signed one out for him if I had known he wanted one."

The incident is still a topic of discussion among the more experienced crewmen, although I doubt anyone actually remembers the name of the first Crewman to take a full complement of bedding on Waincon Exercise.

A few days later, a field parade was held in order to present new corporals with their promotions. Warrant Officer Hagan had not mentioned anything about my being promoted. Consequently, when my name was called, I didn't hear it. After a kick in the rear from the Warrant Officer, my attention span was rejuvenated and I answered the call.

In presenting my corporal hooks, the Colonel smiled and said, "You belong in the Air Force. I think you'll fit much better there." I guess taking a bed on exercise must have left the impression that I valued my comfort. It was the kind of humour that I would miss in the Air Force.

Shortly after returning to Calgary in June, Mother called to let me know that Father had been drinking for a few months and he was seriously ill. Warrant Officer Hagan told me to take leave and visit. Having sold my car, I took a flight to Fredericton. Father was admitted to the hospital a few days prior to my arrival. His lifelong difficulty with alcohol became painfully obvious as he was diagnosed with cirrhosis of the liver.

He didn't recognise us and discussed events of his childhood with an imaginary listener. He spoke to himself and often didn't know we were in the room with him. Once in a while he seemed normal, but it seldom lasted for more than a few hours. My chest felt full of lead as each day he seemed to get worse.

One morning I walked into his room and found him standing on his bed acting as though he was fishing. Mother seemed discouraged. The reality of Father's return to drinking remains a mystery. Why, after almost three years of experiencing the happiness of not waking up sick and hung over, did he suddenly withdraw into a bottle? Regardless of what motivated his sudden relapse, I felt an overwhelming sadness about his condition. Our family doctor informed us that Father's condition would most likely improve. Therefore, after about a month of visiting him in the hospital, I decided to go back to Calgary. My change of trade application had been approved and training for the new occupation was scheduled to begin in late September.

Almost two weeks went by and Father's condition remained the same. Mother spoke of his strange behaviour with a sense of disbelief. The nurses found it equally difficult to deal with often unpredictable outbursts resembling a child's temper tantrums.

On the morning of September 15, 1978, the man with whom I had always disagreed passed away in his sleep. At 51 years of age, it seemed such a short life. I woke up at 4:30 that morning and knew he was gone. Without thinking, I packed my travel bag and got into my formal dress uniform. I just sat on my bed without really knowing what was going through my mind.

The silence was shattered about an hour later when the Duty Officer knocked on my door and asked me to accompany him to the Padre's office. I felt uncomfortable for the Duty Officer, who was afraid to say anything or even smile. It was a sombre mood that often accompanies bad news. The Padre invited me to sit down as he began to explain the situation. He made arrangements for my flight home later that day.

Friends and relatives gathered at the funeral home to pay their last respects to father. He looked so peaceful. Mother sat quietly by the casket when I came in. She looked tired but smiled and spoke softly.

"He's at peace now," she said.

I knew the real meaning of her words. He had never been at peace in life because of his attitudes. Things were never right and he couldn't change them. Now he wouldn't have to.

Clouds threatened rain during the funeral and I remember thinking, "Just like Father to make his last day as miserable as possible." Memories of arguments with him raced through my mind. It was as though I needed to justify feelings of anger that couldn't be explained at the time. It had only been a few days and somehow I already missed him.

Returning to Calgary, reality slowly began making inroads through my emotions. I felt like I was on an emotional roller-coaster. Alcoholism played an important role in Father's life as well as ours. I knew the cause of his death could easily be mine if I let it. Guilt for failing to prevent his relapse almost drove me to drink. I shared my feelings with Lois. She listened intently and offered moral support. A few days later, my change of career plans took me to Falconbridge, Ontario.

TRANSITION TO
THE AIR FORCE

Calgary had been home for almost five years. An emotional bond with Lois left me feeling like I was leaving home again.

An eleven-week course in Falconbridge, Ontario, served as an introduction to as well as qualification for acceptance into the Air Defence Occupation. If I was successful, a transfer to a Radar Site for on-job-experience would complete the transition. There was no way of knowing where my first transfer would take me, but I hoped to get as close to Calgary as possible. When the Course Director assured us that the top three students usually got transferred to one of their three choice locations, I intensified my studies.

Our class was comprised of students who had recently completed recruit training, as well as some of us with military experience. We were informed early in the course that the Air Force is more "refined" than the Army. Therefore, we were expected to behave like "gentlemen", whatever that meant. It would be some time before the true meaning of that message was understood.

During basic training, it was emphasized that tasks and responsibilities would be outlined by supervisors. Armoured Corps training reinforced this thought process, so that decision-making always involved one's supervisor. Not surprisingly, a sense of dependence had blended into the fabric of crewman lifestyle.

BULLIES IN POWER

To be accepted by peers and supported by supervisors, a crewman had to be willing to follow as a team member. Supervisors were only too happy to offer guidance to a subordinate. They also took the time to define a subordinate's task so that details would not lead to confusion during the execution phase.

Suddenly, the introduction of the term "gentleman" indicated that a transition to a more independent decision-making process was necessary. However, time and experience would prove the term and its meaning are nothing more than a facade with which supervisors can defend their inadequacies at a subordinate's expense. If a task is improperly outlined, or a wrong decision is made, the Air Force supervisor can simply blame the subordinate for not exercising the expected "independent" decision-making process.

As a Crewman, I knew what was expected because my supervisor had the knowledge and experience to offer detailed guidance. As an Airman, I was unprepared for the so-called "adult treatment" of the Air Force lifestyle. To be an "adult airman" meant you needed to know how to read your supervisor's mind, or at least make the right decision about what was expected. I would soon understand the meaning of "rank has its privileges", as supervisors often escaped responsibility by virtue of their rank and authority.

While the rank structure for the Air Force is similar to that of the Army, respect is not always earned in the Air Force. On the contrary, the Air Force rank structure relies on the authority of the position rather than the experience or ability that should be reflected by the rank. It was a shock to witness how some of our instructors expected discipline to flow from their rank. They lacked the maturity that comes from having to rely on team work when performing the actual task. In the Army, an instructor needs to teach by example in order to command respect. The Air Force instructor works on the principle of "every man for himself".

I hoped to achieve one of the top three positions on the course. A great deal of technical jargon and a stack of books provided an outline of various aspects of the Air Defence Occupation. The dimmed lights in the operations room, more commonly known as the Data Maintenance Control Centre (DMCC), accentuated the variety of equipment necessary to perform the tasks of this new trade.

Radar scopes of various sizes and shapes attracted our attention like the bright lights of a fairground often mesmerize children. Once the novelty of tracking aircraft with the equipment wore off, the task of committing procedural routines to memory became a priority. As customary on any military course, evaluations were common and required detailed knowledge. While most students enjoyed time in the mess, I spent time in the books and attended self-help group meetings. The extra effort at my studies paid off and I placed third on the course. It meant a posting to one of my preferred locations.

Upon graduation, in mid-December we attended a mess dinner during which our transfer messages were handed out. While my first choice had been Penhold, Alberta, I was given a position in Kamloops, British Columbia. Although it was my third choice, I would only be about a six-hour drive away from Calgary. Looking back, I can see that a twist of destiny played a role in my new assignment. With Christmas holidays on the way, I had enough time to return to Calgary and complete the necessary preparations for the move. There wasn't much to pack and I took advantage of spare time to visit friends while awaiting the scheduled flight to Kamloops on January 3, 1979.

It was early afternoon and there wasn't a cloud in the sky over Kamloops. Looking through the small window over the wing, I could see the city at the junction of the North and South Thompson Rivers. A blanket of snow covered the ground. The aircraft seemed to be getting close to the streets below, but there was no airfield in sight. Suddenly, the wheels hit the ground and the terminal building appeared in the distance. It seemed so small and deserted. The sunshine was certainly misleading as I stepped off the aircraft to feel a startling cold breeze on my face. There was a smell of sulphur in the air. I later found out the smell came from pulp mill emissions across the river.

With my duffle bag over my shoulder and a suitcase in each hand, I made my way out the double doors to a waiting taxi. The driver was friendly as he called attention to the city's points of interest on our way through the downtown area. He referred to our destination as Mount Lolo. At first I was confused because I didn't know that the radar site was located at the top of Mount Lolo. After about twenty minutes over a relatively clear road, we turned onto a snow covered back road. Curves and hills made the last part of the ride seem like a long way.

Arriving at the front gate, I was reminded by the snow banks of the long winters of my youth in New Brunswick. The commissionaire told me to report to the orderly room for instructions. Ice hung from the heating pipes over the roadway. It was the type of setting one might find on a postcard. The roadway went up the middle of the site. On the left was the gym, which also housed the Junior Ranks Mess. A few yards away the Administration building was marked by the traditional flag pole standing just outside the front door. On the right, three barrack blocks provided housing for single personnel as well as the messes for Senior Non-Commissioned Members and Officers. The dining hall was up about twenty yards from the third barrack block. Buildings were close together and snow banks on either side of connecting side walks gave the place a cosy atmosphere.

Once introduced to the administrative staff at the orderly room, I was assigned a room on the second floor of the Junior Ranks barrack block. It was pleasant to have a room to myself for a change. In the Armoured Corps we were almost always two to each room. I settled in quickly and headed for the dining hall. The sun had just gone down and the drop in temperature was noticeable. The branches of fir trees, on both sides of the dining hall entrance, were weighted down with snow. Inside, the staff smiled and there was no line up. It was also interesting to actually walk up to the steam table and have a friendly cook outline the choice of menu.

These new surroundings provided a very positive impression of life in the Air Force. After supper, I took a short look around the gymnasium and Junior Ranks Mess before going back to finish unpacking. I felt as though my head had just hit the pillow when the alarm clock jolted my senses.

While the living quarters, administration, and logistics of the station were located at the lower site, the radar itself was situated at the top of Mount Lolo about seven miles away. Because the road up the hill was dangerous, travelling between the upper and lower sites involved military transport only. Although I wasn't familiar with the schedule, the orderly room clerk had explained that everyone usually had morning coffee in the dining hall while waiting for the bus to come out of the transport compound. I got to the dining hall at 0700 and joined Gord Rude, one of the guys I had met the night before in the barracks. He described the working and living conditions while we finished breakfast.

The ride to the upper site took almost half an hour as the bus crawled up steep hills. Hard packed snow made the road somewhat slippery. Snow banks along the road grew higher as we moved up in elevation. As we approached the top, blowing snow had not only reduced visibility but snow drifts formed barriers across the road. I understood why personal vehicles couldn't be used to travel up those hills, especially during the winter.

A commissionaire signed me into the visitors' register and called the Operations Sergeant for an escort to my new work place. A few seconds later Sergeant Lou Curley introduced himself and led me to meet the staff in the Data Maintenance Control Centre (DMCC). This was the nerve centre of the site.

During the early years of Air Defence Operations, crews of about 30 personnel worked the DMCC. Technical improvements now required less than 4 personnel to perform the same functions. The crew chief of the day was Master Corporal Cecil Gibson, a thin man renowned for his sense of humour. He enjoyed harmless practical jokes and often targeted Lorrie Tate and Tom Poland since they worked on his crew. One of his most popular jokes was to sit with his feet under him and his shoes stuck on the ends of his knees. It gave the impression that his legs were really short. The shock came when he asked an unsuspecting newcomer for help getting off the chair. Working when Cecil was on duty was never boring.

Master Corporal Wally Billick was in charge of training. A tall man with John Wayne type manners, he talked with a slow drawl and walked with a slight slouch. His relaxed approach to often stressful situations was attributed to over twenty-five years of experience. He projected an atmosphere of calm that would later contribute to our successful handling of an aircraft distress call in the fall of 1980.

On-job experience would involve spending time at the various positions in DMCC. Operating the switchboard came first, as it was less complicated and allowed newcomers the opportunity to

BULLIES IN POWER

observe other staff members performing the more difficult tasks. I was anxious to learn everything I needed to know as quickly as possible in order to be assigned to a crew. Tom Poland was tasked with teaching me how to operate the switchboard. Most of the calls to the switchboard seemed to come early in the morning and during noon hour. So when it was quiet, Tom and I talked about life on station. The informal nature of the work certainly fostered a relaxed atmosphere among crew members.

Most of the single personnel living in the barracks were shift workers. Consequently, social activities involved a few off duty personnel getting together in one of the rooms or at the Junior Ranks Mess for a few drinks. Occasionally, a group of married members, living at the station's mobile home park, joined single members at the mess for an evening of activities such as darts or card games. My interest in physical fitness was partially satisfied by a universal weight training machine in the gymnasium and plenty of hills for road work. The cold weather, however, made it difficult to run and the weight training machine was in desperate need of lubricating oil.

After a few days, I sensed a need to establish contact with local self-help groups. Getting to meetings meant driving about twenty-five kilometres to town. Luckily, one of the positive features of living and working at a small radar site is the cooperative spirit that develops among co-workers. A disadvantage, however, is that one's personal life can easily become common knowledge.

Tom agreed to drive me to a meeting on my first Thursday evening at Canadian Forces Station (CFS) Kamloops. I usually felt uncomfortable riding in small cars. However, Tom's Honda Civic seemed to handle very well on the snow covered roads. Saturday afternoon we visited the Honda dealership and I decided to test drive one for myself. I was sold on the idea of buying my first small car. That evening he lent me his car to attend a meeting at the Interior Indian Friendship Centre. I later joined that group because of the friendly greeting received that night.

My new Honda Civic was ready for delivery the following week. I spent my second Saturday in town driving around the city and getting familiar with main streets. While exploring the North Shore area, I came across a sign that drew my attention. Although the Buck

Hawk Pai Gung Fu School was closed at the time, I felt compelled to call for information about enrolment.

Running and weight training simply lacked the motivational appeal that had been important in Calgary. Establishing social contacts motivated my search for a fitness club. I had been in Kamloops for less than two weeks, but I was beginning to feel at home.

I visited the Buck Hawk Pai Gung Fu School early Monday evening. As I entered the front door, I noticed a set of shelves to the left and half-closed sliding doors leading to an office on the right. Ahead was a large divider window beyond which the training area was visible. It was a large room with a set of heavy bags hanging in a row only a few feet from the left hand wall. The right side of the room was covered with large mirrors that went up from the floor almost to the ceiling. At the centre of that wall, a cupboard of sorts held what appeared to be a vase from which burnt fragrance sticks were still smouldering.

Barry Adkins, a soft-spoken and friendly man, smiled as he opened the sliding doors to greet me. After a short introduction and outline of the White Crane tradition, he offered an opportunity to try out Gung Fu for a week before deciding if it was right for me. He certainly didn't fit the stereotype of Martial Arts teachers often seen in movies.

The school's rules were based on health-oriented traditions. Consequently, fighting was strictly forbidden outside the school and closely supervised during training classes. Additionally, only students selected to belong to the fighting team could participate in full-contact training. As a beginner, my classes were scheduled at different times during the day, which would blend well with shift work. Martial Arts had always fascinated me and I was going to experience the unknown side of what looked so easy in movies.

Many of the exercises during that first class were new to me. A lack of flexibility left me feeling very awkward. But there was no criticism of my performance and teachers always corrected with positive feedback. The positive attitudes kept me going back. Tom Laroche and Alan Echino provided instruction in traditional training as well as valuable advice on meditation. As the weeks went by, I began to realize my moods were more settled. That positive side-effect of Gung Fu helped develop a confident approach to everyday activities.

My body went through agony during the first three or four months, but I attended classes every day. I gave up pumping iron and took up meditation. Learning the traditional forms of training became an obsession. At last I had found something that offered positive feedback about my performance.

The school's principles focused on positive goals in everything a student chose to do. Seven days a week I attended two to three classes per day. Barry encouraged students to expand their knowledge in other fields. He suggested involvement with other community organizations where we could develop humanitarian objectives. I soon became an assistant instructor. Self confidence had been slow in coming, but it felt good to be a role model. It also meant developing social contacts.

On-job-training also progressed very well. Much of my spare time was spent either at the Gung Fu School or attending 12-Step group meetings. Abstaining from alcohol was a necessity that called for regular attendance at meetings. Consequently, the parties in barracks or at the Junior Ranks didn't involve me. With the Armoured Corps, those who knew me preferred to see me sober at work than drunk in the Mess. Although most of the people working at the station knew I didn't drink or attend parties, very few knew the reasons why. It was best to keep it that way.

Having flown to Kamloops, I couldn't wait to drive out to Calgary through Roger's Pass. Everyone spoke about the beauty of the mountains and valleys. In late February, I took leave for a few days. While the first part of the trip to Revelstoke was enjoyable, the scenery along Roger's Pass to Banff was breathtaking. Snowy mountain peaks offered a striking contrast to the green forests along the valleys. Streams and waterfalls cascaded down mountainsides. Rivers of Eastern Canada can't compare to the bright emerald green of waterways along that 50-mile stretch of highway.

The trip to Calgary confirmed that time doesn't stand still and people change. Friends had all but forgotten me. The strange, but familiar, feeling of not belonging kept haunting me throughout the three-day visit. The six-hour drive back to Kamloops involved a number of relaxing stops along the way.

In early March, Lou Curley assigned me to "A" crew with Wally Billick and Peter Baillie-David. Shift work was new to me. I enjoyed the access to noon-hour classes at the Gung Fu School. The winter snow had disappeared by mid-March and green grass covered the hills.

It was about five miles from the lower site to the Paul Lake turn off. The road was excellent for running as curves and hills provided a challenge. Nobody said anything about the cattle that roamed around the fields along that road. I soon discovered what the guys meant by 'open range' as I came running around a bend one day and faced a very large bull. He made noises and I didn't wait around to see if he was willing to share the road. After all, who was I to argue with two thousand pounds of muscle supported by four legs and defended by rather large horns. It was a short and fast run that day. Tom Poland laughed, explaining that bulls don't often challenge runners, but they do have the right of way on the road.

Working shifts also left a great deal of time for volunteer work in the community. I became involved with the Interior Indian Friendship Centre where I first met Amy and her son Ken. A tall native woman with a warm smile and a shy nature captivated my attention. She often helped out at the centre. Ken was four years old and reminded me of a boy that our mother babysat for a few years in the mid-1960s. Ken's jovial personality and hearty laughter brought back very fond memories.

There was always something to do around the Centre. I spent time helping

Amy and Ken in 1978

out with some of the projects. Edith Desjarlais, President of the Board of Directors, asked me to fill a position as a Board Member. The experience led to involvement with other community services. Off duty hours were increasingly occupied with volunteer work.

By late summer, 1979, I had also become involved with Big Brothers. Although my first little brother moved to Vancouver shortly after our introduction, it was only a few weeks later that I was introduced to Barry. At 13 years of age this young native had experienced a difficult childhood. His friends were a negative influence at school, which resulted in Barry often getting into trouble. He wasn't a bad kid. He was a kid with confused attitudes and no specific goal to achieve. Once away from the influence of his friends, he began to show signs of maturity.

He became involved in figure skating. At first, he asked whether I felt it was a "sissy" sport. I knew how he felt because I had let the importance of impressions guide my behaviour well into my early twenties. With my own experience in mind, I let him know that his real friends would support his interest in figure skating. He went on to develop his natural talent and became a professional skater. His determination to achieve that goal has been a source of inspiration at times when I felt like giving up my own goals.

Living in barracks meant I had to drive at least fifty kilometres every time I went to town and back. It seemed more practical to find a place in town. I located a one-bedroom apartment near the Gung Fu School and only a few blocks from Amy's apartment.

Inexperienced at living on my own, I visited a friend who worked at a furniture store. An experienced bachelor, he helped select the most practical furniture. Moving out of barracks, I felt liberated from the constraints of specific meal hours and enjoyed the freedom to sleep at my convenience. Being closer to the Gung Fu School, I could attend as many as three classes each day. The dependency that had evolved during military training was being eroded by a growing sense of self-confidence as each new experience led to increased feelings of accomplishment.

The terms of my change of occupation called for completion of all training courses up to my rank level within eighteen months. This meant I would be going on course in the fall. Confirmation of attendance came in early September. The course involved five weeks at Canadian Forces Base North Bay, Ontario.

I had only been gone a few days and already I looked forward to returning to Kamloops. My friendship with Amy appeared more important while on course. I decided to write. For some reason, it was easier to express intimate feelings in letters than in person. Returning to Kamloops in early December, I asked Amy out for dinner. To my surprise she accepted. It was December 7, 1979.

We spent Christmas together that year. Poverty during my youth had made it difficult to enjoy Christmas because I knew how much our mother sacrificed to give us gifts. But I also wanted Ken to experience good feelings about Christmas. My youth was spent feeling different and now I wanted to avoid my father's negative influence. I was determined to guide Ken with positive attitudes rather than the negative criticism that had plagued my development.

Amy agreed to cook the turkey if I helped prepare it. Decorating a Christmas tree for the first time in years awakened many feelings that had been stored deep in the memories of my childhood. Ken's excitement was contagious and, for a fleeting moment, I felt like a kid again. It was the first of many occasions when Ken's light hearted and jovial approach to life chipped away at the defensive outer shell that had kept my emotions undercover.

Amy and Paul at Kamloops in 1980

Over the years, my attitude about Christmas would gradually change and I would grow to enjoy the season of gift bearing.

Amy and I began to see more of each other and soon found ourselves sharing a very close relationship. I invited them over for one of my home-cooked meals. While Ken liked the lasagne, he hated the peas. Amy encouraged him to eat them as a polite gesture. So Ken ate the peas then ran to the washroom to vomit. I felt guilty, but Amy assured me it was alright.

Ken's eating habits were quite different from mine. I often rushed my meals while Ken seemed to take forever to eat. He was sensitive and sometimes tried not to hurt my feelings about my cooking. I remember attempting to make a rice pudding for dessert one day. He didn't know how to tell me he didn't want to eat it. So he went to Amy and quietly asked her to tell me.

Ken's sensitivity also played an instrumental role in helping me change the misguided attitudes I had learned while growing up. The most memorable incident, to affect how I expressed my feelings, involved Ken asking Amy if I loved her more than him. Throughout my youth, Father never showed any feelings of love or affection towards us. Consequently, I didn't think of Ken's feelings when I hugged Amy before leaving for work. It was an awakening for me to suddenly realize that he too had feelings. He too needed to feel loved and part of our relationship. Determined to break away from family traditions, I began reading bedtime stories and taking Ken to the park. He also got his hug whenever I left for work.

Work had become relatively routine. My involvement with various community organizations was well known and encouraged. Captain John Broughton and I discussed my interest in working at an Armed Forces Alcohol Rehabilitation Centre (ARC) should the opportunity arise. He encouraged me to apply for the two-week course in Alcohol Studies at the University of Sherbrooke in early August, 1980. It was the first of a two-year program in which a number of positions were open to military personnel who could speak French. His recommendation was accepted in the selection process and I was scheduled for the course.

Dreams of attending university had faded away during high school. Being selected to attend Sherbrooke was more than luck. Luck or destiny, I was determined not to be intimidated by the advanced academic level of study expected. It was a pleasant surprise to discover that topics discussed were quite easy to understand. Classes and group discussions often went on during evening hours. The study material addressed issues closely related to my own experiences in alcohol consumption.

One might say that the seed of knowledge requires experience in order to grow. In my case, as with many others I suppose, the experience came first and the theory followed. The lectures and group discussions intensified my desire to learn about human behaviour and perhaps some day work in a related field. University studies didn't seem so difficult after all. I completed the course with an A average.

The summer was hot and dry when I returned to Kamloops. Moving up to intermediate level in Gung Fu meant more time would be spent developing skills in various aspects of the Art. The study of reflexology, deep muscle massage and being a part of the fighting team provided the necessary background to become an instructor. A demonstration team was formed to help promote the Art and the school. I jumped at the chance to participate.

Amy was a volunteer with the Crisis Centre. She suggested I get involved as a crisis line worker. At first I was nervous about the possibility of becoming involved with a serious case and not handling it correctly. The staff emphasized that most of the callers were in need of someone to talk to and very few actually felt suicidal. It soon became second nature to sit at the phone and listen to callers who needed to know that someone cared.

Christmas was fast approaching and we planned a turkey dinner once again. This time we invited friends to join us. Lloyd and Bertha made an odd couple who lived in a small apartment on a very limited income. He was a retired camp cook and she was a quiet native woman who suffered from grand mal seizures which prevented her from working. While Lloyd was in his mid-fifties, a lifestyle of hard work and heavy drinking had aged him well beyond his years. He stood about five feet two inches tall and weighed less than 120 pounds. Bertha, on the other hand, was a strongly built woman in her late thirties who stood about five inches taller than Lloyd and outweighed him by at least 30 pounds.

Bertha's condition called for daily medication and almost constant care. Lloyd's deteriorating health often caused him to spend time in the hospital. During his absence, Bertha would stay at the

BULLIES IN POWER

Women's Transition House where staff could ensure she didn't miss her medication or get injured during seizures. Lloyd wasn't able to eat much, but he could cook almost anything and make it taste delicious. His specialty was butter tarts, which were always freshly baked whenever we visited. Sharing Christmas dinner with Lloyd and Bertha made the holiday very special. Unknown to us at the time, Lloyd suffered from stomach cancer which would cause the removal of more than half his stomach in the fall of 1981.

After greeting 1981 at a New Year's Eve dance, the year held promise of career advancement as I was selected for a Junior Leadership Course at Penhold, Alberta, in February. The course involved five weeks of back-to-basic type training in which the focus on dress and deportment provided opportunity to assess one's willingness to take criticism. Leadership skills were tested through various task assignment exercises. With Armoured Corps experience, most of the practical field tasks were easy to execute. However, the theoretical tasks involving administrative duties presented a challenge. Overall, I was assessed above average in leadership potential.

As summer approached, Captain John Broughton informed me that he had submitted my name for the advanced course in Alcohol Studies at Sherbrooke in July. The advantage of having completed the first year provided support for acceptance on the advanced course. There were more students in attendance, as first and second year students would work together in learning the complicated nature of alcohol dependencies.

Once again I learned new information about the influential factors that might have motivated my own abuse of alcohol. The disease model of alcoholism was studied in depth. Years of feeling abnormal were now attributed to a disease, acknowledged by the medical profession, not a mere lack of self-discipline. I came away from the course with a whole new outlook on alcoholism.

Ken's baptism was scheduled to take place in Lytton at the end of August. It was also an opportunity to visit some of Amy's relatives whom I had yet to meet. Amy's aunt Lil lived next to the church and saw us arrive. As was customary, I wore a three-piece suit for church events. Amy wanted to introduce me to Aunt Lil before the service.

When she introduced me, Lil started laughing and said she thought I was the priest. I'd been mistaken for a number of things, but never a priest. We had tea with her and went on to meet other relatives after the service.

On our way back to Kamloops, we stopped at Spences Bridge to visit Amy's father. She told me that her dad was a good judge of character and if he didn't like me he would simply walk into his room and ignore me. I felt very apprehensive at meeting this man. What if he didn't like me? It was his sixty-fifth birthday and I hadn't even brought a gift to soften him up. As we crossed the bridge, a man was walking along the road on crutches. Amy recognized him and we picked him up.

At his house he sat and looked me in the eye and said, "I'm sixty-five years young today." The ice was broken! He had spoken to me! His grey hair was more a sign of wisdom than age, as the sparkle in his eyes left no doubt about his enjoyment of life. I also met Amy's stepmother, Florabelle.

Bad feelings between Amy and Florabelle were made worse later in the fall, when Frank suffered a stroke and Florabelle left him without help for two days. Frank was taken to the hospital, but poor recovery led to his being admitted to an extended care facility. Having met a number of Amy's relatives, I felt more secure with our relationship. Since marriage would have threatened Amy's native status, as well as Ken's, we agreed to maintain our relationship on the basis of mutual commitment.

The completion of addiction studies had generated an interest in pursuing a commission in the Personnel Selection field. However, because of poor marks in high school, it was suggested that I try completing a few more university courses in order to confirm my abilities. Attempts at gaining access to university courses at the local college called attention to the Open Learning Institute (OLI), a university correspondence network in its formative stage.

I first met Iris Rich-McQuay at the OLI office in early September. Her supportive approach led to my enrolment in three first-year courses toward a four-year Degree Program in Psychology and Sociology. While she had suggested starting with one course, I wanted to prove my abilities. Balancing an already tight schedule of shift work, Gung Fu, volunteer work, and university studies proved very difficult at first.

The results of my first assignments were disappointing, but Iris pointed out that English was my second language and I had no experience in writing essays. Amy suggested I drop some of my volunteer work. It was difficult to accept, but she was right. After many sleepless nights and running late on assignments, I decided to devote less time to volunteer work and more time in studies. Gung Fu remained an important method of relieving stress.

In October, 1981, I was awarded my red sash in Gung Fu after successfully completing the evaluation process. This achievement marked an important milestone in my training and reinforced feelings of self-confidence. I wrote my first university exams in December and registered for four additional courses to begin in January, 1982. It was no longer a question of 'if' I could achieve a university degree, but rather a matter of 'when'.

Tom Laroche, Paul (middle) and Barry Adkins 1981

Christmas was only a few days away when Lloyd returned home from the hospital. While the surgery had gone reasonably well, he found it difficult to walk and couldn't eat solid food. Nevertheless, he and Bertha joined us for Christmas. We spent more time together during the holiday because Lloyd felt incapable of taking complete care of Bertha. She had become close to Amy and even called on occasion. This was unusual for Bertha as she had always been too shy to call. It was as though something was motivating her to become more independent after Lloyd's surgery. They would later accompany us to welcome 1982 at a New Year's Eve gathering. Sadly, it would be our last holiday with Lloyd and Bertha. Lloyd would succumb to cancer in early September

Amy at Christmas in 1981

of that year. Bertha would move back to Edmonton to live with family.

In mid-February, rumours of postings were floating around at work. Reality struck later that month when I received word that I was to be transferred to CFS Mont Apica, Quebec, in July. However, a few weeks later a change of heart at the Career Manager's office saw my transfer changed to CFB North Bay, Ontario.

While North Bay appeared to be an improvement over Mont Apica, the transfer could not have come at a worse time. With university courses well under way, I had hoped to remain at CFS Kamloops for another year in order to allow the completion of my first year of university. Hopes of gaining employment as a counsellor at an Armed Forces Alcohol Rehabilitation Centre had led me to apply for assessment. Having received confirmation of selection only a few weeks prior to my transfer message, the opportunity slipped out of reach with news of the transfer to North Bay.

Amy and Ken were apprehensive about moving across the country. Financially, the cost of living in North Bay would be higher than in Kamloops. After discussing the matter with Amy and Ken, it was agreed we would move and make the best of it. The promise of a dog had convinced Ken.

I wrote three exams in April and managed to achieve two A's and one B. Assignment delays in biology made it necessary to schedule the exam for the June session, only a day or so before departing. Travelling to North Bay would take about five days. To make the trip more comfortable, it seemed like a good idea to trade the small Honda for a larger car. Amy had already sold her car to her brother, so we visited a friend at the local Ford dealership. He showed us a used Pontiac Ventura that had recently been traded in. With assurances that the car was in good order and had only one previous owner, the deal was struck. One important lesson was learned from that experience: never trust a used car salesman, even if he's your friend. Although the car was green and white, a more appropriate colour might have been lemon yellow. We would later discover the true condition of the car during an attempt to register it in Ontario.

In preparation for relocation, a request for a Personnel Married Quarters (PMQs) was sent to North Bay. Our common-law relationship did not appear to cause serious concern at the time. We were placed on the waiting list for a PMQ. Shortage of PMQs made it necessary to search for civilian accommodations. So I went on a House Hunting Trip in early June. Although there were plenty of houses for sale, rental accommodation was very limited. Ed Richards had advertised his semi-detached house under rent-with-option-to-buy. Time was limited and, after visiting his home, I agreed to rent for the time being. Ed made it quite clear that a dog would not be permitted. This would be a disappointing turn of events for Ken, as he had been saving bones for the dog we were going to have. I didn't have the heart to tell him when I returned to Kamloops.

There was only three weeks to prepare for the movers picking up our furniture. Amy was visibly depressed about having to leave her home province. She had always lived in British Columbia. It's difficult to explain the empty feeling that precedes a move, particularly if it's a first. We went around and bid farewell to our friends with the promise that we'd return in a few years.

I wrote my exam in biology a few days before leaving and spent some time with Iris, preparing a plan of courses which would satisfy the requirements of my degree. Costs were a serious concern, as the increased cost of rent would create a shortage of money. So I used one of my savings bonds to cover the September courses.

We packed the car while the movers were picking up our furniture. It was our first experience of moving as a family. Military authorities did not recognize Amy and Ken as legitimate dependents. Therefore, we would move on allowances for a single person. Meal allowances for a single person were limited to about $25 per day. Lodging was also limited to about $35 per night. As meals at most roadside restaurants would average about $7 per person, costs would certainly exceed allowances. Determined to make the best of the situation, we set out for North Bay in our used Pontiac on June 25, 1982.

Amy and Paul at going away party in 1982

Hopes for career advancement had convinced me that North Bay held new opportunities. Dreams would turn into nightmares, as administrative staff would seek every opportunity to enforce a strong opposition to our common-law relationship. Our move to North Bay marked the beginning of a very sombre period in our lives that would challenge the bonds of our relationship.

Our relationship is marked by a unique blend of circumstances which need to be described to fully understand the reasons for the decisions that followed our move to North Bay, Ontario. Amy's background remains a very private and closely guarded topic of discussion. Whatever happened during her youth is difficult to define. One can argue that her limited memories may be the result of traumatic stress. To place events into perspective, the following chapter briefly describes the similarities between residential school discipline and military directives. It's also important to note that my protective nature and deep seated hatred of injustice played an important role in challenging military authorities who sought to prey on Amy's passive nature.

AMY: THE RESIDENTIAL SCHOOL EXPERIENCE

Amy's experience in residential school has had a profound impact on how she responds to conflict. Many, like Amy, have lived through the pain but have never been able to share it. Others stand by and witness how government control reflects racial undertones. Those who challenge active injustice are often labelled "radicals".

During military basic training, important lessons are learned through the use of negative examples. If one individual makes a mistake, everyone witnesses the effects. If one member of the squad acts improperly, all members suffer the consequence. Residential school authorities adopted a military approach in which mass punishment provided the means of control. Through the use of peer pressure, individual identity is eroded until individual goals become impossible to accomplish. By punishing the group as a whole, staff and supervisors are able to turn students against each other.

However, unlike military members, native students were not asked if they wanted to volunteer for residential school. They were compelled by law to attend or parents faced legal consequences from government agencies. I was not obligated to join the military and I could also choose to leave anytime by signing a release. At times, we face a choice to stand or run. In 1982, when faced with such a choice, I decided to stand firm and refused to sign a release and run.

The military's non-recognition of "our" common-law relationship required challenge because it was based on the racial bigotry of an outdated conservative era.

The remainder of this chapter explains in Amy's own words the gripping personal description of her initiation to her residential school experience as seen through the eyes, and felt in the heart, of a terrified six year old little girl.

A Personal Experience

I was born in Merritt, British Columbia, and lived on the Shulus Indian Reserve until age six. It was my mother's reserve but she had refused to live on my father's reserve at Spences Bridge.

When I was six years of age, my parents informed me that I'd be going to school with my brother and wouldn't be home for a long time. The day I was to go to Residential School, I remember it was very hot and mother was heating water on the wood-burning stove. She went to great lengths to wash my hair and bathe me in the small round metal tub. She then dried my hair and took great care to braid it. My mom wanted me to be clean, neat and look nice for my first day at Residential School.

When I arrived, I was immediately separated from my brother. He went to the boys' side of the school and I was taken to the girls' side. We were not allowed contact. I felt alone and scared. I was met by a supervisor who led me to a small room in the basement. The supervisor grabbed my back braid and, without so much as taking the time to undo it, she snipped it just below my ear lobe. The front braids were cut in the same manner just above the eyebrow to allow front bangs. I stood there crying silent tears. I felt angry and so very sad. It was a terrifying experience. I recall gritting my teeth to hold back my feelings. This was just the beginning.

The next step of the enrolment involved delicing. It didn't matter if you had lice or not, everyone was made to feel dirty. Before being allowed to take a bath, I was made to first strip wash while in underwear. I was given a bar of lye soap and a floor scrub brush. When the supervisor thought a student didn't scrub herself hard enough, the supervisor would do it. As I look back, it's very obvious the school was administered by military discipline and fanatical religious morality.

Each student was assigned a number. I can still remember the number I was assigned. My identity became number 603. All personal items from underwear to toothbrushes held a personal number. There were many rules and regulations to remember. Perhaps the most important rule was being prohibited from speaking one's mother tongue. I soon learned about that rule. I was deprived of food and only a promise not to speak my native language would allow me to eat.

There were other forms of punishment such as, having one's mouth washed out with soap, beatings with a yardstick or thick strap. The most popular punishment seemed to be being deprived of food.

Every day the routine involved the Big Bell ringing throughout the school at 6 am. Supervisors would come to the dorm to ensure we got up and knelt by our beds to repeat the Lord's Prayer and daily prayer. Then we had to make our beds in strict adherence to the school standard. Corners had to be perfect, bedspread pulled snugly and the pillow set straight without wrinkles or else the bedding would be stripped off and the process of redoing the bed went on. Once the beds passed inspection, we carried on to wash up, brush our teeth and return toothbrushes and towels to the numbered hooks.

Students were divided into three categories: juniors, intermediate, and seniors. As a junior, I had no chores. So we'd wait in the basement until the Big Bell rang. The Big Bell rang to indicate it was time to prepare for breakfast. We lined up in alphabetical order in our respective categories. One supervisor would say grace before and after every meal. After saying grace in the basement, the small bell (hand-held cow bell) would signal us to move to the dining room. There was only half an hour to eat breakfast and finish with grace again. Being thankful was as necessary as obedience to all other rules.

After breakfast, we lined up and left the dining room with juniors in the lead up the stairs and down the hallway to the auditorium where hymn books and prayer books were distributed. We started with a hymn, prayers, lecture, closing prayer, and ended with a hymn, all the while kneeling on the hardwood floor.

The seniors went to public school, so they had to change or wear the school assigned clothes. Students from Grade Eight and up were bussed to public school. Later, Grades Six and Seven would be bussed to elementary school. The intermediate students were old enough to be assigned specific chores such as washing bathrooms, floors, stairways, hallways and kitchen duties. All chores had to be completed before the start of classes.

I failed Grade One. The few memories I have of that first year are of punishment. I remember being beaten for not knowing how to speak, read or write English. For not knowing, I remember being one of the many kids who was put in the corner and made to wear a dunce cap. Wearing the dunce cap meant you were dumb and stupid. It seems this punishment convinced me that I was dumb and stupid.

During my second year, I observed that others like me were punished for not knowing the language. I felt guilty and helpless. I felt their humiliation, as though it was mine all over again. I remember standing by one student who was being beaten with a leather strap and later with a yardstick. I felt shame for being different...for being native. Pain, guilt, humiliation and powerlessness were everywhere, as the only language I knew was beaten out of me. By the time I reached Grade Two, I had lost faith in myself. The experience in Grade One led me to believe I was dumb and stupid. It's a belief that I have carried with me ever since.

Every Saturday afternoon all students had to polish their shoes in preparation for Sunday services. Church services took place in the morning and sometimes in the evening as well. There was also Sunday school to prepare for Confirmation.

While we were in church, supervisors kept an eye out for anyone falling asleep, not paying attention or whispering. If one person was caught, everyone from that dormitory was subject to mass punishment. There would be a line-up in alphabetical order and each would have a turn at getting beaten with the strap or yardstick. Attending church during my youth had such a negative impact that

I find it difficult to hold any faith. Today, I don't attend church as reminders of punishment plague my memories.

By far, the Residential School System's most negative impact has been its effect on family relationships and cultural ties. Those who were unwilling to attend were plucked from their families by the Indian Agent or the parish priest. I remember my brother running away from home the day we were to go to Residential School. Family members caught up to him a few miles away. He screamed and cried, begged and pleaded not to be sent away. At that time it was the parish priest who drove us to the Residential School. My brother sobbed all the way to school. Again, I wept silent tears and felt hurt, anger and a sense of helplessness. Upon arrival we were separated and we weren't allowed to speak to one another. In the school yard we were separated by two mesh fences. Between the two fences there was an open furnace and two buildings: a cannery and a storage area. We used to sneak behind the cannery to exchange a few words and notes. He would always encourage me to be good. There were times we'd use mirrors to get each other's attention across the yards. At meal times we'd exchange smiles and inconspicuous waves in the dining room.

Our mother passed away when I was 13. It meant my sisters Florine and Carol had to attend the Residential School. My mother's death left me feeling responsible for looking after my sisters. Florine and I were in the same dorm. Her long hair had beautiful shades of brown. It was shiny and healthy. I helped her comb her hair in hope it wouldn't get cut. But I knew the day would come when supervisors would want her hair cut.

I spoke to the supervisors about allowing me to cut it, as I felt she wouldn't be as hurt if I did it. One day, despite assurances, a supervisor cornered Florine and cut her hair. She screamed and fought against getting her hair cut. Florine explained, "From that day on, I detested authorities."

Abuse was commonplace, a daily routine. I remember one Sunday morning, shortly after my sister Florine had arrived at school, she and a friend fell asleep side by side on a top bunk in the dorm. They slept through church service and when the supervisor found out she went into a fit of rage. That supervisor reminded me of a raging bull. She stormed into the dorm, grabbed the sleeping girl by the arm and yanked her off the bunk. It's a miracle the incident didn't result in broken bones. Then she reached for my sister. By this time Florine had grabbed hold of the bunk's metal rail and was holding on for dear life. The more she held on, the more furious the supervisor became. Both girls were punished with extra duties. As time went on, my sister hated being there. She found it very difficult to accept the rules.

When I was transferred to the seniors' dorm, I seldom saw my sister. I spoke to her on the phone a little while ago. Discussing memories of the Residential School, she explained that supervisors used to get the whole dorm to punish her. Beatings involved being kicked, poked with rat tail combs, or beaten with thongs.

Florine ran away a lot. The school principal and staff took me with them to find her. I'd have to convince her to come back. I felt guilty, but where could she go? Our mother's house had burned down and we had no home to go to. Our father worked up north and there was nowhere to run. Life was getting difficult for my sister. At one point she even attempted to commit suicide by taking a large dose of pills but was sent to the hospital in time to save her life. This was quite common for students who found it difficult to cope with life at the school.

Amy and her Dad, Frank Walkem in 1965

She and a friend got together and burned the back of each other's hand with a cigarette butt to mark their swearing to be blood sisters. They became partners in disobedience.

When I was in Grade Ten, Dad finally had a house built on his reserve and we were informed we could no longer attend Residential School. This new kind of freedom had its drawbacks. It was difficult to become motivated to do homework without the threat of punishment.

The Residential School System institutionalized native children and created a generations of victims in a state of learned helplessness. We were taught to be silent because only authorities knew what was best for us. The boys suffered sexual abuse at the hands of "the farmer" who used to get free labour from the school. It's the silent crime that left a generation of boys in a state of anger at the double standards of non-native society. Memories of Residential School years seem to be marked by a common bond among native students: is the dependence that accompanies an institutionalized lifestyle. Whether it is expressed in passive silence by girls or angry outbursts by boys, it remains the Residential School heritage. I conclude with a statement reflecting the feelings of many. *Forced to give up our language, family ties, cultural identity, and made to feel shame about our traditional heritage; all that is left is the pain that lives in an emptiness that remains impossible to describe.*

Amy and some of her siblings
BRow Nieces Maureen, Bobbie and Michelle
MRow Sister Grace, Brothers Charles and Billy, Florine and Carole
FRow Nephew James, Amy and Ken

CONSPIRACY AMONG HYPOCRITES

The first day of our trip took us to Calgary. Frequent stops along the highway through Rogers Pass allowed time to gaze at mountain streams and snow-capped peaks before reaching the flat prairie countryside. We would miss the picturesque scenery of British Columbia. Amy and Ken didn't say very much, but the sadness of leaving friends and relatives was visibly disturbing, as they looked back at the increasingly distant mountains. It's a good thing people can't see into the future. I think if Amy had known about the hardships that lay ahead, she might have refused to move to North Bay.

Mountains en route to Alberta in 1982

BULLIES IN POWER

Arriving in Calgary around mid-afternoon, we checked into a motel and decided to visit a few friends. Ben Schultz, Lois' father, greeted us with a friendly hug. Over three years had gone by since my last visit. Ben explained that Lois and Rick had been transferred to Ontario. Lois' mother, Isabel, went along to help them settle in. Although I knew that Lois and Rick had been married for over two years, it was surprising to find out that their move was taking place at the same time as ours. They had left earlier that day. At our room that evening, we watched the sun going down behind the now faraway mountains. A bright red skyline marked the end of the day, and memories of life in Kamloops would soon take their place in yesterday.

We woke up early the next morning and decided to visit the Calgary Zoo before setting out toward our eastern destination. Ken was excited. We spent most of the morning looking at all kinds of animals from goats to lions. The afternoon drive to Medicine Hat was hot and boring. To make matters worse, the air-conditioning in the car stopped working after a few miles. So much for assurances that the car was in excellent condition. With no money or time to get it fixed, we drove with open windows. It felt like we were going through an oven with the heat on. After an early supper in Medicine Hat, we ventured to Moose Jaw where the night air cooled us off. It had been a long day.

An early start on our third day took us to Brandon, Manitoba by mid-afternoon. Two days of driving on the flat prairie highway, during a heat wave, made the trip seem endless. Ken began to wonder if we'd ever get to North Bay. To escape the heat, we decided to stop at Winnipeg and enjoy an air-conditioned room. It was a small motel located along the Trans-Canada highway. The room had two squeaky beds, a television, and an air-conditioner that ran like a lawn mower. But, the price was right for our limited budget.

The following day we finally crossed into Ontario. An early morning rain offered cool relief from the prairie heat. Hills and green forest were a welcomed sight, after almost three days of travelling along relatively flat prairies, where trees are a novelty. As we approached a roadside restaurant, Amy thought it might be a good idea to stop for coffee. As we pulled into the parking lot I noticed a

79

familiar car and tent trailer. The Alberta licence plate confirmed that this was Rick's car. Walking in, I saw Lois talking to her daughter Rosalyn, while Rick was in heavy discussion with Isabel. Although the meeting was brief, we agreed to spend the evening at the Holiday Inn in Kenora.

Ken and Rosalyn soon discovered the indoor pool and wasted no time getting ready to enjoy a swim. Amy, Lois and I accompanied them to the pool while Isabel and Rick took time out to relax. Meeting friends seemed to brighten up the trip. The next day, they went south and we continued east towards Thunder Bay.

After five days on the road we finally arrived in North Bay, Ontario. It was hot and humid. Our furniture had already been placed in storage. Those moving van drivers must have stayed on the road day and night. It was too late to get moved in, so we checked in at the Ascot Motel in downtown North Bay.

There was a fishy smell in the air that would later be explained as shadfly season. For about two weeks in early summer, the downtown area is clouded by swarms of shadflies. These large winged bugs look like giant mosquitoes. They're harmless bugs that litter the streets as they swarm city lights at night, only to fall to the streets by morning. Most people are accustomed to the smell and sounds of these insects being crushed by vehicles and pedestrians on the downtown streets. But we hadn't seen anything like it.

Breakfast was a distasteful experience for Ken as he complained about the smell when we walked out of the small cafe. Approaching the car, he couldn't hold his breakfast down. Luckily, the shadflies are confined to the downtown area, close to the lakefront. Ken's difficulty with the smell soon disappeared as we drove out to meet our landlord at the house.

Our new home, a semi-detached three-bedroom house on McKenzie Avenue, was within walking distance of my new place of duty in the Canadian NORAD (North American Air Defence) underground complex. James and Madeleine Lucas owned the other half of this semi-detached house. He was a recently retired Major from the Personnel Selection Branch. We became friends almost immediately, as we shared common interests in psychology and chess. The neighbourhood also housed a number of military families in rented housing units a few streets away.

Ed Richards, our landlord, was busy finishing up a bit of painting in the kitchen when we walked in. He gave Amy a tour of the house while I called the base for instructions on reporting to work. Reporting procedures involve visiting the various units on base in order to ensure new personnel are familiar with available services. As delivery of our furniture would be delayed for a few days, Amy and Ken returned to the motel and I went on to begin reporting routines. At the Base Orderly Room, I was informed that only one night of motel costs would be covered on my moving claim since Amy and Ken were not considered dependents. So we took the opportunity to visit Grand Falls, New Brunswick, over the weekend. The visit would introduce Amy and Ken to my family for the first time. Returning to our empty house in North Bay, we made use of the sleeping bag and pillows we had brought with us on the trip. It was uncomfortable, but the movers were expected to deliver our furniture early the following day.

Ken and Paul at the Falls in Grand Falls New Brunswick 1982

This first experience of moving as a family left us somewhat disorganized with furniture and boxes everywhere. Suddenly, Phil Mcgrath and his wife Cathy arrived at the door with a pleasant surprise. I had known Phil for a few short weeks in 1978 and 1979. News of our arrival gave them the idea of welcoming us with a spaghetti supper. This unexpected expression of friendship remains one of the most memorable experiences of life in North Bay.

Among the many places I was to visit during the reporting routines was the Roman Catholic Padre's office. It was one of the last places left on the list and I had delayed it for about a week due to my new work schedule. As I walked in the office, Major J.T. Dabrowski greeted me with a handshake and invited me to sit. He was a heavy set man in his mid-forties. He spoke with a heavy accent which I later discovered was Polish. I wasn't prepared for what followed.

My personal life became the focus of his interest. He asked why I had not chosen to live in barracks. I explained that my relationship with Amy and Ken represented a family situation. The tone of his voice became sombre as he began to express a strong disapproval of our common-law relationship. In particular, he was concerned with the fact that Amy and Ken were of Native origin. This, he pointed out, was simply unacceptable and a serious mistake on my part. His solution to the whole situation appeared simple enough to him.

"Why don't you leave your Indian wife, send her and her son back to British Columbia, and move into the barracks. A nice Catholic boy like you can find himself a nice Catholic girl, someone of your own kind."

I don't know what feeling came over me first, shock or anger. During my attempt to explain the nature of our situation, he interrupted with the comment that "Indians and whites don't mix".

He went on, "I can't even marry you, because it will never work."

Hopes of establishing positive relations with this padre were off on the wrong foot. After listening to his definition of family life, I decided to diplomatically terminate the discussion. I had never encountered such bigotry. For a Catholic priest, he certainly lacked the compassion necessary to address modern social conditions. Although he spoke like a priest, he would use his rank of Major to bring pressures on our family situation.

The transfer to North Bay brought more than a change of climate and geography. While common-law relationships had never been formally criticized, ours met strong disapproval. Amy and Ken did not wish to give up their rights. Under section 12(1)(b) of the Indian Act, a marriage to Amy meant she and Ken would have lost rights that most non-native people take for granted. According to Kathleen

Jamieson (1978), a native woman who married a non-native man suffered serious discriminatory consequences.

"She may not own property on the reserve and must dispose of any property she does hold. She may be prevented from inheriting property left to her by her parents. She cannot take any further part in band business. Her children are not recognized as Indian and are therefore denied access to cultural and social amenities of the Indian community. And, most punitive of all, she may be prevented from returning to live with her family on the reserve, even if she is in dire need, very ill, a widow, divorced or separated. Finally, her body may not be buried on the reserve with those of her forebears."(Jamieson, 1978)

It's difficult to imagine anyone having to give up so much simply to fit the military's definition of a "dependent". Such conditions of marriage have never been applied to non-native people. Living common-law was fine with me and I wasn't about to change our lives to meet unrealistic expectations of bureaucratic channels.

I want to clarify a very important fact to those holding the misguided belief that Native Peoples in Canada have more rights that anyone else. Examine *Section 67* of the *Canadian Human Rights Act* which clearly states: *"Nothing in this Act affects any provision of the Indian Act or any provision made under or pursuant to that Act."* It's not by accident that the *Canadian Human Right Act* does not apply to Status Indians in Canada. It means Status Indians are **NOT** protected by Human Rights legislation in Canada. So before you argue that Indians have too many rights, look at the facts.

The Assembly of First Nations and the Government of Canada have been unwilling to allow Status Indians to lodge complaints about ongoing discriminatory practices taking place under the *Indian Act*. The reasons are obvious. The *Indian Act* has no provisions for human rights. If Status Indians are allowed to complain, it would compel the Assembly of First Nations Chiefs to become accountable and responsible for their actions. It would also mean that the Government of Canada could be made to answer for their discriminatory practices. It would mean government authorities, chiefs, and band administrators would have to treat everyone with equality on and off reserves. The fact of the matter was that neither

Amy nor I could file a Human Rights Complaint against the Padre for his comments. If he had voiced the same comments about any other minority or culture, a complaint could have been processed as a human rights violation.

It became obvious that Major Dabrowski chose to exercise the authority of his rank in order to impose his personal convictions. Initially, the incident did not arouse concern. However, his influence would soon generate negative perceptions of our relationship, resulting in imposed administrative ostracism.

The housing officer, retired Major R.J. 'Rolly' Orieux, called a few days later to accuse me of misleading him when I had applied for married quarters. Although our common-law relationship had been clearly indicated on the application and our name had been placed on the waiting list, he argued that I should not have been allowed to apply for married quarters.

Services normally available to families were suddenly denied under the cloak of military non-recognition of common-law relationships. I later discovered that our application for family coverage under the Ontario Health Insurance Plan (OHIP) was also denied by administrative staff. It's difficult to assume what went on behind closed doors between administrative staff and the Roman Catholic padre. However, reflection on those incidents indicates a pattern of events was unfolding which involved the informal channels of the "old boys' network". Clearly, the issue of Amy's native status had attracted attention. Although one would be hard pressed to prove its existence, the results of this informal network are most visible.

While the base administration took a negative interest in our situation, supervisors were more supportive of my efforts with university studies. During air surveillance training, Scotty Nicholson encouraged me to apply for University Training Plan. The idea of becoming an officer had been appealing for years. Perhaps now, with the apparent support of superiors, I could gain access to the yearly competition for a position in the field of personnel selection or social work. Major Denis Kelleher, the Flight Commander, pointed out that if I didn't get selected the first time around it would only be a matter of time before my performance gained recognition.

Amy could not find work, which meant our budget required careful planning. After two weeks in North Bay, time limits for car registration and insurance were closing in. In early August, we decided to use the balance in our bank account to get the car registered. It was then that we discovered the real nature of our "excellent" car. The salesman had sold us more than a used car. The serial number proved to have come from a wrecked vehicle in British Columbia. We had driven an uninsured car that actually belonged to someone else. It could not be registered and the resulting police investigation confirmed the rip-off. To make matters worse, the Ford dealership refused to accept any responsibility for the assurances of its salesman.

In sum, we paid over four thousand dollars for a four-hundred-dollar car. Attempts to get some of our money back failed and the dealership demanded immediate payment of the balance in full. Not wanting to create friction with military authorities, we thought it best to pay them and deal with the matter in court. The court later decided in favour of the dealership. This was a learning experience about the dangers of trusting a used car salesman.

Getting a dog soon became a topic of discussion as Ken recalled my promise. Ed lived in the basement suite of the house and explained his concern with the damages that a dog can do in the yard, not to mention the carpets. After some discussion, Ed agreed to allow a cat on the condition that damages to carpets would be our responsibility. It wasn't a dog, but Ken felt happy to have a pet. We answered an ad in the newspaper which sought to give four-month old kittens away to a good home. The female kitten was named Bear because she had a habit of going up on her hind legs to look out

Ken holding Bear in 1982

the window. She also growled when she wanted food. As the male wouldn't allow us near him, we chose to take Bear home. We had to put her in a cardboard box to take her with us. She was most uncooperative about staying in the car and Ken fought to keep her in the box on our way home. She soon adjusted to the house and the litter.

Bear was also approaching that stage in life when female cats express a natural instinct to mate. We agreed to keep her in the house so that she wouldn't get romantically involved with the neighbourhood males. That didn't prevent her from calling out in the middle of the night. After a few sleepless nights listening to her, we decided it might be best to invest in a surgical solution at the local veterinary clinic. Ken felt sorry for her at first, but a few days later she was back to her playful self. She remained Ken's loyal companion.

Almost three months had elapsed and our efforts at gaining access to the Ontario Health Insurance Plan continued to fall on deaf ears at the Base Administration Office. Costs for visits to the doctor were no longer affordable. Amy had been ill for over a month and required medical attention. I decided to contact the doctor myself. He was furious that the military's refusal to recognize our common-law relationship could affect the provision of provincial health insurance. His contact with OHIP head office in Kingston soon led to an early morning call from the Base Orderly Room.

I had just arrived home from a difficult night shift when the phone rang. I no sooner answered when the voice on the other end ordered, "Get up to the orderly room now!" Trying to explain that I had just come off shift, I was bluntly interrupted, "I don't care about your shifts. Get up here now and move it!" I couldn't imagine what it was about, but his tone left the impression that he was upset with me.

When I walked in the orderly room, Sergeant Guy Cote approached the counter and slapped application forms for family OHIP coverage in front of me.

"Sign these", he stated. He went on, "Fucking Indians get everything around here".

BULLIES IN POWER

At first I was a little confused about the comment and didn't realize he was talking to me. However, when he blurted something about people who don't live like everyone else, I knew he was addressing our situation. His statement, "Indian rights my ass," took me over the edge. I felt the blood rush to my head as a flash of anger temporarily clouded my judgement.

"What's your problem?", I blurted. "That's my family you're talking about, so clean up your act or you'll get a smack in the mouth."

At that point, the Chief Clerk got involved and reprimanded me for addressing a sergeant in such an insubordinate manner. It didn't seem to matter that the situation had been provoked. From basic training, I remembered the emphasis that rank has its privileges. It was clear from that encounter that privilege meant rank served to redefine what was right and wrong.

The issue of native rights had somehow struck a sensitive nerve with the base administration. To have a military member defend the rights of a native person was perceived as disloyal. Amy had already suffered the abuse of government agencies. At Residential School, her language and traditions had been forbidden as the use of corporal punishment and imposed starvation enforced government policies. Native rights have traditionally been defined by government regulations. I was expected to support the directives of bureaucrats who knew very little about the effects of the regulations they were trying to impose and cared even less about the people involved. Denial of housing and medical services was intended to create stress and threaten our relationship. It was generating seething anger.

The limit of one income stretched beyond the breaking point, as monthly bills forced an increased use of our credit card. To make matters worse, OHIP premiums were retroactively applied against my end-month pay in November. We would later realize that our premiums included the employer's share of the costs. It might have been easier to adjust had accounts personnel provided notice of the sudden pay adjustment. Our rent had to be paid through the use of a credit card advance. It was the beginning of a deteriorating financial condition.

Amy became depressed and withdrawn. Her father had suffered a stroke and was confined to an extended care service in Kamloops. She was able to visit him regularly while we were in Kamloops. However, our move left her feeling isolated and alone. Our social activities were limited by financial constraints. Two savings bonds provided assurance that Amy could return to Kamloops in the event her father's condition became life threatening.

In late November, 1982, I submitted my first application for University Training Plan for Men (UTPM). Major Kelleher enthusiastically offered support. Having devoted a great deal of effort to this career goal, it appeared positive. Work in the NORAD complex had become routine. With the new computer system being installed, many new positions were created in the process of modernizing Air Defence Operations over Canadian airspace.

I was selected to work as a Data Quality Monitor (DQM) with the new Regional Operations Control Centre (ROCC). The change of position also meant that I would be under the direction of Lieutenant Colonel R. Greaves of the Electronics Engineering Branch. There were only four Air Defence Technicians working in this predominantly Radar Technician environment. Consequently, we felt a little out of place. The supervisors and upper staff seemed to favour Radar Technicians over Air Defence Technicians, perhaps because of our limited technical knowledge. As I was no longer working under the supervision of the Operations Branch, it was difficult to gain administrative support from upper levels of authority.

Shortly after being assigned to the DQM position I was interviewed by the Base Personnel Selection Officer, Captain Kenneth Madill, regarding my University Training Plan application. During the interview a number of topics were discussed, including my involvement with the North Bay Sexual Assault Centre. For some reason volunteering with this community organization drew an indignant stare from him. He informed me that he would not recommend my application. It appears the focus of his criticism centred on what he argued were "substantial deficiencies" with my intellectual abilities. His reaction was more clearly understood a few years later when he was convicted of sexual offences against juvenile boys in the North Bay area.

He explained, "According to the General Classification Test you took upon enrolment, you would not be able to complete a university level course, much less a degree".

I emphasized, "I've already completed over a year by correspondence with excellent results".

With a sigh he pointed out, "I question the credibility of the institution granting you the credits."

It's obvious he didn't know what he was talking about because all three universities in British Columbia recognized my credits. Captain Madill's assessment could have been challenged by the upper staff of the Branch. However, they chose to fall in line with his opinion. I continued my studies, determined not to give up the goal of obtaining a Bachelor of Arts Degree. After all, there was always next year and another application. If nothing else, the improved education should account for extra recognition on Performance Evaluation Reports.

Christmas with relatives in New Brunswick, 1982

I held some fantasy that if one tried hard enough, success would follow. There are exceptions to every rule, particularly in the military bureaucracy.

The thought of spending our first Christmas away from friends and relatives did not appeal to us. So we decided I should take leave for a few days and drive to Grand Falls, New Brunswick on Boxing Day. Mother was overjoyed when we arrived unannounced. Amy had never experienced a French-Canadian Christmas. For my relatives it was like having Christmas twice when we showed up. Ken enjoyed the company of my nieces and nephews, but Amy felt uncomfortable with all the excitement. My family tends to cling to each other and the novelty of our visit attracted an almost continuous flow of relatives stopping by at all hours. Although somewhat overwhelming for Amy, we managed to enjoy our trip and returned to North Bay in time to greet the New Year.

Disappointed with the results of the UTPM application, and with little hope of improving the situation with Base administration, I decided to request a transfer. Because I had been less than a year at North Bay, the request was turned down. Supervisors suggested I request a retest of my intellectual abilities. Captain Madill argued that I would not be eligible for retest until later that year. Resigned not to give up on the UTPM program, I took the first opportunity to request the General Classification (GC) test. Reluctantly, Madill agreed to allow testing, but the test would be at a higher level of classification. This meant that I would be taking the GC test given to officer applicants. It's surprising that an applicant's entire career is based on the results of this thirty minute aptitude test. Even more amazing is the fact that such evaluations remain credible after an overwhelming body of evidence repudiates them. The results of this second evaluation cast a shadow of bias on Madill's repeated negative assessment. His motives would become clear at a later time.

By the summer of 1983, studies had slowed down because of costs. The Pontiac was falling apart and it seemed fruitless to add more money into repairs. It also seemed that hunk of junk always needed gas. The opportunity of trading it for a new vehicle came while I was at the mall one day. A new dealership was introducing the Hyundai Pony to Canada. The price was right. The deal gave us a new car with the promise of freedom from repairs for at least four years and excellent gas mileage.

Although getting a new car seemed necessary, monthly payments would create even more financial restraint. Somehow, the cost of living exceeded available income. After discussing the matter of housing with my supervisor, it was suggested that I apply for a Married Quarters in writing. The memo went to the Housing Officer, 'Rolly' Orieux, in early September, 1983. At about the same time, I submitted my second application for UTPM. Madill confirmed the results of retesting were more favourable. Although he spoke of average results, I later discovered that I had achieved superior

BULLIES IN POWER

results. He remained adamant about denying access to University Training as he rated our family situation "Below Average".

With almost two years of university courses completed towards my degree, I was denied access to the competition for a commission because of my family situation. Something seemed very wrong with the assessment. The commanding officer's blind support of Madill's recommendation called attention to an underlying current of criticism leading to negative review of my application. It would later become obvious that my family situation was disapproved and that any hope of advancement had vanished when I refused to adhere to the Padre's racist demands.

The written application for housing led authorities to refer me to the Social Welfare Officer, Captain F.G. De Jong. Once again my family situation and educational goal fell under serious criticism. Her report was aimed at supporting earlier suggestions that I give up family and university.

She coldly stated, "His common-law wife is a full-blood Indian and she would loose her Indian status if they married."

She added, "A budget was worked out for him. It is limited, but it did not show financial hardship. If he drops his schooling he could live on it quite easily."

Her recommendation confirms military expectations: "He has to realize that because he has no relatives by blood living with him that he is not entitled to a PMQ."

The term "full-blood Indian" marks the archaic way military authorities continue to refer to native people in terms generally applied to defining breeding in animals.

After almost eighteen months of attempts at improving our situation, I had met barriers that cannot be explained by any other definition than that of a conspiracy among administrative authorities within the chain of command. It was a closing of the ranks among officers addressing our family situation. There was nowhere to turn. The housing request was sharply turned down. The social worker criticized rather than consider the facts. Amy had been depressed for months and took refuge in the house. Ken was finding it difficult at school. Things were not going well at home or at work.

In the midst of all the problems, an airline seat sale was advertised. Amy needed to visit her dad and I knew it. The opportunity of sending her to Kamloops, at an inexpensive rate, was too good to miss. Two weeks in Kamloops would give her enough time to visit relatives and hopefully come out of the depression that had left her socially incapacitated. Meanwhile, I took leave to care for Ken at home. To get a clear perspective on how to deal with criticism of our family situation, it was necessary to visit the local law library.

Research confirmed the problem could best be addressed through a challenge of the padre's racist remarks and the military's non-recognition of common-law relationships. Although Amy's and Ken's native status was the underlying reason for negative criticism, the overt focus on our common law relationship allowed authorities to defend their position. Discussions with a retired judge and a retired senior officer helped define the necessary approach to deal with the problem. The racist comments were legally permitted as pointed out earlier. The padre, being a government employee, made racist comments about persons governed by the ***Indian Act*** which meant Amy and Ken could not file a complaint. That left the military's position on our common-law relationship as the only avenue to challenge differential treatment.

The first step would involve gathering facts. Only written documentation would offer an appropriate source of support. Secondly, I would have to follow the prescribed military Redress of Grievance in order to confirm all necessary steps were taken to resolve the issue through internal channels. Finally, a protective measure had to be devised to prevent retaliation from military authorities. This last step would only prevent my release and could not

Ken getting help from Bear at Christmas 1983

address the career barriers and personal pressures imposed by abusive commanding officers.

Amy's trip was successful in relieving her depression. She arrived at the North Bay airport in a happy mood. Our first task involved addressing Ken's situation. An interview with the teacher offered little hope for improvement. Ken had been inappropriately labelled a "slow learner". It was not the right time to bring up the label. Ken might have been difficult to deal with at times, but he certainly was not "slow". The school's inflexible approach was dealt with swiftly. Within a week, we enrolled Ken at the E.T. Carmichael Public School where teachers were more interested in teaching than labelling.

Ken at Soccer in 1983

Ken's abilities surfaced later that year when he became fascinated with the game of chess. After observing Jim Lucas and I for a couple of weeks, he asked if he could try a game with me. We had not been aware that he actually managed to learn how to play simply by observing us. At school, Ken began to take part in the chess club. One student in Grade Six proved to be his most serious competition. Consequently, he spent lunch hour and a great deal of time after school in practice. Then one day he came home with a big smile and said, "I finally won! She's a good player but I won!" He progressed rapidly from class champion to school champion in a few short weeks. He went on to compete at the district level and won five of seven games against students who were at least three years his senior.

He hoped to win a game against Jim Lucas. He had played him often and never won a game. One afternoon, Ken came in the house with a big smile and quietly said, "I won." He didn't want to gloat because he respected Jim. However, there was no hiding the fact that he was overjoyed. The moral of this story is to beware of labels often placed on people by self-appointed authorities. The transfer to a public school seemed to improve Ken's outlook almost overnight. There was less focus on religious control; educational objectives took precedence.

The second task involved addressing the military's critical assessment of our common-law relationship. Dealing with the issue would call for mutual commitment and support within the family. Once started, there could be no turning back or giving up the challenge. Amy agreed it was the only available solution. I went back to work and began looking up the regulations for filing an official Redress of Grievance. The first step would involve a verbal request, through my immediate supervisor, to discuss the redress with my section commander. Master Corporal Gordon Boddy had been against my relationship and simply refused to bring the matter to the section commander's attention. When verbal requests were ignored, I decided to follow regulations and on December 28, 1983, submitted a written memorandum.

Gord simply tore it up, threw it in the garbage, and argued, "You're not going to win this Paul and I'm not going to waste the captain's time with it."

Three weeks had elapsed and I was no further ahead in attempting to bring the matter up through a Redress of Grievance procedure.

Having been made aware of possible retaliation, I took the judge's advice and notified the Canadian Human Rights Commission of my actions. I explained my concern that internal channels were resistant at the lowest levels and it was expected that I might be released for challenging the matter. At the same time, I submitted a second written Redress of Grievance.

This time I warned, "Gord, you throw this one away and my next submission will be directly to the base commander."

He accused me of wasting his time but reluctantly forwarded the document. It was now January 5, 1984.

BULLIES IN POWER

The letter to the Human Rights Commission drew a reply about a month later. The Commission explained a complaint could not be investigated until all available internal channels had been exhausted. However, I was reassured that my release from the military would call for an immediate investigation. Whereas military regulations indicate a grievance must be acknowledged within fourteen days, it took almost six weeks to receive an answer from a commanding officer. The response, from Colonel J.A. Mitchell, outlined his interpretation of regulations and supported criticism of our family situation.

Major Nickerson called me into his office early one morning to provide a copy of the written response and offer the first of many threats from that level of authority.

He began with, "Paul, you're a good air defence technician. You do good work, but frankly you've become an administrative burden."

The excuse of "administrative burden" is often used when military authorities can't find anything else to justify a member's release. As I stood in front of his desk, my release papers were visible. Something inside changed and I became more confident. After a few seconds of thought, the words seemed to flow with amazing clarity.

"The administrative problem is not my creation. Furthermore, the matter has been referred to the Human Rights Commission and before you action my release it might be best to discuss the issue with the Human Rights Commissioner."

He blew up. "How dare you," he screamed, "take a military problem to an outside agency?"

I calmly replied, "It's not military when it involves discrimination against my family. You left me no option."

With a disgusted tone he blurted, "Get out of my office!"

Back at my desk I read Colonel Mitchell's letter. Describing Amy and Ken, he indignantly points out, "Neither of these persons falls within the definition of dependent as set out in the applicable regulations and orders."

The matter of dependency is an important tool of control for authorities, as they often rely on the family's dependent status to

95

ensure cooperation. To have family members who are not perceived as "dependent" on the military is simply unacceptable.

A few days later I was called to the Major's office again. This time he took a different approach.

"Paul, you know, going out of the military to resolve an internal problem is not wise. This common-law thing will cloud your career. Surely you can see that existing regulations cannot be changed just to accommodate you?"

Now their defence was becoming obvious. They would attempt to make regulations seem justified by isolating my situation and trying to make me feel alone. I needed to keep a focus on the real problem.

"If I had not brought my situation to the attention of the Human Rights Commission, I would have been released. If regulations are discriminatory or outdated, maybe it's time someone called it to the attention of those in position to change them."

The case was simple. A few bigots in positions of authority chose to use the non-recognition of common-law relationships to justify discrimination against Amy and Ken for wanting to protect their rights.

Each level of authority on base and in the underground complex was made aware of my grievance. Nickerson ensured my records were annotated with subtle indications that my relationship was not approved. It soon became known to everyone that authorities had met a stumbling block in a corporal who simply wouldn't break. My request to have the matter considered by higher authorities saw Colonel Mitchell and Lieutenant Colonel Greaves intentionally cause a delay in processing by redirecting the matter to Lieutenant Colonel J.E. Baldwin at Fighter Group Headquarters.

Creating delays through administrative channels is an important mechanism of harassment. Unfortunately, it is a well defended mechanism. Although peers offered moral support, they feared associating with me would draw negative attention from authorities. As a result, my life at home and at work revolved around this Redress of Grievance.

Pressures soon took an administrative form. I was being called in for interviews on my days off. There were times when I waited

BULLIES IN POWER

for an hour or so only to be told I'd have to return the next day, because the Commanding Officer would not be able to see me that day. Major R.J. Parent soon took over from Nickerson and continued to apply a critical approach to our situation.

Supervisors had access to our home phone number. It was impossible to prevent harassment. Amy soon became disappointed and depressed as most interviews were conspicuously taking place during my off hours. When I attempted to explain that I needed my days off, I was abruptly reminded of my options.

"You're expected to be available 24 hours a day in the military. If you don't like it, just get out."

Over four months had elapsed and my grievance had simply circulated between various offices at CFB North Bay. Regulations were not respected by authorities, but little could be done.

The Human Rights Commission monitored the situation. As each level of review responded to my grievance, I forwarded a copy to the Commission. Colonel P.A. Hamilton, the Base Commander, provided a response to my grievance in early April. It was nothing more than an endorsement of earlier decisions against our family situation. At my request, Colonel Hamilton submitted the grievance to Air Command in late April, 1984.

It had taken four months to get through the first level of authority. Regulations clearly affirmed that the first level of authority should have been complete within thirty days. The naive hope that higher headquarters were beyond the influence of base authorities slowly disintegrated and shattered the illusion of a fair hearing. The issue had already been outlined through informal channels of the "Old Boys' Network".

After a few months of waiting for an answer from Air Command, I decided to approach the local Member of Parliament. Jean-Jacques Blais, a Liberal MP with the Trudeau Government, also held the post of Defence Minister. Although I was not registered with the constituency, I attempted to make an appointment with his office to ask for assistance.

According to his assistant, "Mr. Blais is much too busy to look into a trivial problem that can be addressed through your Redress." So much for Liberal Party representation! Mr. Blais' humiliating

97

defeat at the polls, later that year, suggests his constituents may have considered their concerns more than "trivial".

With each university course completed, I felt one step closer to the goal of a university degree. Financial pressures often led to depressive mood swings that challenged my interest. Amy and Ken played an important role in bringing me out of those darker moods. Only Amy knew that I carried a mask of confidence.

At work, peers began to avoid me. It's difficult to explain why I felt compelled to turn the focus of peer discussions to my problem with military non-recognition of common-law relationships. Perhaps, it was an unconscious effort to dispel an overwhelming feeling of inadequacy in dealing with authorities.

I felt as though authorities held the upper hand. "Paul, you can't fight city hall" people would say. I was beginning to feel alone. If things are wrong, why is it so difficult to gain support in establishing change? Everyone agreed with my challenge, but very few, if any, felt I had a chance of causing a change. It would take some time to build confidence in myself. Confidence is the only mechanism that can dilute negative thinking. It soon became obvious that if I was to keep friends I would have to change the topic of my attention and become more positive.

Ken helps blow candles at Amy's Birthday July 1984

In early July, the Human Rights Commission accepted a formal complaint since it became obvious that internal military channels were uncooperative in dealing with the issue before them. Theodora Preito was assigned to investigate the complaint and report to the National Capital Regional Director, Mr. Charles A. Lafreniere. Although remedial action could not be initiated until the grievance was complete, there would be a record of events leading to the eventual processing. An insulting response came in early September from Major-General Donald M. McNaughton, acting Commander of Air Command. He had simply mimicked previous interpretations.

"This headquarters is not aware of any decision to date by appropriate authorities in NDHQ, the Minister, the Governor in Council or the Human Rights Commission which would cast doubt on the validity of the existing housing accommodation policy. Therefore, the allegation of discrimination is without foundation."

Major-General McNaughton was well aware that his delayed response contributed to the very administrative barriers precluding "appropriate authorities" from reviewing any possible change to existing policies. There was an indignant challenge in his argument. Not wanting to disappoint him, I promptly submitted a request to have my grievance considered by the Chief of Defence Staff.

Why was there so much resistance to the modernization of policies that pertain to changing social conditions? Rank and control were obviously more important than addressing obvious bigotry perpetrated by a senior officer. Authorities would not openly admit their expectation to control families through the military member. However, it was made obvious in a media comment from a public affairs officer in early 1986. Major Robyn Alford emphasized, that if common-law couples were allowed to live in married quarters, there would be "no legal control over them, and that is not deemed to be in the best interest of the service."

Since 1976, the Federal Superannuation Act has defined legal responsibilities for military members engaged in common-law relationships. It's interesting that our common-law relationship suddenly became the focus with "legal control". Matters of native status have traditionally been associated to "legal control" among various government agencies dealing with native peoples.

Could it be the "legal control", so fervently sought by military authorities, was not aimed at common-law relationships, but rather at compelling Amy and Ken to give up their aboriginal rights as natives? One can also suggest that authorities wish to maintain social control through racial barriers. Take a close look at Canadian

Armed Forces senior officers. How many are native? If a non-native is denied access to competitions for commissioning because he chose to defend his spouse's aboriginal rights, what measures are applied to prevent natives themselves from entering the officer ranks? Therefore, Alford's comment about legal control reflected "deeper interests" than those of the service.

Financial conditions were deteriorating rapidly and Christmas was approaching once again. It was a painful reminder of the many Christmases of my youth, when financial conditions left us feeling the shame of poverty. Frustrated with the lack of response from the Chief of Defence Staff, I approached the newly elected Member of Parliament for the Nipissing Riding, Moe Mantha, in early December 1984. He decided to address the matter to then Minister of Defence, Robert C. Coates. Coates would respond with the usual political shuffle in late January 1985.

"Inasmuch as I may be required to consider Corporal Lagace's grievance, I know you will appreciate that it would be inappropriate for me to make any comment on this matter at this time."

Once again the question of addressing delays was shuffled by incompetence. Coates never did make a decision on my Redress as he resigned from the federal cabinet for taking a side trip to an exotic dance club while visiting Europe.

The holidays had come and gone without much fanfare. Amy and I had managed to get a few gifts for Ken and made the best of our situation. Costs for rent and utilities were going up and my pay never took us to the end of the month. The holiday expenses left me without the means to begin another course. I took advantage of free time to get involved with more volunteer work at the Sexual Assault Centre. Amy became involved with a school program for unemployed women. Her confidence was in desperate need of a boost. She enjoyed the social contact and explored avenues of education at the college level.

Christmas with Mom and brother Pierre in 1984

It was a cold winter that year. When I walked to work, my hands and feet went numb as temperatures often dipped to minus 40 degrees. I didn't mind walking, but I certainly could have done without the wind and snow. With little hope of improving career prospects, I requested a career review. Perhaps there was a possibility that my interests and education could be applied in another occupation.

Throughout the difficulties, one of the stable features in my life had been my continued effort to maintain a high level of fitness. I trained at the Base Gym almost daily. One of the senior staff members, Warrant Officer Gus Paris, often encouraged me to consider becoming a Physical Education and Recreation Instructor (PERI). During the career review interview with the Base Personnel Selection Officer (BPSO), Captain Madill, the possibility of becoming a fitness instructor was explored. He explained that I would need to complete a five-week Unit Physical Training Assistant course (UPTA) at CFB Borden before I could apply to change my occupation to Physical Education Recreation Instructor (PERI).

His concern also focussed on my age in relation to the physical demands of the course. "You'd be one of the oldest students on the course." Nevertheless, he agreed to recommend that I attend the UPTA course scheduled to begin in March. In order to prepare for the course, I was assigned to work under the direction of Gus Paris at the Base Gym. Gus worked with a very simple and effective philosophy: "Know your stuff, never bluff, and practice what you preach." He lived by it and I was expected to adopt that philosophy in daily training.

He often said, "If you're not fit to do the exercises, then don't expect your students to do them."

After telling me that I would have to complete fifty consecutive chin-ups before going on course, he reached up to the bar and proceeded to do fifty. It left no doubt that he lived by the standards he taught.

Being assigned to the gym had relieved the stress of being called in on my days off, not to mention that I got a rest from the shift work. In the meantime, Amy had become more active with an academic program through the college. She felt more at ease with my schedule and it allowed us to share the stability of evening hours as a family. For six weeks Gus showed me how to prepare sports and fitness programs. Physical conditioning went well and I exceeded all expectations prior to departing for Borden.

Amy was a little worried about my going on course. Being away from home for five weeks didn't exactly turn me on either. However, the opportunity of changing occupation seemed the only way out of work conditions in the underground complex. As an Air Defence Technician, my career was going nowhere.

For five weeks in Borden, I worked hard and enjoyed everything about the course. Although I was the oldest in training, it soon became apparent that Gus also wanted me to be the best conditioned. During the final week of the course, staff members at the school interviewed all students in order to assess who was interested in changing occupations. During my interview, Sergeant Joe Beauchenes agreed that I had the physical talents to be an excellent Physical Education Recreation Instructor (PERI). However, my educational achievement confirmed that the most appropriate channel to become an officer was to focus all my energy on completing my degree.

"You'd be better off to pursue your education than tie yourself down with a year of difficult training just to change trades."

I returned to North Bay as a qualified UPTA and even more determined to overcome the setbacks of official criticism.

Going back to work in the underground complex I had to decide whether or not to take a change of occupations. After I discussed the matter with Amy, she said very little except that my education offered more hope of becoming an officer. So it was decided that I would remain an Air Defence Technician and continue as many courses as time and money would permit.

Bills had accumulated to a point where it was necessary to consolidate. At the same time, the bank decided to call our loan. With no way to pay them, I approached the Base Accounts Officer and Deputy Judge Advocate for advice.

Trying to work out a budget, the accounts officer pointed out that my income didn't meet our expenses. For over two years I had tried to convince authorities of that fact. It wasn't that we spent too much. It was that costs of living on one income were simply too high. We couldn't move to less expensive housing because there were no vacancies in the city. Although there were unoccupied married quarters, they were reserved for 'married personnel'. Now I faced personal bankruptcy.

With conditions deteriorating, it appeared the only possible avenue was to go public with our situation. I pointed out to the Deputy Judge Advocate, "It may be the only way to motivate change." Getting public attention on the matter of housing was not what authorities needed at that time. Suddenly, there was a possible solution through the Canadian Forces Personnel Assistance Fund (CFPAF). A $5000 loan was arranged through CFPAF as well as an additional $6500 loan through the Military Credit Union. Authorities had made it possible for me to pay the bank and credit card balances. It was a temporary solution that hardly seemed cause for joyous gratitude.

After eight months of waiting, the Chief of Defence Staff, General G.C.E. Theriault, responded to my grievance.

He states, "I have given careful consideration to your grievance and I have examined the issues that you have raised."

Then he proceeded with an expanded copy of previous views: "The CF do not recognize common-law relationships and the persons with whom you reside do not satisfy the definition of dependents."

Once again the matter of "dependents" was placed at the forefront of the argument against our relationship. General Theriault maintains that "to recognize cohabitational arrangements would preclude the fulfillment of the military ethos....I do not consider that you have suffered any personal oppression, injustice or other ill-treatment."

It's difficult to understand how our relationship could impede military ethos. "Ethos", is defined as the "characteristic spirit or attitudes of a community"(Pocket Oxford 7th edition, Oxford University Press, 1984). It's obvious my challenge of racially-motivated discrimination was the impediment of pompous "military ethos," a clear reflection of the spirit or attitudes among the upper ranks; our relationship had not offended the community we lived in.

General Theriault's response presented nothing new. So I submitted a request to have the grievance forwarded to the Minister of National Defence. This step in the chain of command would take the issue to a political level. My request didn't get very far. I received notice two weeks later that an appointment had been made with the Deputy Judge Advocate on Base. Colonel Mitchell questioned my ability to read and understand the Chief of Defence Staff (CDS) General Theriault's letter. The instructions from Colonel Mitchell were insulting.

"Cpl Lagace is to take his copy of the CDS letter with him to that interview during which the DJA will go over the CDS response paragraph by paragraph."

Two years of university courses, completed by correspondence, and I didn't know how to read? Amy was appalled at their arrogance. I must admit, I was angry with the continued delay tactics. The Deputy Judge Advocate was somewhat perturbed at the idea that he was placed in the middle of inappropriate measures that only served to delay the Redress of Grievance procedure. While he agreed that such measures were inappropriate, there was nothing he would do about it. I submitted a second request to have the matter forwarded to the Minister of National Defence. It would take another three weeks before the Base Commander processed the request.

With summer approaching, Jim Lucas had been playing his bagpipes in preparation for upcoming marching band festivities. Jim appeared a little tired on the morning of the parade in New Liskeard. It was a sunny Saturday and I was cutting the grass out front. He

Ret'd Major James Lucas and wife Madelaine

came out all dressed up in traditional Scottish kilt, carrying his bagpipes. I could tell he enjoyed this important expression of his heritage. Madeleine was her usual quiet self as they got into the car and backed out of the driveway. It was the last time we would see Jim alive. The heat and humidity went up quickly. By noon the temperature hit almost thirty degrees Celsius. The difficult parade march uphill was too much for Jim. At the end of the parade march, he sat down to catch his breath. A massive heart attack saw him pronounced dead at the hospital.

Ken had been invited to attend the Sams' family reunion in Lytton that weekend. We met him at the Toronto airport on Sunday afternoon. On our way home, we explained what had happened to Jim. Ken didn't say very much and quickly changed the subject.

The following day Amy and I got ready to attend the funeral home. Ken asked to come along. Seeing Jim in the casket, Ken looked at Madeleine with tear-filled eyes and quietly said, "He's not coming back is he?" It was the kind of direct honesty that exposes reality and cuts through the masks that adults often use to cover emotions. Our good friend, advisor, and chess partner would be missed. I was suddenly reminded of my father's death. I felt alone for a few days.

Our income tax refund had arrived early in June. Although we planned to deposit the amount on our loans, Jim's sudden death convinced us to plan a much needed trip to visit Amy's dad in Kamloops. Frank's condition had deteriorated and Amy worried that his time was limited. I couldn't remember the last time we had taken a family vacation. My application for a month's leave was initially turned down. However, after it was pointed out that I had not taken summer leave in years, the application was reluctantly approved. A friend agreed to care for Bear while we were gone. After packing the tent and camping gear, we headed west.

Our first overnight stop at Pancake Bay campground provided an opportunity to take a relaxing walk on the beach along Lake Superior. A cool breeze chilled the night air as the sun went down. Ken had just come back from swimming in the pool and we were lying down in the tent when I saw what looked like a big dog on our picnic table. Without thinking much of it, I got up to see if the owner was around. When I opened the inside screen of the tent door, I suddenly realized it was a black bear. I don't know who was more frightened. He went running off into the woods while Ken looked on and laughed. Camping out proved to be an enjoyable experience as each day brought new sights.

Amy's Dad at Overlander Extended Care in 1985

We arrived in Kamloops after six days on the road. Visiting Frank at the extended care facility, Ken was shocked by his condition. Two strokes had left him paralysed and weak. It was a difficult time for Amy. Frank's weight loss had changed his features. The gleam in his eyes was gone. Although Amy pretended she was happy to

Amy and Emily in 1985

see him, the look in her eyes spoke a painful truth that she simply couldn't hide. Each visit seemed more painful.

Having agreed to let Ken spend time with his paternal grandparents, we drove out to Merritt a few days later. Leaving Ken with his grandparents, Amy and I decided to visit Vancouver Island. It was an opportunity for Amy to get together with one of her long-time friends. While they had kept in touch with letters, they had not seen each other for over twenty years. The reunion brightened our trip and we enjoyed a week of their hospitality.

Returning to Kamloops, we spent another five days with friends and visited Frank every day. While we were on Vancouver Island he had developed pneumonia. Although we had left telephone numbers on file at the front desk, there had been no attempt to contact us when Frank had been rushed to the hospital. This upset Amy as she realized he could have died and she would not have been informed. Prior to our departure, a special effort was made to ensure that any change in Frank's condition would be reported to Amy directly.

After a month of camping out, it was comforting to arrive home and sleep in our own bed. Going

Ken wins Cub Car Rally in 1985

back to work, however, was not a welcomed experience. Expecting to hear that my grievance had reached the Office of the Minister of National Defence, I asked Master Warrant Officer Gary Carlisle for a progress report. He was new to the section and wasn't aware of the situation. A couple of days later he informed me that authorities could not confirm the location of my grievance.

Frustrated with the delays, in early August I decided to write directly to the new Minister of National Defence, Eric Neilson. It would take six weeks to get a reply from the Associate Minister, Harvie Andre. In typical political fashion Harvie Andre proceeded to call me a liar and argued that changes to the Indian Act in 1985 somehow offered remedy for my grievance. The military's non-recognition of common-law relationships was not related to the Indian Act. His suggestion that changes to the Indian Act in 1985 could address injustices dating back to 1982, only emphasizes his lack of concern for the matter brought to his attention. His closing statement provides additional evidence of incompetence.

"Please be assured, however, that your grievance will receive a thorough, objective and fair review, should you still request that it be submitted for my consideration."

He was not aware that my grievance had been submitted for his consideration some three months earlier. I followed up with a letter to the Minister in order to address the inconsistencies of Andre's response. Suspicions were confirmed over two months later when a letter from an assistant to the Associate Minister of National Defence gave me a patronizing brush off.

"Mr. Andre's responsibilities as Associate Minister of National Defence include matters related to applications for Redress of Grievance and, accordingly, he will be considering all the issues raised in your application at the earliest possible opportunity."

At no time did Eric Neilson or Harvie Andre address the intentional delays in processing, much less the subject matter of my grievance.

Administrative authorities repeatedly referred to my records in defending their policy of treating me as a 'single' member. It didn't seem to matter that attempts at changing the inaccuracies of my

BULLIES IN POWER

records had consistently been refused. During the completion of personal information sections of my Annual Performance Evaluation Report in October, 1985, I made note of my family situation. Once again, the attempt was short-lived as administrative staff argued over the legal terminology.

Captain Kaulback explained, "By DND legal terminology he is single. Also, unless the son is his "blood" relative he cannot list him as a dependent."

On most military documents the military member is in a no-win situation. If I didn't indicate family circumstances on the forms, disciplinary action could be taken. However, when all appropriate information was provided, administrative channels refused to accept it. So my Performance Evaluation Report was processed with the personal information section incomplete.

Almost three months after submitting a third University Training Plan Application, the Selection Officer conducted an interview. The sudden release of Captain Kenneth W. Madill, for convictions on sexual offences against male juveniles, resulted in a temporary Selection Officer conducting the interview. His review of my records confirmed that I had been "under-rated" in previous assessments. However, he too felt that my family situation was somehow "Below Average". Nevertheless, he agreed to recommend the processing of the application and informed me that a medical examination had been scheduled at National Defence Medical Centre in Ottawa the following week.

It was early December and blowing snow made the road trip from North Bay to Ottawa seem endless. At the Medical Centre, it was discovered that I was developing peptic ulcers. How could it be possible that years of daily exercise couldn't prevent this physical manifestation of stress? It was explained that physical exercise reduces the effects of stress but it doesn't completely eliminate it. The doctor asked about conditions at North Bay.

After discussing the difficulties of our situation, he asked if a transfer to Kamloops would help relieve the stress. With Amy's father in poor physical condition, he agreed to recommend a transfer. I didn't hold much hope for his recommendation. During the return trip to North Bay I became angry with the whole sordid affair. By the time I arrived home, depression was setting in. The redress procedure had failed to address our housing problem and now ulcers threatened my health.

I had felt like calling public attention to the housing situation, but resisted because it seemed too drastic. A few days after returning from Ottawa, a reporter called to ask about our problems with the housing office on Base. I wondered; how did the media find out? After considering the situation for a few seconds, I agreed to discuss the matter with her.

Rose Simone visited us at home early one evening and explained that we didn't have to say anything if we didn't feel comfortable. It was no longer of concern how she found out about our problem. The Redress of Grievance procedure had served as a retaliatory tool for military authorities to frustrate us in an attempt to discourage efforts to change the discriminatory policy against common-law relationships. There was nothing more to lose. I gave Rose all the information available on the matter. She indicated it would take some time to prepare the story for print. When I didn't see anything in the paper over the following week, I assumed she had decided not to go ahead with it.

A few days before Christmas, Master Warrant Officer Gary Carlisle called me into his office. His smile told me good news might be in.

"Paul," he said, "how would you feel about a posting to Kamloops?" I almost fell off the chair.

"We can be packed by early tomorrow morning," I replied in gleeful jest.

He handed me a copy of the message from the Career Manager's Office. What a Christmas present! Amy and Ken were excited about the move scheduled for June, 1986. It's not known how the decision came about, but the doctor's recommendation may have been a motivating influence.

The holidays may have been limited by financial conditions, but there was no lack of joy in our home as the posting message promised improved conditions ahead. I had almost forgotten about the newspaper article.

Then one evening Rose Simone phoned to let us know the story would be published in the January 30th edition of the North Bay Nugget. "It will also go with Canadian Press", she added. Rose had done her research meticulously. The article provided a detailed look at the military's lack of flexibility when dealing with human rights. A spokesperson for the Canadian Human Rights Commission confirmed the matter was being held up by the military Redress of Grievance procedure.

On February 12th, the Toronto Star published an article which called attention to the discriminatory nature of the military's non-recognition of common-law relationships. It also pointed out that the Canadian Human Rights Commission seemed powerless against military authorities hiding behind the cloak of internal grievance procedures.

The following morning, Major R.J. Parent called me into his office.

"Speaking to the media without permission is a serious violation of military regulations," he emphasized.

He went on to outline the need for discipline and obedience in the military. His argument faded into an irrelevant exaggeration of the situation.

"What if you were called upon to fight a war? Would you call the media to voice your personal views against it?"

Although his argument made sense to him I suppose, it certainly lacked a sense of reality to me.

I pointed out, "I've never neglected my duties, and I don't see how my family's rights compare to the issue of war; unless you perceive those rights as some sort of national threat."

I enjoyed playing his game of 'let's exaggerate'. With a frustrated look on his face, he barked, "Get out of my office!"

As I reached the door he warned, "No more media contact without permission."

The matter of getting permission didn't appeal to me. Common sense told me that a request for permission to speak with reporters would result in another merry-go-round of administrative delays.

That evening a friend encouraged me to establish contact with Members of Parliament who were assigned as critics to the Ministry of National Defence. I immediately sat down and wrote a letter to Leonard Hopkins, the Liberal critic. About a month later, his administrative assistant, Linda McGreevy, confirmed he would be able to address the matter to the Minister of National Defence, as soon as he returned from Germany.

In late March, I received a reply from Len Hopkins in which he included another brush off letter from Harvie Andre's special assistant, Linda M. Johnson. Once again, she gives an assurance that Harvie Andre will reply at the earliest opportunity. Harvie Andre had been in the possession of my grievance since early July, 1985. It's difficult to understand how the matter could escape his notice for over nine months. What could be keeping his decision?

In mid-February, 1986, the Human Rights Commission decided to act on the complaint which had been on file since July 16, 1984. It was reassigned to Michelle Crete and a notice was sent to the Department of National Defence. Media focus on the military's unreasonable delays justified intervention by the Commission. Having received a copy of their intention to proceed with the complaint, we felt our situation might be remedied prior to our move to Kamloops. This might allow us to move as a family rather than being limited to 'single' allowances.

In late March, I decided to address the matter to Derek Blackburn, NDP Member of Parliament and also critic for the Minister of National Defence. In the meantime, on April 11, Len Hopkins forwarded Harvie Andre's reply to the earlier inquiry. In this reply, he states that my grievance was submitted to him "in late February of this year."

A month later, I received a letter from Derek Blackburn which also included a copy of Harvie Andre's reply to him. This time, Andre states that my grievance was submitted to him "in late March of this year."

BULLIES IN POWER

Harvie Andre was either mistaken or simply dishonest. I can trace the route of my grievance since addressing it to the Minister of National Defence in May, 1985. It would appear that someone held it somewhere until late February, 1986 if you speak to Len Hopkins, or late March, 1986 if you speak to Derek Blackburn. It would appear that Harvie Andre really never knew where my grievance actually sat.

By the time the discrepancy of Harvie Andre's replies was brought to Derek Blackburn's attention, Mr. Andre was shuffled to another Ministry. His replacement, Paul Dick, would take over the shuffle and blend it with some brush offs of his own. A few months later, Paul Dick explained the inconsistencies of Andre's statements as an insignificant mistake.

He then added, "Rest assured that this grievance will be addressed as expeditiously as possible."

The assurance turned out to be more political 'hot air' than political practice.

In preparation for our transfer to Kamloops, I made an appointment with a clerk at the Base Administration Office in order to discuss arrangements for moving our furniture. The clerk's inexperience in dealing with the 'unique' circumstances of our family situation led him to suggest that I write a memo to the Base Personnel Administration Officer, Captain R.J. Woroschuk. The aim of the memo was to request a PMQ at Kamloops or a House Hunting Trip (HHT) to secure a residence prior to the move. It seemed logical to me that if a PMQ could be approved, there would be no need to take a HHT. Captain Woroschuk jumped at the opportunity to criticize my attempt to follow his staff's directives.

"Cpl Legace has been informed on many occasions of his ineligibility for a PMQ...This point should be reiterated one more time by his supervisors."

His reply left the impression that I had nothing better to do than disturb his daily workout in self-glorification. My supervisor, Master Warrant Officer Gary Carlisle, was not impressed by Captain Woroschuk's attempt to flex his ego. A message was sent to Air Command requesting authority to proceed on a HHT to Kamloops.

Approval of the HHT, in late April, allowed me to travel to Kamloops in search of accommodations. Amy and I agreed to cash in our bonds and gather as much cash as possible in hope of buying a house. The price of homes in Kamloops was out of reach, but it was possible to purchase a mobile home. Although mobile home pads were in limited quantity in the city, there were a number of empty pads at Canadian Forces Station Kamloops. After my request for a pad was approved by the Commanding Officer, Major Ray Dunsdon, I made arrangements to complete the purchase of a new mobile home.

With our limited down payment and an assortment of bills it's a miracle that the bank's loans officer approved the loan. The HHT had been successful and Amy was excited to see pictures of our home.

Once again we had to move across the country on the limited allowances of a 'single' person. To reduce costs, we were prepared to camp out and avoid restaurant meals. Amy graduated from her college program in mid-June. Ken was ready for the school transfer and looked forward to returning to Kamloops.

Amy's Graduation in 1986
Canadore College Advanced
Automated Office Program

Gary Carlisle was aware of criticisms from authorities and looked for a way to ensure that my performance would be reflected in my evaluations. As a DQM, I had managed to locate and resolve a number of computer software problems. To avoid a confrontation with authorities, he indicated that a letter would be sent to my new supervisor outlining the positive results of my efforts during the first part of that year. His support offered a ray of hope for my career, as

BULLIES IN POWER

it seemed obvious the only barriers I faced were related to criticisms from senior officers. Everything was progressing too well.

Finally, the day came when movers started packing our furniture. It would take two days. We slept on the living room floor that first night. The following afternoon, Gary pulled into the driveway with a worried look on his face that served as an introduction to the message he handed me. After reading it twice, disbelief changed to anger as it was clear the purpose and timing marked an intentional act of harassment. Major Dunsdon had waited until the day we were scheduled to depart North Bay to inform us that he had rescinded approval for the mobile home pad.

Referring to the House Hunting Trip (HHT) in May, he explained, "At that time trailor pad was available and approved."

Six weeks later, something had motivated a change of plans as the message advised, "He will have to move onto a pad located in the city of Kamloops."

Gary's efforts to deliver the message allowed us to deal with this issue prior to departure. I can only imagine the problems that would have awaited us had we left North Bay without knowing that we had no place to live. The movers were told to hold loading the furniture. Internal channels needed strong influence to act immediately. The news media offered the only possible source of support. Once informed of the situation, military authorities acted quickly. Less than two hours later, the Chief Clerk delivered a message that our mobile home pad was re-approved. A confrontation had been averted.

Gary remained with us while events unfolded. After the matter was resolved, he wished us luck and the movers finished loading the truck. That evening we cleaned the house. A sense of relief was in the air as our experience in North Bay would soon be part of memories of four painful years.

THE OLD BOYS'
NETWORK IN ACTION

The early morning humidity hung thick in the air as the sun broke through a rising fog. Waking up to Bear's call for food, we soon fed her and finished packing the car. It was shadfly season again, but we decided to have breakfast in town before heading west.

Leaving the smell of shadflies behind like a bad memory, we began feeling the excitement of a new beginning in Kamloops. Amy glowed with happiness. We soon found ourselves at Pancake Bay for our first night on the road. Although the wind made it difficult to set up the tent, it also helped fight off the mosquitoes. Overall the trip to Kamloops took six days, with stops at the familiar places of our previous trips. In Moose Jaw we splurged a little and stayed at a motel close to the downtown area. The rain would have made it difficult to set up the tent anyway. It was nice to take a shower in the privacy of our room, not to mention the comfort of sleeping in a bed.

Camping can be a very pleasant experience if you do it by choice. Moving on a single person's allowance took the element of choice out of our experience. In Calgary we set up the tent at the KOA campground. It was sunny and hot, but the facility was great. Ken and I enjoyed a dip in the pool while Amy took a rest in the tent. The excitement of being so close to our destination left us tossing and turning most of the night.

116

Camping Across Canada in 1986

An early start from Calgary gave us time to visit the Lake Louise area by mid-morning. A clear blue sky exposed the beauty of snow-capped mountains overlooking the sparkling clear water rushing down a roadside stream. Driving through Rogers Pass was like waking up from a nightmare and realizing it was just a dream. North Bay had not been pleasant, but knowing it was over brightened the road ahead like a rainbow after a rain shower.

Arriving in Kamloops, the mobile home salesman seemed surprised to see us. He explained our home would not be available for another week. Amy was a little disappointed. Our contract confirmed we had arrived on time. It was now up to the manager to correct the problem. He made a few telephone calls and assured us the home would be delivered within a week. In the meantime we would stay at one of their vacant mobile homes in a nearby park. It wasn't what we expected upon arrival, but not much could be done to change the circumstances.

I drove Amy and Ken to our temporary home and reported to the station. The staff at the orderly room was pleasant and helpful in addressing the delay of our home. It was late afternoon and my supervisor, Warrant Officer Peter

Camping Across Canada in 1986

Hayes, was on his way down from the upper site. A short man of slight build with thinning hair, wearing black horn-rimmed glasses, introduced himself as he walked into the orderly room. He spoke with a heavy British accent as we discussed the problem at hand.

The most practical solution, under the circumstances, was to take a week of leave. With nothing to do but wait, Ken could visit his grandparents in Merritt. His grandparents wanted him to stay for a few weeks to help with the gardening as well as keep them company. They had missed having him around.

Amy's father, Frank, had suffered another stroke that left him confined to his bed. Amy visited him every day while we waited for our home to arrive. Finally, the new home was delivered. It was worth the wait. While Amy had seen pictures of a similar home, the excitement of walking into our own place was almost overwhelming. It looked bigger than expected. Perhaps the sunken living room and vaulted ceiling, enhanced by three large bay windows out front, accentuated the open design. Unlike traditional mobile homes with dark wall panels, the lighter coloured walls and cabinets in this home offered a brighter atmosphere.

There were only five families living on the station's mobile home park. They came to introduce themselves and have a look at the home. People on a small station tend to be more friendly than larger base communities. John and Donnette were both military members who had recently been married. They lived closest to us and often came over for a visit.

The Bourguignons lived up the street. Their two sons were about Ken's age. They looked forward to meeting Ken. Their stepfather, Claude, seemed a most abrasive individual who had very little good to say about anything. Although he was uncomfortable to be around, his wife and two boys seemed pleasant enough.

Denis and Eleanor Gamache lived at the far end of the park. They had five show dogs and spent their weekends going to dog shows. I had known them during my first stay in Kamloops. They too had been transferred in 1982 only to return two years later. The Rainvilles occupied the home next to the park's laundry building.

McNair Park, as it was named, had once been occupied by more than sixty families. The laundry building had served most of the residents. Few mobile homes, in the early days, were equipped with laundry machines. Reminders of those busy days were still visible as empty holes in the walls marked the rows of washers and dryers that once filled the now empty room. Only two machines were left in operation.

Time changes everything. We had been gone for four years and Kamloops had changed. People we knew had either moved away or passed away. It took a few weeks to re-establish old connections with those few friends who remained. Barry Adkins still ran the Gung Fu School. I went down the long flight of stairs that led to his new office. The school had been expanded to include a gym facility downstairs, where a training ring and various exercise machines were located. A kit shop displayed an assortment of training equipment as well as a selection of health food supplements.

Barry was sorting a box of equipment that had just arrived. He looked up and a smile broke across his face as he greeted me with a hearty handshake. It was the kind of welcome that marks the unique bond of friendship and respect shared between a student and teacher.

Tom Laroche no longer worked at the school. It appears after defending his World Kickboxing title for three years, he decided to retire from the ring and work with a youth correction centre at Logan Lake. Yes, things had changed, but the positive energy that once motivated my daily workouts was still very strong in the school.

Before we knew it, August rolled in. The skirting around the mobile home was now completed and I was ready to continue with my studies. It was also time for Ken to register into his new school. He wanted to attend St. Ann's Academy. This Catholic school holds a very high academic standard along with a well-earned reputation for positive development of student potential. Of particular interest to Ken was access to St. Ann's in-class computer training.

Ken and the Bourguignon boys were the only students who lived on the station. Because the station was located twenty-five kilometres from town, a military vehicle provided transport for dependents attending school. Shortly after Ken's registration, I was called into the orderly room and informed that Ken would not be able to ride the military vehicle because he was not considered my dependent. Not wanting to create a fuss about it, I accepted their decision and Amy agreed to drive Ken to school.

The cost of living had been reduced when we moved from North Bay. Now I could register for as many courses as time would permit me to work through. The start of third year courses required more time at the college library. Amy began looking for work. Coming off night shifts at nine in the morning and going on evening shifts at three in the afternoon made it impossible to go to the library at the same time as Amy drove Ken to and from school. We needed a second vehicle but couldn't afford the costs of another car. While out for a walk in mid-September, I stopped at a motorcycle shop and tried out a scooter. It was just what I needed and didn't cost much to run. The Kamloops climate allowed about nine months of driving during the year.

Learning to drive a scooter wasn't as easy as the salesman made it appear, but after a few days of practice, I felt more confident. It took a few weeks to take the practical exam. The guys at work joked about my new "machine". "Why don't you get a real bike?" they kidded. They soon got used to seeing me come through the gate riding the "mini-hog". At about ninety miles to the gallon and under a hundred dollars per year for insurance, appearances didn't really matter. It got me to and from the library, which accomplished the intended goal. With three courses in progress, there was little time left for other activities. Plans to complete my degree were now coming together and an end was in sight. At that rate, I hoped to apply for a commission before the radar site's closure in 1988.

The Redress of Grievance seemed to drag on and the Human Rights Commission had not been able to motivate military authorities to render a decision. A Human Rights Conciliator had been appointed to attempt to bring about a settlement of the complaint. With no success, it became necessary to bring the matter before a Tribunal. Finally, in October, a response came from Colonel L.C. Friesen at Air Command Headquarters. He briefly stated that the Associate Minister of Defence had denied my Redress of Grievance.

There were no reasons outlined for the denial and it would take months to research the wording of the minister's reply. It was clear that he supported the non-recognition of common-law relationships, even though every other branch and level of government recognized the responsibilities of people involved in such relationships. After I informed the Human Rights Commission of the response, it was necessary to submit a request to have the matter referred to the final level of authority. The Governor in Council offered the last hope of gaining support in motivating a change of policy within the military.

In the meantime, John R.A. Douglas, a lawyer from Prince Edward Island, was appointed as Human Rights Tribunal Chairman to inquire into my complaint. Legal Counsel, James Hendry, would represent the Commission and me before the Tribunal. The emotional impact of delays in processing had been diluted by bureaucratic procedures. A feeling of helplessness was slowly taking over the issue. Amy recognized the turmoil. She pointed out that I couldn't allow myself to become obsessed with a situation that was out of my hands. My studies were more important.

Amy became involved with the Interior Indian Friendship Centre and applied for a term position working with an adult students' program. Ken's interest with computers, and the requirement for my writing longer essays, led to the purchase of a personal computer. I wasn't too excited about having to take time to learn how to operate this modern contraption. But time saved in processing my essays with the computer made up for the effort to learn. Ken enjoyed the access to games.

In the short time since our move, we had managed to acquire a scooter and computer without experiencing financial difficulty. Already it was December and exam week was rapidly approaching. Taking every spare moment to prepare was worth it. Our return to Kamloops seemed to improve my concentration. Exam results showed a welcomed improvement as I received two A's and a B.

Christmas at Mount Lolo in 1986

Christmas dinner was shared with Amy's brother Charles and his family. John Sam also joined us for a few days in order to visit with Ken. After the holiday season, studies resumed. With Amy working, the added income would help clear up the small bills. Early January saw the start of a new course. It was also the time of year when my Performance Evaluation Report (PER) needed to be signed.

A PER usually reflects a member's performance throughout the previous year and plays a key role in selection for promotion. At that time, military personnel were not allowed to see the entire report. In fact, the supervisor's narrative and the personal data were the only parts that an individual could see. The point scores and commanding officer's narrative were kept hidden. These were the most important sections of the entire document.

I had just received copies of my previous reports through the privacy act. Although Gord Boddy had assured me that the reports he wrote were "average", the scores and commanding officer's comments left me well below average. I was furious that he had deceived me. It appears that Lieutenant Colonel Greaves had been able to impose low scores on my reports until Gary Carlisle

BULLIES IN POWER

became my supervisor and argued in favour of a fair assessment. Unfortunately, Gary's input was limited to my final report out of North Bay.

Reviewing the previous reports, I made up my mind that I would not sign any document that I couldn't see in its entirety. Consequently, when Warrant Officer Hayes presented me with that year's report, I explained that unless the entire document was made visible there would be no signature. He argued that procedures prevented members from seeing the entire document. I didn't even read the narrative. The PER went ahead without my signature.

During the winter, Frank's condition became worse. Now bedridden, often unconscious for days at a time, he was unaware of the world around him. Amy visited him, but it was obvious his condition saddened her. There were times when she also blamed her stepmother. "If Florabelle hadn't been so concerned with getting drunk, she might have helped Dad when he suffered that first stroke." Those were times when I think she was most frustrated with seeing her father in such a helpless condition.

By mid-February I had managed to get ahead on my assignments in anticipation of the trip to Ottawa. The Tribunal struck a sensitive nerve with the Station Commander. I knew there was opposition among senior ranks to common-law relationships gaining recognition. However, there had been no documented proof that my Redress of Grievance or Complaint to the Human Rights Commission was actually being held against me. That is, until one of the clerks at the orderly room informed me of a letter which accompanied my annual Performance Evaluation Report.

Regulations clearly indicate that attachments to a PER are not allowed. So how did Major Dunsdon justify a contravention of regulations? The clerk had taken a copy of the letter and handed it to me. It briefly outlined my refusal to sign the report, which could have been indicated on the appropriate comment section of the report itself. Of concern in this letter was the direct reference to the grievance and complaint related to common-law relationships.

Dunsdon states: "Cpl Lagace has pushed a grievance through the complete DND grievance procedure that was denied at every level. He is now continuing his grievance in hearings before the Canadian Human Rights Commission."

The use of the word "pushed" suggests he was very much aware that my grievance had been resisted by authorities. He then infers a connection between my attitude and the grievance.

He states: "His attitude appears to be confrontational on any regulation or procedure he does not personally agree with."

Dunsdon's personal views continued to influence his judgement up to the day we left when the station officially closed in 1988.

The tribunal hearing would take place in Ottawa. The flight was pleasant, but Ottawa weather lacked the western appeal. Prior to my arrival, I had not been aware that another complainant was also involved. When James Hendry mentioned the name John Schaap, I thought his name sounded very familiar. Meeting John later that evening, I was shocked to see a familiar face from the past. John had been a Crewman in training with me. It seems shortly after his transfer to Gagetown, New Brunswick in 1980, he had filed a grievance because the housing officer had refused to place his name on the Married Quarters list because he lived common-law. Although he had since married, his complaint had been processed. I detected he felt uneasy about testifying on the matter. He was worried about the effect it would have on his career. I understood his concern.

On March 9, 1987, the tribunal hearing provided an opportunity for the matter to finally be heard. The informal setting did not preclude a courtroom atmosphere during the proceedings. Brian Saunders represented the Department of National Defence while James Hendry represented the Human Rights Commission, John Schaap and me. The initial arguments from Brian Saunders called for a dismissal of the complaints because it was felt that the tribunal did not have jurisdiction over the Department of National Defence application of Queen's Regulations and Orders. That motion didn't float.

After all the legal jargon was complete, it was time for John and me to give evidence. John went first. His relationship had been relatively short and so was his testimony. He was visibly nervous and had difficulty answering questions. Brian Saunders didn't seem too concerned with John's testimony. When he was finished, it was decided that a recess was appropriate. We would return after lunch.

Having heard John's testimony, I expected the questions would be somewhat similar. However, the focus of Department of National

BULLIES IN POWER

Defence's (DND) argument called attention to the unfairness of the Indian Act. After James Hendry's examination of the facts, through my testimony, Brian Saunders would attempt to confuse the issue by asking why I had not challenged the Indian Act.

"The Indian Act never denied us housing," I calmly replied.

It was an unexpected response that served my intention to return the line of questioning towards addressing DND's policy. Although the hearing seemed complicated by technical jargon from both sides of the argument, I came away feeling confident that a favourable ruling would follow.

The flight back to Kamloops allowed time to work on the final assignment of my geography course. Amy greeted me at the airport with her usual friendly smile. Her passive approach to the entire process reflected the nature of her residential school experience. Accounts of child abuse cannot compare to the often heartbreaking descriptions of native students suffering abusive treatment at the hands of school authorities, sanctioned by government agencies. While legislators worked to expand French language rights across Canada, native students were being beaten and starved to prevent them from speaking their native language. Politicians spoke of equality for all Canadians, while native populations were rendered helpless by a systematic dismantling of their cultural identity.

It wasn't that Amy didn't want to challenge the unfair regulations. She simply couldn't. The invisible authorities, who had established themselves as controlling agents over her life at school, remained a powerful influence over her decision to quietly accept bigotry. Amy's support played an instrumental role in maintaining the determination necessary to challenge the unfair practices of military authorities. I might not have been able to reverse the damage of residential school abuse, but I certainly wasn't about to impose additional abuse.

A wall of secrecy surrounded the Associate Defence Minister's 1986 response to my grievance. Without knowledge of his reasons for denying redress, it was difficult to justify consideration from higher authority. After a number of unsuccessful attempts at gaining access to the Minister's response, it seemed appropriate to discuss the issue with our local Member of Parliament, Nelson Riis. About a week later the station administration officer advised me to contact the Assistant Judge Advocate General (AJAG), Major N.G. Girard, regarding concerns with unfair delays in processing. This small ray of hope suggested that internal channels might be open to reviewing the situation.

My appointment to Master Corporal, in early May, gave reason for even more hope. There would be no acknowledgment from the AJAG's office that my concerns were ever reviewed. Consequently, in early July of that year, I submitted my grievance to the Governor in Council. A reply from Nelson Riis, in late August, confirmed my suspicions.

"It is quite apparent that it is the military's intent to handle your appeal internally and that all other interventions are given little recognition."

My grievance would remain "under consideration" at the Governor in Council's office until 1989, when it was no longer applicable.

Denis and Eleanor Gamache were transferred that summer. He had been the park's mayor since 1985. Now he wanted me to take the traditional key to the park and play the role of token mayor. With only four families in the park, the mayor's position was reduced to a mere technicality. For a few weeks it was a popular joke on site that our commanding officer held a seat on Kamloops City Council and I was the mayor of McNair Park.

Life on the station offered a taste of wilderness without actually being isolated. The fish pond, only a few hundred feet away, allowed Ken to discover the excitement of catching his first trout. I remember the screams of joy as he came running up the hillside with a fish in one hand and the pole in the other. He glowed with pride as he huffed and puffed his way to the front porch.

"Look! Look!" he said excitedly, "I caught one and it's big isn't it?"

"I guess it's big!" I agreed.

Fishing had never been one of my favourite sports, but he could be proud of that catch.

"What do we do with it now?" he asked.

Without much experience at cleaning fish, I suggested we cut the head off and clean out the insides. Since it was my suggestion, he pointed out I should do the beheading and he would do the cleaning. Using the small axe, I chopped the head off.

BULLIES IN POWER

He seemed to feel sorry for it as he quietly asked, "Do you think it felt anything?"

His question seemed like a plea for forgiveness. I remembered my father's cruel response to my question about a dying rabbit that my brother had shot. As it screamed, I asked if it was suffering.

Dad looked annoyed as he blurted, "If you don't want to eat, you stupid fathead, go back to the truck and shut up."

I wasn't going to hurt Ken that way. Ken felt sorry for the fish and I knew it.

"You caught this fish and now we're going to eat it. Chances are, the size of this fish means that it was getting old and would probably have suffered a slow death anyway. So all you did was helping nature."

It may have helped relieve his feelings of guilt, but it was the last time he would catch fish. He still went out to practice, but adopted my way of fishing. Like Ken, I feel sorry for the fish so I never bait my hook. It's a very successful way to enjoy the motions without actually hurting anything, especially the fish.

We had access to the gym and swimming pool, which Ken and I often enjoyed. Amy didn't mind accompanying us after supper once in a while, but she seldom did any swimming. It was also the point of social contact for people residing on site.

Once in a while Andre Bigras dropped in from work. A quiet individual, who confided his lack of confidence in handling responsibility, Andy had remained a corporal for over twenty years. He worked at the supply section and was considered different by most station personnel because of his somewhat unsociable character. A confirmed bachelor, he seldom attended social functions and didn't seem to have many friends. For some reason, he felt comfortable with Amy and me. He joined me for coffee break whenever my days off provided the opportunity. We spent many coffee breaks sitting on the porch discussing everything from our childhood to politics.

Visiting Frank at the extended care facility had become a daily ritual that left Amy depressed. His condition became worse and in early September he suffered another stroke. Nursing staff explained that Frank had very little time left and perhaps someone should notify family members of his condition.

Amy's sister, Grace, had never been close to her father, but she decided to accompany Amy during those last few visits. Then, on September 22, the call came as I was about to go on guard duty. It was a busy morning at work because of a station defence exercise. Amy's voice was shaking as she quietly informed me that Frank had passed away. Grace had accompanied her for that morning's visit.

I don't know if it was relief in knowing that Frank's painful existence was over or emotional turmoil with Amy's grief, but I simply couldn't control the feelings. Warrant Officer Peter Hayes quickly closed the door and asked what was wrong. The words couldn't come out as I tried to explain that Amy had asked me to meet her at the hospital. After a few moments of confusion, Peter got the military police to drive me down the hill.

Although we knew it was just a matter of time, the reality of Frank's death evoked ambivalent emotions. There was a sense of relief but also the painful need to let go of him emotionally. I think Amy unconsciously wanted the opportunity to say goodbye to the "dad" that she knew, before the strokes left him unaware of how much she actually loved him.

Frank's funeral arrangements were plagued with turmoil as relatives found it difficult to agree on details. Amy had been very close to her father and had visited him regularly. Even his wife, Florabelle, had avoided visiting Frank. Amy and her brother Charles had been the only regular visitors.

Contact with his band, to arrange for a burial plot, proved most difficult. The band's administration office at Spences Bridge was reluctant to assume responsibility for the task of preparing the plot. Frank had been a member of that band for over seventy years. It wasn't the time to play family feud. Last minute pressures cleared the way for a plot to be prepared, just in time for the funeral. The stress of family discord wore Amy down emotionally.

The casket was lowered into the grave and the minister said the usual prayers. Then, it was time for relatives to approach the grave and drop the traditional handful of dirt in silent acceptance of our eventual return to the ground. There was a pause, as everyone seemed to wait for others to step forward. Amy decided to go ahead. As she dropped the handful of dirt on her father's grave, she held on to me and wept silently.

BULLIES IN POWER

After a few moments, she looked down at Frank's casket and tearfully said, "He's gone. He won't suffer anymore."

I knew she already missed him as her tears had triggered mine. Relatives and friends gathered at the community hall for the rest of the day and talked of Frank's escapades.

"He loved to drink and was a lady's man", they said.

Amy's brother, Charles, had stayed away from the funeral because of an argument. I could tell she felt sad for her brother, but there was little we could do for him. Later that afternoon, I saw Charles leaving his father's gravesite. He had said goodbye according to native tradition, by leaving food on the grave so the deceased doesn't go hungry on his journey to the spirit world. My heart was heavy for him, yet I knew his grief would eventually pass.

It would take a few months for us to adjust to Frank's death. The grieving process for a loved one is said to involve a number of stages. Amy found it difficult to get over the anger and resentment. She bitterly blamed Florabelle for Frank's suffering. After a few weeks, Amy began sharing her feelings more openly, thanks to a friend who had suggested she attend a group for people experiencing difficulties dealing with the loss of a loved one.

At work, Peter took time to discuss our situation and offered his support. His sensitive approach was a refreshing change from the abrasive nature of supervisors in North Bay.

In early October, I asked for a few days off to travel to Spences Bridge. Amy had arranged for a headstone to be prepared for Frank's gravesite. We would have to transport and set it. She had not been to her dad's grave since the funeral. After setting the headstone, she went around and showed me where her brothers and sister were buried. It was a time for memories that had been locked in her past. Emotions were different as Amy's anger seemed to be replaced with a sense of acceptance. I remember thinking that there had been so much loss in her life.

Returning to Kamloops, she spoke of her childhood and how her father had been a source of support to her. It was as though a heavy weight had been removed from her shoulders. The sun was bright and for the first time in weeks, I actually felt hungry. We stopped at a roadside restaurant in Cache Creek. It was so good to see Amy smile. It had been so long. Such intimate moments are precious in any relationship. Life would go on.

My course assignments were late. November was approaching and I needed to spend time at studies. I took advantage of quiet hours on evening and midnight shifts to catch up. Three unsuccessful attempts at becoming an officer had convinced me to place career plans on hold until my degree could be completed. During a day shift in mid-November, Captain Cliff Halpen approached me about the upcoming Officer Candidate Training Plan (OCTP) competition.

He emphasized, "You don't require your degree to apply and you'd make an excellent candidate."

After some discussion and his assured support, I decided to submit an application.

In early December the career manager's visit provided an opportunity to discuss our transfer the following year, if the OCTP application was unsuccessful. Chief Warrant Officer Pete Henderson had been a source of support when times were tough in North Bay. He understood our situation and had been receptive to the suggestion of our 1986 transfer to Kamloops. During his briefing, he addressed the station closure and indicated most postings preferences would be accommodated wherever possible. He was aware of our willingness to go to Canadian Forces Station (CFS) Holberg.

He assured me, "It won't be a problem to get you there, since it's an isolated transfer that people want to avoid."

Once again, the Christmas gift came in the form of a screening message indicating my selection for transfer to CFS Holberg. It was customary to ensure family members were prepared for an isolated location. So the screening would confirm the health of family members, as well as ensure no hardships would be caused by the transfer. After attending Ken's school to get the approval of his principal, I then received medical clearance from our family doctor. Having obtained approval from necessary authorities, the completed forms were forwarded to National Defence Headquarters (NDHQ). We knew our Pony wouldn't do in Holberg so we decided to trade it on a new Nissan King Cab pick up. It would be more practical on the gravel roads of Northern Vancouver Island.

We spent the holidays in quiet relaxation at home. Once again, John Sam came to visit Ken for a day. Everything seemed to be going too well. Luck didn't hold out. On the first day back to work after the holidays, Peter informed me that the commanding officer had not recommended my OCTP application. During an interview, the following day, Major Dunsdon made his reasons clear.

"Why don't you just get married and avoid all these problems?" he argued.

Acknowledgement of my education and community involvement provided little comfort, as Dunsdon offered a serious criticism of my challenge to the common-law policy.

"He has had a tendency in the past to buck or ignore the system if he does not agree."

In addressing leadership, he emphasized; "MCpl Lagace was promoted to MCpl in 1987 and his leadership potential cannot yet be assessed."

It's difficult to understand how Dunsdon could overlook an "above average leadership potential" assessment from my 1981 Junior Leadership Course (JLC).

His recommendation, "that at least one or two PERs as a MCpl be assessed prior to a recommendation for OCTP", confirms the intent of his actions.

My age and time-in-service criteria would not permit future applications for commissioning under the OCTP program. With less than a year of university to complete, I no longer qualified for the University Training Plan for Men (UTPM) program. When informed of this being my last opportunity for commissioning under the OCTP program, Dunsdon smiled and blurted, "Too bad".

Ironically, Dunsdon's stringent criteria on leadership and performance did not apply to Corporal John Middleveen's application for commissioning that year. John had never attended the Junior Leadership Course (JLC) and his potential had never been assessed. Dunsdon's motives for ignoring the results of my JLC remain a mystery. Additionally, John failed the first phase of the Basic Officer Training Course (BOTC), which would normally disqualify a candidate from obtaining a commission. However, John was commissioned and allowed to proceed on his first year of university training. One can argue that my qualifications were not the issue of concern to authorities. It's clear my redress and complaint were.

It would be necessary to complete my degree in order to apply for special commissioning.

During an interview with Lieutenant Jodoin, later that day, I was reminded of the importance of obeying orders.

"To be an officer, you have to accept the rules even if you don't agree with them", argued Lieutenant Jodoin.

His narrow focus on obedience lacked experience in reality. This archaic image of military authority was traditionally extended to include one's family situation.

"Your common-law wife would not fit well into the officers' mess," he added, because "you must display a willingness to accept regulations whether you like it or not".

In other words, I had failed to impose a marriage ceremony on Amy and that was perceived as a challenge to the "moral image" of what an officer has to represent. He was being honest in what he knew of informal expectations. As a young officer, he displayed the expected support of superiors. I knew he didn't agree with the commanding officer's approach to my commissioning application, but he would not acknowledge his disapproval.

Operating the site's switchboard often meant having to monitor calls in order to confirm line operations. A few days after the interview with Dunsdon, I briefly overheard him in a phone discussion with the commanding officer of CFS Holberg. It appeared the matter of my transfer to Holberg was cause for concern.

"In Lagace's case, you have to apply regulations to the letter", stated Dunsdon.

He went on, "Common-law is not recognized, so don't recognize it."

Within a week, the orderly room clerk at Holberg informed me that Amy and Ken would not be permitted to reside on the station, because they were not considered "legal" dependents. However, it was necessary for me to move on the station, since the commanding officer would not allow any personnel to live off station. This was a definite indication that our family situation was being challenged by authorities, again! During that week, two sets of documents were mysteriously dropped off at our home. It was unusual for documents to be delivered at home. Ken received the documents and became aware of difficulties accompanying our transfer.

Semi-isolated conditions at CFS Holberg involved special arrangements for dependent education. Under the non-resident school fees agreement, the Department of National Defence paid $255.30 per month per student to the province for dependent education. Because Ken was not considered a legal dependent, it was implied on the document that, if we moved to Holberg, we would have to pay those fees. Accompanying the school fees document was a routine order entry which outlined the allowances for moving family pets.

It's ironic that military personnel could move any number of family pets, at public expense, without proof of ownership. On the other hand, allowances were not provided for a common-law spouse and dependents because their relationship to the military member seemed less formal than that of a pet. This attempt to harass us had been successful. Ken was now aware that his education would involve extra expenses, which he also knew we couldn't afford. It was also clear to him that the Department of National Defence (DND) regarded his existence as less important than a pet. We could move our cat at public expense, but he and Amy wouldn't even be allowed to live with me.

The situation was becoming increasingly untenable. To make matters worse, NDHQ refused to accept the completed screening documentation. Their message left no doubt about the intended treatment of our family situation.

"Common-law not recognized as legal marital status by Canadian Forces. Therefore any screening action for common-law wife and her dependent son is member's responsibility and not the Canadian Forces."

Pressures continued as authorities sought opportunities to apply regulations "to the letter". Although sympathetic, Chief Warrant Officer Pete Henderson could not resolve the problems that a move to Holberg would have generated. Finally, on January 28, 1988, I received word that we would be transferred back to North Bay instead of Holberg. Ken made no comment, as he had become withdrawn and quiet. Amy tried to keep a positive outlook, but I could tell she was disappointed.

Everything seemed to be going wrong all at once. With hopes for a commission crushed and a transfer to North Bay scheduled for June, I continued my studies while Amy worked part time with a native education program. I also kept the Human Rights Commission informed of events as they unfolded. At Lieutenant Jodoin's suggestion, I agreed to discuss my career potential with the Base Personnel Selection Officer at Chilliwack.

In early March, Captain B.E. Belec confirmed the obvious. Allowing media attention to focus on our common-law situation, in 1986, had been a serious insult to authorities who now questioned my loyalty. Now there's a fine lot to be assessing my loyalty when they failed to deal with their own deviance from regulations. Nevertheless, I came away from the three hour interview with a deep sense of loss. Prospects for career advancement were dim. The cloud over my career remained firmly attached to the matter of our common-law relationship.

The return trip from Chilliwack tired me out as the roads were treacherous and my mind kept reviewing Captain Belec's argument. While a commission seemed out of reach, he felt positive that education and experience would provide an excellent opportunity for me to work as a counsellor with an alcohol rehabilitation clinic.

On March 11, the tribunal chairman finally rendered a decision on the common-law issue. His support of the DND position was harshly criticized by the Editor of the Canadian Human Rights Advocate, Kathleen Ruff.

She stated, "Douglas turns the clock back to a past era of intolerance which places women in common-law relationships in an extremely stigmatized and vulnerable situation."

Although the decision would be appealed to the Federal Court, military authorities took refuge in that decision to exact penalties against members involved in common-law situations. In Debert, Nova Scotia, a commanding officer ordered the military police to escort a young woman and her child off the base while the common-law husband was at work. A few days later, the young corporal was notified that he would have to move his mobile home off base, since his common-law spouse would not be allowed on base.

In Greenwood, Nova Scotia, a different type of harassment was taking place as the common-law wife of a military member was subjected to a daily routine of completing forms, to obtain clearance from the military police in order to drive her husband to work on Base.

BULLIES IN POWER

Nothing was working right because authorities had the freedom to control public information and the application of rules. Only embarrassment would motivate authorities to change attitudes. The only way to gain influence would be through the establishment of a network of military personnel willing to take the risk of gathering information against senior ranks. That information could then be released to media contacts in pieces so that the puzzle would form slowly and prevent tracing the information to specific sources.

The aim of embarrassing military authorities would serve two purposes. First, authorities lacking the trust in their peers would direct suspicion at peers rather than subordinates. Consequently, a process of backstabbing would begin. Second, public confidence in military authorities would be eroded. For years, military authorities have functioned under a cloak of immunity and a somewhat unrealistic public belief that they could do no wrong. Albeit subversive, my goal was focused on the infusion of reality into the façade that protected abusive authorities.

Meanwhile, the Douglas decision would make life more difficult as the station closure drew near and Major Dunsdon seemed to have a free hand to impose his authority. His political ambition was focussed on the mayor's seat in the upcoming municipal election. Consequently, he maintained close relationships with influential community members. Visits and social functions would involve municipal 'dignitaries'. The fact that NDHQ turned a blind eye to Major Dunsdon's activities only extended the power of his authority over subordinate officers on site.

In late March, Ken's teacher became concerned with his behaviour. He had been withdrawn and showed signs of depression. It was felt the problem was serious enough to advise us. We tried to discuss the matter with Ken, but he maintained that there was nothing wrong. Impatience often led to angry outbursts between Ken and me. He had neglected his homework and I was angry. With all the difficulties taking place, Ken's feelings were the last thing I thought about. Being sorry for yelling at him simply wasn't enough.

Emotions were in turmoil in our home and we needed advice on how to deal with the crisis. Counselling was arranged through our family doctor. We would attend a local counselling centre during early evening hours so that Ken's school schedule would not be affected.

Ken's Confirmation in 1987
L-R Ken's Dad John Sam, Ken, and Godfather Ed Holm

At 13, he was emotionally vulnerable and we didn't realize his state of mind was seriously affected by the barrage of critical events and negative perceptions of our situation. As rules of confidentiality are undermined by the military chain of command, it was imperative that military channels not be involved. Under normal circumstances, medical personnel on site might have been trusted to assist with this crisis.

Sergeant Paul Livingston, the senior medical assistant, was known for his inability to keep his mouth shut on any sensitive matter. To confide in him could have had devastating effects. If Dunsdon had become aware that we were undergoing family counselling, there is no doubt it would have rekindled his attack on our situation and provided leverage to justify release action. Authorities had shown a lack of sensitivity with our situation. The counsellor and doctor agreed military authorities could not be trusted.

Amy felt helpless and, for the first time in years, I felt a strong urge to get drunk and avoid reality for a while. I knew from experience that getting drunk would have led to a violent confrontation and military

BULLIES IN POWER

authorities would have accomplished the goal of provocations. Counselling sessions revealed Ken felt responsible for financial and administrative pressures imposed by military authorities. Helping him became our first priority. It meant that military activities would no longer be part of our family life.

Closure of the radar site involved a number of activities. A mess dinner had been scheduled for April 8th. As I had been selected to attend this compulsory function, our family counselling session had been scheduled for the 15th. However, a last minute change of plans saw the dinner re-scheduled for the 15th. Getting excused from the dinner was the only option left, as counselling sessions were difficult to re-schedule. When I discussed the matter with the station Master Warrant Officer, Ed Skretka, he explained that only a medical doctor could excuse me from the dinner. Once again, regulations were being applied "to the letter".

So I approached our site medic, Paul Livingston, about seeing the doctor. After I refused to provide details and explained the problem was personal, he reluctantly made an appointment. Doctor J.L. Mabee, a civilian doctor employed on contract for the site's military personnel, provided an excusal form and ridiculed military authorities for their immature attitudes. The excusal would not satisfy our inquisitive medic. When presented with the document, he immediately called Doctor Mabee to question the matter. Needless to say, the excusal was not accepted by Dunsdon, who used an obscure regulation to override the doctor's recommendation. Ed Skretka later informed me of the cancelled excusal and that the dinner was compulsory. I thought, why am I arguing with these idiots? With all the available alcohol, attending that dinner with an urge to get drunk would have been insane. We maintained our priority and kept our counselling appointment.

The following week was particularly difficult as exams kept me busy almost day and night. James Hendry provided a bit of good news when he confirmed the tribunal decision would be appealed to the Federal Court. In preparation for our transfer, it was necessary to apply for a mobile home pad on base at North Bay.

As expected, the housing officer, Roger Levesque, cynically replied, "Since your documents show that you are single we regret to inform you that you do not qualify for a trailer pad on base."

Consequently, I would have to take a House Hunting Trip to North Bay in hope of locating a pad off base.

As if matters weren't bad enough, on April 24th Ed Skretka advised me that I would be charged for failing to attend the mess dinner. I couldn't believe it! The following day, Dunsdon found me guilty and imposed a hundred dollar fine along with a severe reprimand as punishment. Dunsdon had been embezzling thousands of dollars through messing accounts while military authorities looked the other way. Now they would look the other way while he took even more money through the abuse of his position. His actions confirmed that our family crisis would have meant nothing to him, except as a reason for further harassment. The only recourse was to apply for redress of grievance. As with the first redress, it would take months to receive a reply. At least military authorities couldn't say they were not aware of Dunsdon's activities.

I spent the first week in May looking for a trailer pad in the North Bay area. The only pad available was located in Redbridge, about 25 kilometres from North Bay. Returning to Kamloops, another disappointment awaited. The station accounting officer, Captain Carl Hussey, had decided to cancel our dental coverage. According to Canadian Forces policy, our common- law relationship did not entitle us to dental coverage. That was the straw that broke the camel's back.

A review of events since our arrival suggested that there was too much to be explained by coincidence. I filed a retaliation complaint against Dunsdon, through the Human Rights Commission. The offence involved a criminal investigation which led to an interview with Corporal D.L. Ayers of the Kamloops RCMP. He then interviewed Dunsdon. However, unlike other criminal investigations, it appears the accused is not compelled to answer any questions. It was explained that unless Dunsdon confessed to the offence, there would be no prosecution. Getting him to confess was as likely as getting crows to turn white.

Dunsdon's high profile in municipal politics obviously sheltered him from serious investigation. Although many personnel on site offered words of support, it was obvious from their behaviour that fears motivated most to avoid speaking openly. Andy Bigras knew the situation but visited almost every day. He wasn't influenced by the commanding officer's subtle threats.

My brother, Pierre, had travelled to Kamloops for a visit and chose to stay with us while we prepared for our move. It was a relief to have him help with the removal of skirting around the mobile home. After dismantling the makeshift porch, the movers came in to estimate the moving contract.

Amy and Ken spent a great deal of time in the city during the day. I had been assigned to work with Master Corporal Claude Rainville, in the traffic section, shortly after returning from the trip to North Bay. With limited television channels, our evenings were enjoyed by the pool or visiting friends in the city. The last two weeks before a move always seem to drag on. Finally, the day came when movers packed and loaded our furniture. With only the empty mobile left on site, Amy and Ken went through the front gate of the site for the last time as we went to check into a motel for our last night in Kamloops. Amy seemed glad to be away from the site, but sad to be leaving Kamloops again.

Two years had gone by so fast and yet so much had happened in such a short period of time. It was hot and Bear didn't like the back of the truck. With all the camping equipment and assorted things that the movers wouldn't take, there was little room for her cage. Ken had set up a mattress in the back and looked forward to keeping her company on the trip.

Shortly after breakfast the next day, I accompanied the mobile home movers to the site. As they left, I took one last look at the countryside. Yes, it had changed from that first afternoon in early January, 1979, when I saw it for the first time. My heart was heavy with tarnished memories that would never be restored. I met Amy and Ken at the motel where we silently loaded our things in the truck and left.

THE CHALLENGE: TURNING THE TIDES

This road would take us from a place we didn't want to leave to a place we didn't want to go. For almost two hours Amy remained silent. Events of the first trip to North Bay buzzed around in my head. The turmoil of relocating home and family left me questioning career goals, but with my degree almost completed a thread of hope remained. More importantly, job options and family commitment made leaving the military an impractical alternative.

Resigned to make the best of it, we began another camping trip that would take us across the country. Lakes and hills of the countryside went without notice, until I suddenly realized we were approaching the Rogers Pass area. No matter how depressed life can appear, the breathtaking scenery between Revelstoke and Golden, British Columbia, captures the attention of anyone driving through.

Amy broke the silence to call attention to Ken and Bear. Both had fallen asleep on the mattress. Resting her head on Ken's foot, Bear appeared more relaxed about the trip. As we left the Rocky Mountains behind, a sombre feeling washed over us. Choking back the emotional impact of reality, we looked at each other with silent understanding of the uncertainty that laid ahead. Few words were spoken on that first day. Calgary played host to us again. Too tired

BULLIES IN POWER

to set up camp at a campsite, we stayed at a motel and had supper at a nearby restaurant.

Bear seemed to suffer most from the unbearable prairie heat. After two days of trying to find a cool place for her in the back of the truck, we began to worry that she might become ill. In Winnipeg, the rain increased the humidity level but did little to cool the air. We sought refuge in an air-conditioned motel, where Bear spent the night sleeping on the floor in front of the air conditioner.

We took every opportunity to minimize costs by cooking meals at roadside campsites. Camping just outside of Thunder Bay, at the end of four exhausting days, the last thing we needed was rain. But we got it anyway. An early start the next morning allowed us to make it to North Bay late that evening. We arrived before the mobile home movers. It would take another two weeks to settle our mobile home in Redbridge and take delivery of our furniture. In the meantime, we stayed at a motel.

Once again I was assigned to work in the Regional Operations Control Centre (ROCC), but this time as an Identification Technician. It was an unfamiliar task that required training. Corporal Cathy Hilts was assigned to prepare me for an operational qualification. A short stocky woman with a quiet demeanour, she certainly knew her job. Nothing seemed to disturb her calm approach to often stressful conditions.

At work, I listened to Cathy's explanations attentively and made every effort to avoid conflict with authorities. Meanwhile, at home, I worked on a social psychology course that had accompanied me from Kamloops. The course exam was scheduled for early August. With only a few weeks to complete an already late final assignment, I had no time to work at setting skirting around the home. As the exam date approached, I spent most of my off hours studying at the library.

We had been compelled to settle our home about 25 kilometres from the base. Consequently, it was agreed that the phone would be in Amy's name so that supervisors would not be able to harass us by calling me to work on my days off.

Following my initial grievance in 1983, it had become common practice to call me in with no concern for time of day or my days off. The process had served to harass the entire family. This time, there would be no home phone number provided and supervisors were advised of the necessary barrier between my work and home responsibilities. Interference would be addressed as harassment. Shortly after arriving at North Bay, the commanding officer, Lieutenant Colonel W.D. Reimer, began to pressure supervisors for my home phone number.

"It is military policy that you have a phone in case you are required at work," Captain Natalie Leblanc argued.

Somewhat naive about the "Old Boys' Network", she simply could not believe that any commanding officer would use his position to harass anyone. There was no means to compromise. Past experience proved supervisors could not prevent senior officers from having me report to work on my days off. So our phone number remained a secret.

Training progressed exceptionally well and within a few weeks the identification of air traffic was becoming very familiar. In order to attend the social psychology exam I would require a day of leave. While it was unusual for a military member to require leave to attend recognized university exams, my situation appeared different.

The motives for differential treatment became obvious when my request for leave was denied. Facing the possibility of missing the exam, it was clear Lieutenant Colonel Reimer had exercised the authority of his rank to create an impossible situation. There was no time to address the matter through the redress procedure. In discussing the issue with Master Warrant Officer Guy Baker, I explained my entitlement for leave during the summer months. He argued that I was on training and would not be granted leave until qualified as an Identification Technician. It was then necessary to affirm the possibility of filing a human rights complaint for harassment and grievance for the inappropriate use of administrative policies. Leave was reluctantly approved a few days prior to the exam. There was no question that Lieutenant Colonel Reimer and Master Warrant Officer (MWO) Baker intended to make life miserable at work. As

BULLIES IN POWER

for Social Psychology 450, I achieved an "A" on the exam and the course.

The Human Rights Commission advised us that the retaliation complaint against Major Dunsdon had not been supported by the Royal Canadian Mounted Police (RCMP) investigation. A letter from RCMP headquarters confirmed the result of their investigation. Investigators argued that Major Dunsdon's actions were part of his job. However, it was soon discovered that he had not followed regulations in processing the Officer Cadet Training Plan (OCTP) application.

A Human Rights Commission investigator would later uncover the inadequacies of the RCMP investigation. When addressing the subject of the OCTP application to DND officials, their reply confirmed that Dunsdon had refused to follow regulations.

Officials at NDHQ smugly argued, "that there is no application for O.C.T.P. on file as required and it is therefore assumed that no formal application was submitted by the complainant."

Fortunately, my copy of the completed application, with Dunsdon's comments on it, was proof that I had in fact applied. Without that document, it would have been difficult to support the career damage complaint filed during the summer of 1988. Dunsdon would later admit to the evidence of inappropriate behaviour in dealing with our situation.

Why was there so much difference between the results of the RCMP investigation and that of the Human Rights Investigator? The event didn't change. It is my well-researched opinion that the Kamloops RCMP was reluctant to address the complaint seriously because Dunsdon was a prominent figure in the community. However, the Commission investigator was not influenced by Dunsdon's role in the community.

As the commanding officer of the radar site and alderman on Kamloops City Council, Dunsdon had become a familiar member of the community. His contacts with the local RCMP may have influenced a biased support of his credibility over mine. Let's face it, the RCMP is human too.

It's difficult to blame subjectivity on any particular individual. There is no evidence that the investigation even took place, as the reports are not accessible. It seems unfair that Dunsdon would have access to my statements, but I would not be given the opportunity to review his explanation. Under the circumstances, we had no choice but to accept the RCMP's closure of the file.

Matters of the cancelled dental plan, denial of access to a mobile home pad on base in North Bay, and the denial of family allowances for our move were all addressed through a complaint filed shortly after our arrival at North Bay.

The difficulty in dealing with multiple incidents of discrimination is that the Human Rights Commission addresses each incident by itself. For example, the military's discriminatory policy affected my career as well as financial allowances. Separate complaints were necessary to deal with each situation.

As victims, the reason for filing a complaint is to stop the problem from growing. Complaints addressed individual situations, but failed to prevent the continued pattern of discrimination that would take a different tangent as each situation was reported. The pattern was becoming more pronounced.

I had addressed the issue of housing, but military officials increased the need for more complaints by expanding the field of application of their discriminatory policy. The strategy served to compound the problem, thereby making a solution that much more difficult to define. I had been compelled to file complaints for housing, dental, moving allowances, career damages, and harassment. The process had not yet addressed the first complaint.

Meanwhile, a few months had elapsed since our arrival at North Bay. During in-clearance routines, I had refused to pay mess dues because of our limited budget. After all, we had been forced to live out of town and simply couldn't afford to attend the mess. So why pay dues to support a social establishment that we couldn't attend? After three months, the accounting staff sought to collect dues by imposing an administrative deduction.

Through Lieutenant Colonel Reimer, the process began. It didn't seem to matter that we were financially broke. Supporting alcohol consumption took priority over family needs. There had not been a response to the redress of grievance, filed after the mess dinner

BULLIES IN POWER

incident at Kamloops. When all else fails, simply refuse to pay. That usually gets somebody's attention. It did.

In mid-November, 1988, the Acting Commander of Air Command forwarded a stinging response. Short of calling me unpatriotic, Major General J.R. Chisholm presented a review of "custom and tradition" which places mess dinners at the forefront of service members' lives. Colonel P.A. Riis, Radar Control Wing Commander, added his own rhetoric on mess dues by calling attention to the purpose of Canadian involvement in two World Wars. In questioning the legitimacy of mess dues I was somehow denigrating those who had fallen on the battle fields to protect our freedom.

It's ironic that our freedom of choice always seems to be defined by authorities who fail to recognize the difference between their privilege and our rights. Mess dues suddenly become something that others have died for. I shudder to think what life would be like without having to pay for a mess, where military members can go to have a few drinks. Also unthinkable, is the idea that military officers would find it necessary to display their pomp in a civilian establishment.

Messes have been a financial cost to the majority in support of a minority's need for covert alcohol consumption. Civilians know very little about the extravagant costs involved in providing mess dinners. More importantly, mess dinners are partially funded by public funds. As taxpayers and military members, we got to pay in both capacities. And that, according to Major General Chisholm and Colonel Riis, is why we fought two World Wars.

Officers are often too far removed from the reality of financial limits to allow common sense to interrupt their fairy tale image of military pageantry. After all, senior military officers don't have to worry about financial limits because social activities are paid by taxpayers. Lower ranks pay their own way when attending social functions while senior officers are privileged to claim the costs at public expense. As my grievance was getting nowhere, I terminated it in favour of devoting more time to working on the New Boys' Network.

Lieutenant Colonel Reimer imposed the administrative deduction without concern for family needs or the fact that I could not attend

Amy tries out new shovel in Redbridge Ontario, 1988

social functions at the mess. In retrospect, it's obvious that military authorities display a need to control by virtue of position. Similar behaviour patterns and attitudes are commonly found at the heart of dysfunctional families where an insecure parent dominates by force.

Because we lived in Redbridge, Ken's after-school activities were taking toll on the truck. Public transit wasn't accessible. By early December, winter had stormed in with bitter cold temperatures and more snow than previous years. Ken decided to enrol with his school's cross-country ski team. Although he would have preferred to learn downhill skiing, we simply couldn't afford the costs. I felt sad about that financial reality. Ken never complained. He took advantage of the opportunity to get as much cross-country training as possible. I borrowed skis from the Gymnasium sport stores and went out with him a few times. Even Amy tried the sport. During such outings we lost ourselves in joys of the moment where pressures of military authorities couldn't reach us.

Christmas holidays reminded us of family members near and far. Amy's niece had been under the care of Social Services in Kamloops, British Columbia. At 14 years of age, Michelle's life at home had become difficult and she chose to seek refuge in a group home. When a social worker called us about taking Michelle into our home, we simply couldn't refuse. Within four days Michelle arrived. I've never seen social workers move so fast.

It would take some time for the paperwork to catch up, but we were happy to have this grown-up addition to our family. Ken was particularly happy to have someone his own age to relate to.

Christmas was made even more joyous by a phone call from James Hendry. The Federal Court of Appeal had ruled in favour of recognizing common-law as a marital status. The precedent-setting ruling called on Department of National Defence (DND) to move from its archaic practice of non recognition of common-law relationships.

Lieutenant Colonel Reimer was not aware of the ruling when I returned to work later that week. I had been at work less than an hour when Master Warrant Officer Baker called on me to attend Reimer's office. The smell of alcohol permeated the small office. Reimer spoke with a slight slur as he informed me of his intent to see me out of the military.

"We don't need guys like you in the service, and I'm going to make it my business to have you released."

A flash of anger swept over me like a tidal wave. My head felt ready to burst. A tremendous urge to strike out almost took over. He then called attention to my grievance and how my actions had offended many senior and "respectable" military members at NDHQ.

Obviously, he had mistaken my calm demeanour for naivety. Under the calm exterior there was a growing rage that threatened to explode. Listening to a flow of criticism any longer would have led to a physical confrontation. So I chose to leave his office and call James Hendry to ask that such harassment be stopped.

Taking the threat of release seriously, the Human Rights Commission lawyer brought the matter to DND authorities. A few days later I received a message of transfer, along with instructions to attend a five-week Nuclear, Biological and Chemical Defence (NBCD) course at Canadian Forces Base (CFB) Borden. With less than a week to prepare, there was no way to postpone the two university courses already in progress. So I took the study material with me and worked on assignments during spare time.

John Sam's plan to visit Ken for a week made it necessary for Amy to drive to Toronto during the fourth weekend of the course. It was an opportunity for the three of us to spend a day together in the Borden area.

The following day, as I accompanied Amy and John to the truck after our morning coffee, a familiar car pulled up beside us. To our surprise Lois stepped out and was equally shocked to see us. As Amy and John headed out to North Bay I spent the day reminiscing with Lois. The years had not affected that special twinkle in her eyes. We talked like only close friends can and shared emotional experiences while the afternoon wore on.

We parted as we always did: with a warm hug and assurances of visits. I tried to study that evening, but my mind kept wandering over events of my past and expectations for the future.

The following week I returned to North Bay, having achieved one of only two A's among the 16-student class. With a transfer to Base Nuclear Defence assured, I now focused on two university exams with only two weeks to prepare. Sleepless nights in study provided the reward of two more A's.

Meanwhile, in the Regional Operations Control Centre (ROCC), I began my out-clearances in order to transfer to my new position on Base. During the final morning in the Operations Room, Master Warrant Officer Guy Baker nervously informed me of Lieutenant Colonel Reimer's release from the military. It was not my concern and I didn't ask for details.

A sense of relief breezed through me as I left "The Hole" for what I thought would be the last time. Authorities have never liked the nickname "Hole" for this underground complex. However, many in the Air Defence occupation apply a slightly different connotation to "The Hole" than just a complex about nine hundred feet underground. Perhaps the most appropriate explanation of the nickname is if the earth was to get an enema, "The Hole" in North Bay is where God would stick the tube.

Captain Jene Kleinschroth, a portly man in his early fifties, introduced himself with a warm smile and hearty handshake. As the base nuclear defence officer, he was to become the first commanding officer to acknowledge the true nature of my situation.

BULLIES IN POWER

Introducing me to my new supervisor, Sergeant Mike Christie, Jene jokingly remarked, "Maybe now some work will get done around here."

For the first time in years I felt welcomed. Irene Anderson greeted me with a caring smile and an offer of clerical support on any tasking that might require typing. As the secretary for the base operations officer, she also performed clerical duties for nuclear defence training programs.

Major Scott Archer wasted no time in offering his support. He confirmed, "My door is always open, Paul. Any problem you have I want to help you deal with it."

I had heard those words from other officers, but this fellow was different. Evidence of his support would become apparent later that year.

The Federal Court decision had taken effect and we were offered a Married Quarters (MQ). Expenses in Redbridge had exceeded my income since the move in 1988. With Michelle and Ken needing to get closer to school, moving into an MQ seemed our only hope for improving access to after-school programs. Once our mobile home was sold, we moved into an MQ. The redress of grievance for housing was finally settled after almost six years in processing.

It was mid-August and less than a week after the move from Redbridge that my brothers and their families decided to come out and visit for a few weeks. No sooner did one family leave, another arrived. Amy was becoming irritated with the lack of privacy. For about two weeks we had kids sleeping all over the place from the living room to the basement. To cap off the summer, we agreed to visit Niagara Falls for a few days with my brother Allain and his family. There's nothing like a vacation together to build tension. Luckily, Allain's need to return home cut our trip a few days short. The rush around family visits left Amy in need of time to recuperate, like maybe a decade or two.

Summer had come and gone with as much notice as the blink of an eye. Mike was busy preparing a schedule for training base personnel on shelter operations. Jene asked if I would take on the secondary duty of Unit Drug Education Coordinator (UDEC) for the Operations Branch. It meant going on a one-week course at Arnprior.

149

Already it was apparent that Jene and Scott supported my interests with drug and alcohol education programs.

My directed study in sociology was almost completed and there was plenty of time to get involved with other interests. Shortly after returning from Arnprior, in late November, I was informed by my sociology tutor that my directed study had earned a B. I wasted no time registering for the directed study in psychology. After eight years, an important goal approached completion.

The directed study in psychology called for extensive research which could only be accessed at the college library. I decided to take leave for six weeks. I wanted this study to be my best work. I spent an average of 16 hours a day to reading and writing about alcoholism.

By late February, 1990, a sixty-page research paper was ready for submission. I anxiously waited for my tutor's call. Two weeks went by and I began to worry. Finally, early one evening in mid-March, the phone rang and I instinctively felt nervous tension. It was the long-awaited call.

"Written with the quality of a Master's Thesis," he stated.

I had done it! My degree was completed. Amy glowed with happiness. Ken and Michelle were happy to hear they wouldn't have to put up with my need for absolute quiet in the house. Jene and Mike congratulated my perseverance.

"So are you going to apply for your commission now?" asked Jene.

After being disappointed four times, the thought of being rejected scared me. Each time I had been encouraged to apply and each disappointment had been followed by deeper states of emotional turmoil and depression. Despite Jene's positive outlook, I turned down the proposal of another application.

After a few weeks of almost daily assurances from Jene, that an application would certainly get me commissioned, I fell for it. "I have it from very high up that your application will be rubber stamped, Paul," he argued. Hopes for positive results led to my fifth commissioning application in late April, 1990. Neither Jene, nor Scott, were aware of the barriers that lay ahead. Completing a

BULLIES IN POWER

Bachelor of Arts degree and strong support from my commanding officer should have provided access to the competition.

While anxiously awaiting the screening interview with the Base Personnel Selection Officer (BPSO), I received word from Open University that all requirements were complete. My degree would be presented at the next convocation.

By late June, I was beginning to wonder if the interview with Captain David Wong (BPSO) would ever take place. Finally, on June 21, after a two-hour interview, I was informed that my application would receive favourable support. Wong felt confident I'd make a good officer. After almost ten years of rejections, it was a relief to hear positive feedback. Although the application would require the Base Commander's support, it was expected to be a simple formality.

Colonel A.J. "Butch" Waldrum had been very active in community activities and provided strong support for improvements to the military lifestyle. However, his liberal facade proved to be more political than practical. The following day, Jene came in the office with a look of disappointment on his face.

It appears, in discussing my commission with Colonel Waldrum, Jene was told, "Not in a million years will he be commissioned".

Two days later a message from National Defence Headquarters (NDHQ) indicated my choice of occupation was closed indefinitely. Wong pointed out that Waldrum was transferred in early July and that my application would certainly be forwarded by the new Base Commander.

In the meantime, a selection of alternative occupational choices would increase chances of selection. It was only a couple of weeks to wait, so I went along with the plan.

A few days later, Jene approached me about becoming the Base Newspaper Editor. Traditionally reserved for officers, it appears Waldrum thought the position would allow me the opportunity to show my leadership abilities. Had Waldrum changed his perception? It would later prove to be another administrative trap.

Jene explained, "It could be the chance you need right now."

It seemed like a good idea. Besides, this secondary duty included a one-week course at Ryerson School of Journalism in Toronto. My schedule would require planning in order to keep up the duties of

Sergeant (Ret'd) Paul M. Lagace, CD., B.A.

Unit Drug Education Coordinator (UDEC) and Base Newspaper Editor, while maintaining a daily fitness program and performing my primary duties in the nuclear defence section. Evenings were occupied with the ministry of corrections as a volunteer probation officer. What more could be done to display those "officer-like qualities"?

The application for special commissioning was finally sent to NDHQ in late August, 1990. However, it was two days late for the selection board. Although my application would be held until the next selection board, hopes for a commission vanished. Amy had warned me that I was being led into another trap. Each rejection seemed to take a little more out of me. Once again I became depressed for a while.

Was it simply an administrative error that my application took over three months to reach NDHQ? Could it be coincidence that the first occupation selected just happened to close two days after Colonel Waldrum harshly opposed my application? Might it be more bad luck that, once forwarded, the application was two days late for the selection board? Jene explained the pattern of mishaps as a sequence of bad luck. The look on his face and his tone confirmed that he didn't believe himself. He had been reassured, by a Colonel in the Personnel Selection Branch at Ottawa, that my application would receive approval. Now he felt used.

In hindsight, it's crystal clear that the aim was to ensure another rejection on record with an "unsuitable" rating. It had been difficult to trust Jene's encouragement and assurances of support. After all, a few years earlier, Captain Cliff Halpen had offered similar encouragement for the previous application. It's my belief that officials at NDHQ were playing a cruel mind game. I was repeatedly led to the edge of success with empty promises only to be rejected with criticism and blamed for failure. It would later be proven that this latest rejection played a key role in an elaborate plan among senior officials to cover-up Major Dunsdon's refusal to process the 1988 OCTP application.

During the summer, Amy registered for a two-year social service worker program scheduled to begin in September at Canadore College. Moving to Married Quarters brought us closer to college

BULLIES IN POWER

and public transit. The truck was giving us problems, not to mention the lack of seating space for Ken and Michelle, so we decided to trade it for a new car. They were now able to sit in the back seat without the usual complaints about crowding.

Living in town also allowed more flexibility for participation in after- school sports. Amy enjoyed her studies, even though she worried about the quality of her work. Her mid-term report left no doubt about her abilities. Having achieved A's on most of her courses, she now worried about keeping up with the marks.

Although Canadian Forces regulations now recognized common-law relationships, the application of the Federal Court ruling was limited to housing. To deal with the complaints for denied moving allowances during our 1986 and 1988 transfers, the Human Rights Commission appointed Brian K. Stewart as conciliator. His attempts at conciliation met with bureaucratic resistance from military officials. The 1988 career damages complaint remained under investigation.

Over the years, Christmas marked a time for good news. In late December, 1990, I received a letter from the principal of Open University. Amy noticed my excitement as I read the letter. My Grade Point Average (G.P.A.) had earned the Governor General's Silver Medal Award as top graduating student that year. The letter also pointed out that I was the first recipient of the award at Open University. A formal presentation was scheduled to take place at Vancouver during the official convocation in March, 1991.

University Convocation in 1991

What a way to celebrate the holidays! Unfortunately, Amy's exam week was scheduled at the same time as the convocation and she wouldn't be able to accompany me to Vancouver. I wanted Amy to share the experience since it was her support that helped make the accomplishment possible. In compromise, we agreed to have the event video taped.

Returning to work after the holidays, I wasted no time in sharing the good news with Jene and Mike.

Jene emphasized, "They can't turn you down now. You've proven your potential and they'd be crazy not to offer you a commission."

I was sceptical about the possibilities of a commission. A few weeks later, I signed my annual performance evaluation report. For two years I had worked hard and Mike had ensured my reports reflected the effort. The new Base Operations Officer, Major Michel Prud'homme, had been in conflict with Jene and Mike since his arrival.

Jene had decided to retire when it was made clear that he had been misled by senior officers. Mike took an assignment to Alert. A strong proponent of French language, Prud'homme had also pressured Irene to quit. Conditions in our unit had deteriorated rapidly. Prud'homme went about his daily routine and I managed to stay out of his way. The last thing I needed was to butt heads with someone in a position of authority. I was busy enough with secondary duties that our paths seldom crossed.

In early February, another transfer was planned for us. The Career Manager, Chief Warrant Officer Pete Henderson, asked if I would be willing to move to British Columbia. Not knowing how long I could avoid conflict with Prud'homme, I accepted the transfer to Holberg. Changes in the Air Defence structure had reduced Holberg radar to a Detachment of two crews involving about 35 personnel to man the Operation site. Families were now housed in the Comox Valley area, while personnel worked a seven-day rotation.

I expected to go unaccompanied for a year while Amy and Ken remained in North Bay. Michelle had already moved to Vancouver shortly after locating her biological father. He and his wife looked forward to getting to know Michelle. Teaching her about responsibility also meant she needed to experience making decisions. Although I felt she should have completed high school before moving, the choice had to be left with her. At 16, she was old enough to make her own decisions. After all, it wasn't our intention to turn our home into a prison.

I was apprehensive about leaving Amy and Ken in North Bay. I thought, "Perhaps I will be commissioned before the transfer." Hope and luck appeared to be antagonistic partners in my career. What I hoped for always seemed to fall prey to bad luck. Shortly after returning from the convocation, Prud'homme received a message that I had been found "unsuitable" for commissioning. The grievance and complaints to the human rights commission had weighted against me.

According to the report, my personal file reflected a history of problems with non-adherence to regulations and poor judgement. It's difficult to understand how the board came to that conclusion. They must have been looking at a very short history because the previous rejection, in 1986, had focussed on my "average" but "not outstanding" performance reports. Now that my performance reports were outstanding, it seems Lieutenant Colonel M.R. Spooner, Major B.J. Cockerline and Lieutenant Commander G.J. Droszio refused to accept the positive side of my records. Instead, they focussed on inappropriate references to the redress and the excused mess dinner of 1988. Both incidents involved harassment. More importantly, these officers had been involved with the issue of my redress of grievance and human rights complaint.

Obviously, archaic traditions and self-righteous pride among senior officers took precedence over common sense once again. Frustrated, I spoke to Bob Wood, the local Member of Parliament. He decided to bring the matter to the Defence Minister's attention. Discussing the "not suitable" message with Major Prud'homme, he requested a chronological review of events dating back to 1982.

"Bringing the sequence of events to the attention of authorities," he explained, "will hopefully help to correct the problems with your career."

Major Prud'homme submitted the documents to the Base Commander, Colonel E.J. Jackson, who simply ignored the matter entirely. The Associate Minister of Defence, Mary Collins, provided more rhetoric about two months later.

According to Bob Wood, "The Minister is satisfied that your complaints are being dealt with as quickly as possible."

The Honourable Mary Collins might have been satisfied but it wasn't her career that was being washed down the bureaucratic tubes.

Receiving Fitness Award from Captain Jim Hue at North Bay

Results of Amy's first-year studies proved impressive as she achieved a 3.2 Grade Point Average. Although she felt confident about handling the rigours of the second year in college, financial difficulties associated to the separation convinced us to move to British Columbia as a family. Amy would attempt to transfer her college credits to Malaspina College in Nanaimo. Unfortunately, the attempt was unsuccessful, as Malaspina didn't offer a similar program.

The decision to move as a family involved taking a House Hunting Trip (HHT) to secure accommodation. During the five-day trip, in early June, we managed to purchase a home in Courtenay. As CFB Comox provided logistical support for Detachment Holberg personnel, it seemed logical to settle as close as possible. Additionally, there was less than three years remaining on my 20-year engagement. The career manager was confident that, if I extended my tour at Holberg until closure in 1993, I would be assigned a position at CFB Comox until my release in 1994. Holberg offered the only alternative to an increasingly difficult situation at CFB North Bay.

This would mark our first move with the recognition of family status. In early July Brian Stewart notified us that military authorities had agreed to settle the claims for moving allowances. Unsuspecting of any ulterior motive by military officials, I would later discover the settlement of moving allowances was a legal ploy to prevent any future reference to those incidents. The career damage complaint was left as an isolated incident which meant the motives for Major Dunsdon's actions were clouded by legal secrecy.

We wouldn't have to cook our meals at campsites or search out a low cost motel and tenting. Ken was unhappy about having to leave his friends. Amy pretended the move didn't bother her, but I knew her studies meant a great deal more than she let on. Bear wouldn't travel with us this time. Instead, we decided to place her in a kennel for a couple of weeks until we settled at our new home. The 12-hour flight would be safer than a cross-country drive. We decided to follow a route across the Northern United States.

During the last few days before moving, we took time to have a few of Ken's friends over to enjoy marathon games of Dungeons and Dragons that sometimes lasted through the night. I felt sad for Ken. He would miss his friends. There had been so few of them over the years. Uprooting him and Amy at this time left me feeling guilty. But, it was too late to reverse the decision. We had bought a home and it offered the possibility of a brighter outlook in a new place. With retirement around the corner, it was time to prepare for the transition into a civilian job.

Once the movers finished packing our furniture and effects, we spent our first night in a motel. It was different this time. Ken had his own room and we had ours. The next day we began our trip across the country. It was hot and humid. Thinking of Bear, it was a relief to know she wasn't going to go through the stress of our last move. Ken slept quietly in the back seat. Amy smiled as we headed west.

DECEPTIVE PROCESS BECOMES OBVIOUS

We didn't have to sleep in a tent. Cooking by the roadside was a choice rather than a necessity. Expected to be our last transfer, it wouldn't be a rushed trip. Crossing the border at Sault Ste Marie, the chosen route took us across the Northern United States. A newly purchased video camera recorded roadside points of interest. The three-thousand-mile drive offered a sort of vacation. Each day the Western sunset glowed a little brighter. Leaving Shelby, Montana, Amy thought it might be nice to take a couple of hours to visit her cousin in Cardston, Alberta. After catching up on family news, we headed north towards Calgary.

At the Best Western, the only room available was the Presidential Suite. It was getting late and we didn't want to spend time looking around for less expensive rooms. The experience of having a whirlpool in the bathroom was more luxury than expected. We also enjoyed a spectacular view of snow-capped mountain peaks from our bedroom window.

Ken had adjusted to the freedom of his own room and television as part of the suite. Two bathrooms reduced the frustration of planning our morning schedule. Of course, the video camera recorded memories of that luxurious stay in Calgary.

BULLIES IN POWER

We left late the next morning, bound for Lake Louise and on to Kamloops. After eight days on the road, the ferry crossing to Nanaimo brought us within sixty miles of our new home. A long wait for the ferry at Vancouver's Horseshoe Bay delayed our arrival to Nanaimo, so we decided to stay there overnight. There was no need to report for duty until the afternoon of the ninth day, so we slept in until noon and completed the short drive from Nanaimo after lunch.

Shortly after we arrived at our new home in Courtenay, a long-awaited letter outlining the settlement of complaints, related to moving allowances, provided hope for positive change in regulations. Although a claim for the 1982 transfer had been rejected, there would be compensation for losses incurred during the 1986 and 1988 transfers. Compensation for additional expenses, resulting from having been compelled to settle our mobile home in Redbridge for a year, was also included. By mid-August a cheque for $13,000.00 arrived.

It couldn't compensate for the effects of difficulties that had accompanied years of financial limitations, but it did provide a sense of satisfaction at having accomplished a goal. Much of the money went to our mortgage and household bills, since a tight budget was an accepted way of life.

Amy's family reunion took place at Spences Bridge in early August. We decided to attend and renew old acquaintances. Seeing Amy enjoying the company of her relatives, for the first time since Frank's funeral, confirmed the unspoken bond between the members of this extended family. Of course, the central feature of such gatherings involves the traditional meal. Although my appetite is well adjusted to any type of food, the smoked fish and bannock triggered an almost gluttonous display of my eating habits.

To supplement the main courses, there were all kinds of side dishes along with desert trays filled with "belly puffers". Concerns for waistlines were laid to rest by Amy's cousin Verna who assured us all food items had been turned upside down to drop the calories out. Staying at her Uncle's Motel for a couple of nights brought back many memories for Amy. She recalled working at the Sportsman

159

as a teenager. The place had aged over the years, but her memories were as though only a few days had elapsed.

The weekend was capped off with meeting Ken at the Lytton Hall that Sunday afternoon. He was returning from a two-week nature trip up the Stein Valley. A large group of youths, interested in preserving that important wilderness area, took part in a guided tour of this yet undisturbed natural habitat. A picnic gathering at a lakefront brought young and old together in celebration of a successful visit with nature. Entertainment included songs performed by those who took part in the trip. Ken sang with his peers while his grandma proudly looked on in admiration of her grandson's recognition of his heritage. We returned to Courtenay late that night. There were a couple of days to rest in preparation for my first shift at Holberg.

The work schedule involved a six-hour trip to Holberg in military vehicles. That first trip seemed endless as the last sixty kilometres from Port Hardy to the radar site was over a rough logging road. Nature's green blanket over the hills and valleys was interrupted by the obvious intrusion of clear cut logging operations. A wet climate helped to heal parts of the landscape, but the scars will remain visible for many years. Wildlife blended with a scenic countryside to relieve boredom.

Arriving on site around noon, my stomach growled for lunch. Derrick Hiscock and Alistair McKenzie explained the shift routines over a quick lunch. I was excited about working in this more relaxed environment with guys I knew from previous years in North Bay.

The deputy detachment commander, Master Warrant Officer Peter Hooker, wasted no time in calling me to his office for a pleasant introductory interview.

"I've heard a lot about you," he said, "and not all good either."

He spoke with a slight British accent.

"I don't care what other people have to say about you. As far as I'm concerned, what matters to me is how you do your job. That's what your performance evaluation will be based on."

His words reminded me of Jene Kleinschroth and Mike Christie a few years earlier. Peter and I would become friends over the next year. His commitment to honesty proved itself many times over the months that followed. I felt welcomed in my new workplace.

It was a short work week. I left that Friday, with the supply truck, to prepare for a five-week course that would qualify me for a promotion to Sergeant. I didn't mind the course, but it was to be held at North Bay. Only a few short weeks ago I had left North Bay, hoping never to return. Now I was going back to live in barracks on base. I couldn't turn down the course without good reason, so it would add another experience to my repertoire of useless military training.

September nights in North Bay are marked by dramatic drops in temperature. Barracks were cold and the flight from Comox had left me feeling flu-like symptoms. During the following two weeks I couldn't shake the flu. My roommate, Gary James, finally decided to ask the course director if the heat could be turned on in barracks.

Darryl Levitt had been given the high profile position of course director. His attitude had changed over the years. He had become more supportive of superiors and less concerned with assisting subordinates. In short, Darryl had become a bit of a brown-nosed suck-hole. He didn't want to make waves and simply stated that base policy would not allow the heat to be turned on until the first week of October. It had already snowed once and the barracks were like a cold storage.

The following day Gary addressed the matter of people on the course experiencing problems as a result of cold temperature in barracks. I listened as Darryl seemed annoyed that anyone would question "policy."

"If you have medical problems just see me about getting an appointment with the doctor," he said bluntly.

So I raised my hand and requested an appointment. Obviously, Darryl had no intention of applying common sense to the situation.

His face flushed as he began to scream, "Paul you're not going to change base policy. The heat doesn't get turned on until October and that comes from the Base Commander himself. So don't waste your time trying."

I couldn't care less about base policy. All I wanted was to feel better. He stormed out of the classroom. Later that morning Gary informed me that an appointment was set for eleven o'clock.

At the hospital, preventative medicine staff seemed concerned with the number of barrack block occupants reporting to the hospital with cold symptoms. It appears students on the other two floors were experiencing more serious problems with the cold. I pointed out the lack of heat might be the root of the problem. He immediately called the Base Utilities office.

Chief Warrant Officer Worth and I had been in Egypt together in 1976 and we knew each other well. This burly man had a bellowing voice that could intimidate anyone who didn't know him. Hearing the voice echoing through the telephone, the medical staff quickly passed the phone to me and asked me to explain the situation.

"What's the problem over there, Paul?" he asked in his usual loud tone. After a brief discussion, he confirmed my suspicions.

"The heat can be turned on at any time", he bellowed. "We simply have to be told when it gets too cold. Otherwise, Base policy states that the heat will be turned on by October 1st, regardless of the temperature. The heat will be on in your barracks by two this afternoon."

Darryl had been unwilling to ask about the heat. Instead he used policy to defend his fear of dealing with a common sense issue. On my way back to class, he came out of his office to inform me that he couldn't get anywhere with the heat problem. When I explained Chief Worth had approved turning on the heat, Darryl almost jumped out of his skin. Caught in a lie, he began to rationalize his incompetence by criticizing me.

"You shouldn't have done that Paul. You know policies are there for good reasons and you can't go around questioning all the time. You're going to have to change your attitude if you expect to get promoted."

"Don't worry about it Darryl, it's no big deal", I replied.

My attitude didn't give me a cold. The lack of heat in barracks did that. So if I had to change common sense for Darryl's brand of leadership and management, I didn't want a promotion. It was obvious that one had to be prepared to suffer in silence to gain approval. It's the authoritarian way of exercising control and foster dependence in subordinates. I managed to complete the course ranking third out of ten.

BULLIES IN POWER

Human Rights Commission conciliator, Brian K. Stewart, had been unsuccessful in reaching a settlement on the complaint related to Major Dunsdon's refusal to process my 1987 application for OCTP. Three years had elapsed and military authorities were fully aware of investigation results. In fact, it was well-known that Major Dunsdon had refused to adhere to regulations by not processing the application.

The question for legal authorities remained; how to cover it up? Legal services personnel at NDHQ had managed to delay proceedings while they put a plan in motion. Since the facts couldn't be changed, rationalization would provide escape from responsibility. It was determined that an argument had to be devised to show that I would not have been selected, even if I had been allowed to participate in the program. Dunsdon's refusal to obey regulations would be explained through the subsequent denial of access to commissioning. In the Human Rights Commission conciliator's report of late August, 1991, the pattern of deception would soon become very clear.

Jene Kleinschroth had encouraged my application for Special Commissioning because he had been informed, by a Colonel at NDHQ, that the application was simply a formality. The completion of my degree and confirmed support from NDHQ left him feeling confident my application was already approved. So why had there been another rejection with the usual "unsuitable" rating? Documents reflecting the selection board's decision might offer the answer. A request for those documents went out under provisions of the Privacy Act.

More serious questions were also becoming obvious. Who was the colonel that spoke to Jene about encouraging my application? Why would a colonel be interested in my career? If he was serious about offering a commission, why would he get Jene to encourage me to apply? Something didn't seem right with the whole sequence of events leading to that fifth application. A few weeks later, documents of the selection board's decision arrived.

According to the board's assessment, I had a "history of lack of discretion, poor judgement, and disregard for rules and regulations."

A cold shiver ran through me. It suddenly made sense. The intent of having me apply for commissioning was to deny access using the same excuse that Dunsdon had used for not processing the 1987 OCTP application. After all, what judge would believe me even if I called attention to this elaborate plan? Legal personnel at NDHQ would later argue that Dunsdon's assessment must have been accurate since a selection board came to a similar conclusion four years later.

The conspiracy to discredit any evidence of official wrongdoing involved inadequacies in Human Rights Commission Investigation Procedures, as well as an elaborate scheme by DND officials to block legal avenues that might have exposed the pattern of injustice.

First, the Human Rights Commission provided investigation results to military officials in March 1990. Is it coincidental that Jene received instructions that I should apply for commissioning at that time? I think not. It was the initial step in ensuring that another rejected application would be on file.

Second, military authorities used delay mechanisms to slow down procedures aimed at addressing complaints about moving allowances and denial of the Dental Plan. For example, an insincere claim of wanting to negotiate settlement of all complaints together delayed the process for months. Was it coincidence that the only complaint remaining, after other complaints were settled in 1991, was the denial of access to competition for commissioning? When it was clear that career damages would not be ignored, military officials decided to settle all other complaints.

In hindsight, that seemingly cooperative effort would later prove to be part of the plan to prevent evidence from being introduced at a tribunal to follow in 1992. But I'm getting ahead of myself.

There was no snow for our first Christmas in Courtenay. Ken didn't like his school and missed his friends in North Bay. He found it difficult to accept his responsibilities at school which led to arguments about incomplete homework and poor grades. During the holidays he decided to visit his relatives around Vancouver and spend a week or so with his dad. He felt we were too demanding and wanted to see if it might be better to live on his own. His cousins provided first-hand experience about the joys of living on his own. It was enough to adjust his perception of reality. He returned home after the holidays with a different view of life at home. He understood the harsh conditions of life on his own.

I worked a long set of shifts during the Holidays and spent only a few days at home for Christmas. The extra time at work meant a little more money in allowances. We certainly needed it. Amy found that first winter depressing. There was no snow and it seemed to rain every day. By late February 1992, she had adjusted to the weather and Ken appeared to enjoy school a little more. The cool breeze that seemed to go through the walls left no doubt that our house needed renovations. So we decided to invest in exterior siding and thermal pane windows. The expense was well worth it.

It was time to begin renovations inside. Although summer was fast approaching, our spare time and money was taken up replacing wallpaper with a fresh coat of paint. Amy had begun taking the wallpaper down and it looked easy enough. Doing home renovations had not been one of the more important lessons of my youth. After all, father never had the patience to teach me anything. Even if he had been patient, I doubt if my willingness would have endured the thought of doing manual labour.

Working in the garden also became an important source of satisfaction. It was our first attempt at such a large garden and soon involved more hours than expected. With only six days

Amy and Paul in Comox
British Columbia 1992

off every two weeks, it was difficult for me to maintain the garden. Strawberries added to our collection of fruit-bearing plants in the back yard. Amy spent more time out there than I did.

Since initiating the career damages complaint in 1988, very little progress had been made through the Human Rights Commission. Finally, after four years, the Commission decided to request the appointment of a Human Rights Tribunal to hear the evidence.

Judge Alfred Lynch-Staunton was appointed Tribunal Chairman and hearings were scheduled to take place at the University of Victoria during the week of November 16, 1992. That gave me over four months to prepare for the most important challenge of my career. Proceedings were expected to take about five days. Human Rights Commission Senior Counsel, Rene Duval, would present the matter before tribunal. My task in the matter involved gathering documents and providing the names of possible witnesses who could help clarify the facts of the case. Witnesses included supervisors dating back to 1982.

After interviewing a few witnesses, it was determined by the Commission that none could offer any new evidence that wasn't already available in documents. So, except for the actuary presenting account of damages, I would serve as the only material witness for the Human Rights Commission.

I felt uncomfortable about excluding Jene Kleinschroth and Mike Christie from the proceedings. They had witnessed a number of incidents that corroborated my perception of bias among senior officers on base and at NDHQ. Rene felt the case was strong and witnesses would only add delay to proceedings. Consequently, Jene and Mike were not called to attend proceedings.

Harassment of military members on Base Comox had been the focus of media attention during the spring of 1992. Expecting media contact, I thought it best to adhere to regulations and request approval for response to media questions on the matter. Lieutenant Colonel (LCol) King, at CFB Comox, offered a rhetorical reply to my request. In short, it was a circle jerk reply. Although a simple yes or no would have served the purpose, LCol King recoiled and called attention to regulations without giving an answer to the question.

BULLIES IN POWER

Imagine going to a restaurant and, after selecting the meal of your choice, the waiter refuses to take your order. Instead he reads the menu and assures you the food is good. So there it was. Regulations said I had to ask permission and LCol King confirmed it. But he lacked the backbone to give an answer. It was clear I had to ask permission and I had done so. Consequently, any media questions would not be answered. The media didn't get involved anyway. I had become so gun-shy about my actions that fear of criticism had taken control.

It was determined that during the hearings we would stay at the Empress Hotel. Rene wanted to meet with me the day before the hearings in order to go over some of the material. I had spoken to him on the phone, but I didn't know what to expect. His round spectacles, heavy French accent and straight posture gave him the distinguished appearance of classical lawyers one might see in old black and white movies. Confidence rang through his voice as he explained the way these proceedings usually took place. He had addressed many such hearings and his experience left no doubt about the plan of action. He emphasized the need to remain calm no matter what took place.

Department of Justice lawyers might attempt to discredit our case by provoking angry responses. Along with a positive attitude, my uniform would have to be impeccable. Boots shined to a high gloss and the crease in my pants pressed to a sharp edge. I was ready for the next morning.

Making a final adjustment to my tie, I walked off the elevator and met Rene in the hotel lobby. My briefcase weighed heavy on my shoulder as it held all related documents dating back to 1982. As I stepped out of the cab in front of the Begbie building, the driver explained how to locate the Moot Court facility. Inside, the building appeared deserted.

Rene pulled his cart of document holders behind him while we sought out the room where legal minds met to do battle with words. I felt like we were walking onto the set of "People's Court".

Although the room appeared to be in a formal setting, Rene emphasized this type of hearing has traditionally been somewhat more relaxed. He began to lay out his material on one of the desks.

I sat in a second row seat behind him. He turned and motioned me to move up.

"You'll sit beside me and take notes of things you feel may be important to discuss later".

I don't know if he did that to relax me or if he simply felt it was important to cover all angles of information.

He emphasized, "Don't show any reaction to statements made by witnesses. It's important that you simply take notes without displaying any emotion."

Department of Justice lawyer, Donald J. Rennie, walked in with Captain B. Cathcart of the Office of the Judge Advocate General. They looked around the room briefly. The tribunal clerk and recorder were making final administrative preparations necessary to receive the Chairman. Heat and humidity had invaded my uniform and I began feeling uncomfortably warm.

We were called to order for the Chairman's entrance. I recognized him from the hotel lobby earlier that morning. He was a portly man in his late sixties or early seventies, whose thick handlebar moustache characterized the style of his youth. The stern look on his face hinted a conservative nature anchored in traditional values of a past era. As he assumed his seat at the elevated desk overlooking the room he quietly said, "Please be seated."

Throughout that first hour or so both lawyers argued over legal concerns, clearing the way for testimony to begin later that morning. The first witness was called to present a report of financial damages resulting from denied access to commissioning in 1988. After an hour of testimony, explaining age charts and income comparisons, the end result left me confused. However, the direct damages, outlined in lost wages and pension, involved over 600,000 dollars.

It's difficult to believe that officers can benefit so much by virtue of a military commission. All I wanted to do was work in the field most closely related to my education. One might have expected that concerns for cost effectiveness would have encouraged military authorities to apply my education in an appropriate field. After all, training an officer cadet to do the work I was already trained to do involved four years of education and at least two years in language

BULLIES IN POWER

school. But then, who was I to question the wisdom of those who justified the waste of tax dollars?

Finally, after years of delay, I was called to give my side of the story. Rene Duval's Examination in Chief drew attention to the pattern of events that had started in 1982. Donald Rennie, counsel for the Respondent, objected to the review of events. His objection revealed the real motives for settlement of previous complaints. In order to keep the information from being revealed at the tribunal, military authorities had chosen to settle all other complaints except for the issue of career damages.

The settlements of 1991 were little more than barriers precluding reference to the related incidents. It was expected the Chairman would see through the charade and call the facts to question. When he pointed out the conspicuous nature of Donald Rennie's objection, I felt a sense of relief. Could it be that this relic of yesterday's system would display the wisdom necessary to uncover the pattern of discrimination that had plagued my career for years? Only time and his decision would tell. I would later discover the chairman's relationship with military authorities cast a shadow on the outcome of the proceedings.

From the outset of the hearings, during breaks the chairman casually engaged in conversation with Major McCormack and Captain Jackson, witnesses for the Armed Forces (Respondent). While in conversation with McCormack and Jackson, on one of the breaks the chairman boasted about his retirement from Reserve service at the rank of Colonel. His frequent association with McCormack suggests a mutual goal may have developed. The chairman began to openly refuse to accept testimony that might contradict the military's argument.

Unless my testimony agreed with what counsel for the Respondent wanted to hear, the chairman became annoyed and directed me to agree. At one point, when asked if I took steps to compel Major Dunsdon to process the OCTP application, I testified that "I couldn't". Donald Rennie then stated; "You didn't". I replied, "I couldn't". The chairman then ordered me to agree that I didn't. The fact of the matter is that corporals don't tell the commanding officer what to do. From that point, it was obvious the chairman was determined to manipulate evidence.

The planned cover-up of an obvious pattern of retaliation and harassment was now hinted. In cross-examination, Donald Rennie began to focus on positive comments made by Dunsdon on the application. This line of questioning was drawing attention away from the actual result of the negative comments. Positive comments had no substance. They led nowhere and held no value. It was the negative comments that had impact on the application. The serious flaw in his line of questioning went without concern, as the chairman seemed wrapped up in the web of deception.

It was clear Mr. Alfred G. Lynch-Staunton had fallen prey to his own conservative nature and began to show signs of agreement with those empty explanations. His attention to positive comments, by Dunsdon, slowly cracked my confidence that the pattern would be unveiled.

Statements about negative reports from supervisors suddenly became a focus of defence. I had not been aware that such reports existed! Who could confirm the authenticity of those statements?

The supervisors had not been called to provide input at the Tribunal. There had been no reason to believe supervisors had harboured negative perceptions of my performance or attitude. All written documents supported my testimony about the positive nature of supervisor reports. Only Dunsdon testified that there had been negative comments. He couldn't be specific about any particular incident. In fact, his testimony was plagued with contradictions about what might be defined negative. To the chairman, this testimony was the gospel according to Major Dunsdon.

Then there was testimony from Captain Francois Jodoin. Oddly enough he suffered from selective memory loss. He couldn't remember any discussions with me in 1988. But he did remember a number of things that he had not said during that discussion. Lynch-Staunton saw nothing wrong with Jodoin's contradictions. He would accept that the conversations had not taken place and then refer to those conversations to argue that I had misinterpreted Jodoin's statements. I guess it's one of those circumstances that only

BULLIES IN POWER

officers can understand. To me, it confirmed Lynch-Staunton's bias in interpreting evidence.

I had refused to sign an incomplete PER in 1987. Even though Dunsdon's comments were not known, it was argued that the PER most likely got me promoted to Master Corporal. Once again, Dunsdon's statements went on record without question. The facts confirmed the PER never reached the merit board until late 1987. By then, I had already been appointed the Master Corporal. The course of this tribunal hearing had rapidly changed and the attempt to make me appear ungrateful seemed to work.

Much of the so-called "expert" testimony from military officers focussed on rhetorical assumptions about my capabilities to succeed in completing the Basic Officers Training Course (BOTC). By their account, it would have been impossible for me to complete this first step in the commissioning process. Having completed all previous military courses in one of the top three positions, it's difficult to believe the BOTC would have presented a problem. What difference would it have made anyway? John Middleveen had failed his attempt at BOTC and it didn't prevent him from becoming a commissioned officer.

I recalled Captain Ken Madill's 1982 statement that I would not succeed in completing a University course, much less a degree. It's ironic that military officials failed to remember how that perception had been misguided. I guess Dunsdon simply wanted to save me from the embarrassment of failure. What a humanitarian gesture! In my opinion, that self-centred egomaniac didn't have a humanitarian bone in his body. He neglected his responsibilities and refused to forward the application to NDHQ. He then had the audacity to testify that he refused to process my application because of his concern with my attitude!

Captain Cliff Halpen and Warrant Officer Peter Hayes had been the motivating influence behind my submitting the application in the fall of 1987. So how could this pompous ass argue they were not supportive? To make matters worse, his testimony was accepted without concern for inconsistencies. The Commission had refused to call Halpen and Hayes as witnesses.

On the other hand, I was expected to prove every statement ever made about the interpretation of documented events. His twisted recollection of incidents echoed with a patronizing tone. It was implied that I had misinterpreted everything that happened, including Dunsdon's neglect of duty. How could I be so insensitive? Lynch-Staunton, like many others in positions where respect is expected, sought to protect the decadent role of bullies in power.

Rene Duval seemed unimpressed by Lynch-Staunton's apparent resistance to challenge the traditional image of military authorities. Rene's passive approach to contradictory evidence was confusing. Why wasn't he calling attention to inconsistencies in the Dunsdon testimony? His approach would later confirm my suspicion of questionable practices in addressing a controversial case. Rene may have been more interested in setting precedents than resolving the case. His initial enthusiasm was more for the sake of posing than legal representation.

Returning home after four days of emotionally charged legal arguments, there was little to do but wait. In discussion with Rene, a few days later, Lynch-Staunton's indisputable penchant to protect the traditional image of military officers had to be noted. Was it possible that his judgement could be affected by the wishful expectation that military officers still possessed the integrity and honesty of his generation? It couldn't hurt to address my feelings in a written submission to Rene Duval. The letter would be held until the tribunal decision was rendered. Hopefully, the decision would be handed down quickly.

Preparations for official closure were underway at Detachment Holberg. A new automatic radar would be installed as a replacement for the old one. This would mark the end of an era in air defence history. Our last Christmas at Holberg called for a special gathering of both crews in early December. Even Mother Nature contributed a snowfall to inspire the right atmosphere for the occasion. Family members could not be included at that time, but detachment commander, Captain Ron Godin, assured everyone the final party would involve family members.

The Canadian Forces Reduction Program (FRP) allowed military personnel the opportunity to take early retirement without penalty

BULLIES IN POWER

to their pensions. Additionally, a special leave package provided extra incentive. Consequently, a number of personnel took the package and retired early. As my term of service would expire in April, 1994, I didn't qualify for the special leave package. Besides, a positive decision from the tribunal would provide a long-awaited commission. Only four Air Defence Technicians had chosen not to embark on early retirement.

The career manager took time to visit in late January, 1993. Planned transfers involved the possibility of my going to Clear, Alaska. This unaccompanied transfer did not sit well with Amy. Of course, Chief Warrant Officer Richard Poulin assured me a position at Victoria's Alcohol Rehabilitation Clinic (ARC) after my tour at Clear. To sweeten the offer, he indicated I would be attending Counsellor Assessment at ARC shortly. All I had to do was accept the transfer to Clear. There were a few problems with this "deal."

It was well known that Chief Poulin was scheduled to retire on FRP within a few months. The new career manager would not be compelled to keep promises made by the previous manager. As my term of service would expire within a year, it meant I could be facing the end of my contract without the promised position at ARC. Perhaps, most importantly, insincere verbal promises had been repeatedly broken over the years. Why should I believe anything this human puppet had to say? After discussing the matter with Amy, a decision was made.

I couldn't accept a transfer to an isolated place simply on the promise, by an outgoing career manager, that a good transfer would follow. The fact that he kept referring to the possibility of changing circumstances and constant repetition "you didn't hear that from me" left the impression that his motives were suspicious.

Would I be transferred to ARC in Victoria after doing a year in Clear? What about the expiring term of service? Would authorities provide an offer to extend my term of service in order to accommodate a transfer to ARC? With nothing in writing to support any of those promises, and the repeated references to possible changes in operational commitments, I wasn't about to move to a place like Clear, Alaska. I had made it clear in writing and emphasized the point to the Chief Poulin and Captain Cote that I would not accept an extension of service unless I was commissioned or received a counselling position.

Shortly after the career manager's visit, a message confirmed that I would be assessed for employment at ARC. The assessment involved attending the 31-day program as a client. This was good news and indicated the possibility of a transfer to ARC. Amy was pleased with the turn of events. At about the same time, a screening message announced a transfer to Alaska.

The thought of twenty feet of snow and temperatures hovering around minus 40 degrees for nine months of the year didn't appeal to me. A brief call from Chief Poulin explained the clerical error. A few hours later the screening message was formally cancelled. So I wouldn't be going to Alaska after all.

Everyone else seemed to know where they were being transferred after the detachment closure. There had been hints that I might find myself on the move to North Bay again. After two tours of duty at North Bay, it didn't make sense to transfer us across the country with less than a year left on my term of service. Besides, I wasn't well liked by authorities in North Bay. But then, rumours on Base Comox indicated I hadn't made any friends among the higher ranks there either. It appears my involvement with the Human Rights Commission fostered discomfort among senior officers.

It's difficult to understand how one person can cast such a large shadow over authorities. So where would I go? Resigned not to worry about it, I looked forward to attending the Alcohol Rehabilitation Clinic (ARC) at Victoria.

Captain Ray Mostowy, ARC Director, explained I should travel to Victoria a few days early in order to meet counsellors and become familiar with the assessment process. It would also provide an opportunity for a visit with Amy's cousin Verna. Ken looked forward to the drive back. It wasn't very often he got the chance to exercise his newly acquired driver's licence.

Verna's busy schedule at university didn't allow much time to visit, but it was long enough to catch up on the latest family rumours and politics of the Cooks Ferry Band. After an early supper, Amy dropped me off at ARC and Ken gleefully slipped into the driver's seat for the three-hour drive back to Courtenay.

For the first time in years, I had nothing to do. Sitting on my bed, later that afternoon, thoughts began racing through my mind. What if the Tribunal decision was rendered during my stay at ARC? With no outside contact for the first two weeks of the program, it would be impossible to deal with the results of the decision. I recalled the words of a close friend, "What can you do about it now?" he'd say. Nothing! Therefore, outside issues would have to be set aside for the next 31 days.

It was sunny and cool outside. The thought of being free from worries left me feeling restless. Years of constant pressure, to accomplish too many tasks at once, had left little time for enjoyment of accomplishments. A walk might fill the void. If nothing else, it might change the course of the depressive mood I seemed to be slipping into. The streets were quiet. I was reminded of my first few weeks in Calgary as I walked by a small shopping centre. The smell of pizza, coming from the open door of a small restaurant, triggered an urge to eat. I wasn't particularly hungry, but I stopped anyway.

Walking along the waterfront on my way back to the ARC residence, I enjoyed the colourful sunset and the smell of the ocean breeze. There was no television in residence. So I went to bed early, but my mind kept racing for a few hours. When I managed to finally get to sleep, nightmares of past drunken experiences kept waking me up. Perhaps dreams are a subconscious mechanism to address a need for change in daily activities. As my sponsor advised on a number of occasions; "When in doubt, go to a meeting." That evening I went to a meeting.

At ARC, the program involves working on individual issues for the first three weeks followed by a combined spousal program during the final two weeks. Treating alcoholism as a family illness makes recovery a family affair.

During the early phase of the program, counsellors pointed out that my "perfectionist" standard was unrealistic and impractical. Okay, so I like things to be done right the first time! After two weeks, it was obvious issues of control dominated my relationships at work and at home. By participating in group sessions during the day and attending meetings in the evening, a sense of tolerance and serenity developed.

Amy arrived at the end of the third week, when individual and group sessions focus on working with family members. The next two weeks opened new areas of communication with Amy. This necessary hurdle improved our relationship.

Amy and Paul at Alcohol Rehabilitation Clinic for Paul's Counselor Evaluation in Victoria British Columbia 1993

Over 16 years of sobriety and I felt like a newcomer just sobering up. We found time to go on early evening walks. Quiet time together helped to review the feelings that had kept us together through some very tough times. We cared so much about each other's feelings that we avoided discussing how we really felt. There were times when my protective instincts prevented Amy from expressing herself. A stronger bond formed between us over those two weeks. Amy also became more vocal about her expectations. On the last day, it was difficult to say goodbye to peers and counsellors. There was an atmosphere of emotional closeness within the group. The short five-week program was an experience that seemed like a lifetime of emotional growth.

Back at Courtenay, life continued with the detachment in process of moving equipment to Comox. I was assigned to work with the Base Alcohol Counsellor; expectations of a transfer to ARC were high. A few days after our return from Victoria, a message from NDHQ outlined release procedures upon completion of my term of service.

It stated clearly that, April 29, 1994, marked the expected last day of service. Definitely not a message of hope for a transfer to ARC. Oh well, with only one year left in my service contract, I expected

BULLIES IN POWER

to remain in the position of Assistant Base Alcohol Counsellor. Conducting Group sessions provided valuable experience in preparation for release and the eventual search for employment as a counsellor.

The usual stroke of luck brought news of a transfer scheduled for late June. North Bay!!! How could it be? Realizing that logic has never played a role in career management, this move seemed to defy sanity. Captain Ron Godin contacted the career manager who informed us that I was also being promoted in early June. What was going on?

During the tribunal, Major McCormack had given me his phone number and told me to call if I needed information. So I called. He let me know that an offer of Indefinite Period of Service (IPS) would allow me to serve until age 55. Once again, the familiar statement, "But you didn't hear that from me".

I didn't want to work as an Air Defence Technician for another 15 years. My goal, in completing a degree, was to gain access to a commission or work in the counselling field. Returning to the hole in North Bay wasn't my idea of good news, regardless of the promotion. Besides, taking on the position of sergeant fell short of the goal of a commission.

In hope of gaining support for common sense, I decided to call Member of Parliament Nelson Riis to ask for intervention. This was at about the same time as the Somalia incident became news. Riis found it sad that Master Corporal Clayton Matchee had attempted suicide after being arrested for the beating death of a Somali youth. Not being one to keep my tongue tied, I suggested he look a little closer at the situation.

"What do you mean?" he queried.

"I would suspect he was beaten to keep him quiet and it was made to look like an attempted suicide," I replied.

"You can't be serious," Riis argued.

"Why don't you visit him when he arrives at National Defence Medical Centre and see for yourself if he's bruised?"

A few days later, Clayton Matchee's condition was reported to have been bruised and battered. Charges would go ahead against the three others involved in the beating of the Somali youth. Only Private

177

Kyle Brown would be sentenced to jail for manslaughter. It was time to discuss the matter with others more closely involved. Once again, information would serve the new boys' network. Everyone knew that a cover-up would take place. It was important to ensure that evidence was preserved for reference.

Riis asked questions about my transfer but received very little response about the reasons. In all, the effort was wasted.

Moving meant selling the house. Amy and I would have to work on the completion of renovations before placing the house on the market. A phone call from Cook's Ferry Band Chief, David Walkem, brought good news for Amy.

Amy's childhood was marked by difficult conditions of poverty and abuse under the residential school system. Her mother's death left the family in turmoil. Siblings were dispersed among the homes of relatives. At 13, there was nothing Amy could do to prevent Social Service officials from apprehending her two-year-old sister Ellen.

Over the years, Amy often wondered about the blanket of secrecy that covered her sister's adoption. The tragedy, of native children having been adopted by non-native families, left many native families in search of siblings. For almost three decades Ellen's location had been kept secret by government regulations. I can't imagine the feeling of emptiness Amy must have felt over the years whenever she thought of her sister.

The harsh reality, of government policies to extinguish native culture, marks the lack of concern officials have had toward native family relations. In late 1991, David Walkem began inquiring about Ellen. It took almost two years to break through the barriers of government bureaucracies.

David's call came late in the evening and he wanted to talk to Amy. The look on her face told me something was up. There were so many questions, but David had not met Ellen yet. So for the next few days, Amy glowed with happiness. The sadness, of not knowing her sister's whereabouts for over 28 years, was suddenly replaced by a growing anxiety at the prospects of meeting Ellen.

Plans for a visit were set for Easter weekend. Unfortunately, selling the house meant one of us would need to stay home. Although

BULLIES IN POWER

I would have liked to meet Ellen at that time, I think Amy felt more comfortable taking the first visit by herself.

I couldn't change the fact that we had to move and the house would have to be sold. I didn't want Amy to delay her visit with her sister. So we agreed it would be a good time for me to spend the weekend alone and finish installing a ceiling in the basement. Ken would go along to visit his grandparents at Merritt. Little did we know the house would be sold by the time Amy returned from visiting Ellen.

The tribunal decision had slipped my mind until Eddie Taylor called the day before Amy's trip. His sombre tone told me it wasn't good news. In fact, he pointed out my copy would arrive by courier and I should read it through before discussing it. I guess he knew the decision would infuriate me. As Amy and Ken were packing the car, the courier delivered a package from the tribunal office. Knowing the decision was not positive, it seemed like a good idea to wait until Amy and Ken were on the road so I could focus on reading without interruption.

As soon as they left, I opened the package and began reading. Rage filled my chest and threatened to blow my lungs out. The word "preposterous" appeared early in the decision. According to Alfred Lynch-Staunton, a man of my experience should know better than to criticize an officer of Major Dunsdon's calibre. What about Dunsdon's experience? His repeated refusal to adhere to regulations seemed unimportant to Lynch-Staunton. This representative of archaic attitudes sought to protect the image of military officers as he consistently refused to consider the facts surrounding the situation. It's been argued that justice is blind. I had always thought the meaning of this blindness was to prevent the tarnishing influence of bias. In this case justice may have been blind, but the decision is a reflection of selective hearing and a narrow-minded approach in assigning weight to evidence.

Throughout the decision, blatant bias attacked common sense. Lynch-Staunton's perception, that Dunsdon couldn't do anything wrong and I couldn't do anything right, was a slap in the face. I managed to read the first 20 pages before throwing the document on the table and going for a walk. The walk turned into a long run.

Renovations went well after a few hours of blowing off steam. With the ceiling installed, all that was left was replacing the ceiling light bulb with a fluorescent light fixture. Surprisingly, time had slipped by and I suddenly noticed it was dark outside. The clock displayed twenty minutes after midnight. Over nine hours had disappeared. Hunger took hold of my stomach with an empty growl. It was time to relax and have a bite to eat. Work would continue the next morning. Walking by the table, I saw the tribunal decision sitting there. Picking it up, I thought about reading some more. It would wait.

The telephone woke me up. A real estate agent asked about showing the house that afternoon. It was already ten thirty. Rushing to clean up the dishes and tidy up the basement, the house was ready. During the first visit, another agent called. Three couples looked at the house by the end of the day. Not much got done that afternoon.

Sitting at the table, the dreaded document sat there as though it stared at me. I picked it up and convinced myself to read it. Not much sank in during the first reading. So I read it again and made notes. Disappointed and frustrated, it was time to go for another walk. Again, time had slipped by without notice. The walk helped to relieve emotional turmoil. A deep sleep didn't seem to provide any rest. Once again, I woke up to the telephone ringing. An offer had been made on the house. The real estate agent wanted to discuss the offer that evening.

Amy and Ken left Spences Bridge early in the morning and would probably arrive sometime in the afternoon. I agreed to meet with our real estate agent, Victor Simonson, after supper. Amy's approval was needed before accepting the offer on the house. Victor had just finished explaining the offer when Amy came in. Within a few days the house was sold and there was no turning back.

Returning to North Bay appeared closer to reality. It was time to think positive and look for ways to make the move a productive experience. Amy's studies had gone well before our move to Courtenay. The thought of completing her diploma generated anxiety and excitement all at once. Inquiries with Canadore College confirmed she could continue at the second year level.

A request for married quarters didn't seem too positive, as the housing office at CFB North Bay explained our position on the list left us with a six-month waiting period. A house hunting trip would take Amy and me to North Bay in early June. Perhaps, by then, a PMQ might become available and we could avoid having to travel to North Bay in search of a place. In the meantime, the finishing touch on renovations called for laying tiles on the basement floor and painting the back steps off the deck.

Detachment Holberg's closure parade saw the presentation of my promotion to Sergeant. It was to take effect on the 1st of June. It wasn't clear why I was being promoted with less than 10 months left in the service. But, what the heck, the little bit of extra money would help.

We attended the final closure party later that evening. It was an excellent gathering. Perhaps the best feature of the party was the cost. Fund-raising allowed members of the detachment and their spouses to attend free of charge. This final function held a much different outcome than the last mess dinner at the Kamloops closure in 1988. For one thing, Captain Ron Godin didn't find it necessary to show off, by inviting municipal politicians in "grand-stand" fashion, as Dunsdon had done at Kamloops in 1988.

It was now early May and time to appeal the tribunal decision was running out. Eddie Taylor explained it was necessary to wait for the Chief Commissioner, Max Yalden, to make his decision on whether or not he would support an appeal. There was only 30 days to provide notice of appeal.

Finally, on May 7th, Eddie informed me the Chief Commissioner had not made his decision but, if I wanted to, I could appeal myself. Oh great! Fine time to tell me, I thought. It was Friday afternoon and the last day to file the appeal was Saturday. There was no way of processing the documents until Monday morning. By then, it would be over 30 days and quite likely too late.

Eddie explained that since the final day fell on a weekend, the last day would be Monday and everything would be alright. I was angry. Why put off filing the appeal until the last day? If I had known I could file the appeal myself, it would have been done two weeks earlier. I was beginning to wonder whether or not the Human Rights

Commission legal branch agreed with an appeal. I processed the documents on Monday morning with assurances from Eddie that it was within the time limits.

About a week later, a letter from Donald Rennie informed me the notice of appeal was two days late. In short, it was clear the issue of timing would be a factor of concern in the appeal. More bureaucratic arguments! Once again, Eddie assured me the matter of timing would be handled by the Commission. Within a few days, the Chief Commissioner decided he wouldn't support an appeal. That left me on my own. Of course, the legal branch would provide any advice necessary to help me in presenting my argument.

After letting me hang in waiting for 29 days, without mentioning that I could file the notice of appeal, I couldn't help but wonder whose side they were on. All I could do was hope the tribunal president would agree to appoint a review tribunal to hear my appeal. It would take another few months for the appointment of a three-member panel to hear the appeal. By then, we would be in North Bay.

Plans to travel through the United States on our move to North Bay wouldn't include visiting friends and relatives. Instead, we took advantage of time off for the long weekend in May, and decided to visit Kamloops. On our way back, we stopped at Chilliwack and spent time with Amy's sister Ellen. She certainly had Amy's quiet demeanour. There was no doubt they were related. A brief stop at Michelle's place in Vancouver left us just enough time to catch the last ferry to Nanaimo. It was our last weekend off as the house hunting trip and Ken's graduation would occupy much of the month of June.

At work, the following Tuesday morning, Captain Godin called to inform me that my request for permission to speak publicly about difficulties with the Redress of Grievance had been strongly disapproved.

He emphasized, "In speaking with Commander Price, of the Judge Advocate's office in Victoria, he made it clear that if you choose to speak out or publish anything about your situation there would be serious disciplinary action."

The threat may have been meant to discourage any media contact, but it pushed Amy into an angry response.

BULLIES IN POWER

"How dare they," she argued, "say we have to keep quiet while they throw our lives in turmoil?"

A brief phone call to the local paper saw her speaking to the editor within a few hours. It's the kind of story the media loves to publish. Just in time to publish while we were on our house hunting trip.

During the first week in June, we were off to North Bay in search of a place to live for early July. Arriving in North Bay, it was cold. The flight left Amy feeling flu-like symptoms. I was worried that she would have another one of those terrible migraine headaches. They were coming more often and required longer stays in the hospital. She didn't feel like looking around for a place to rent. So I got a paper and searched out the ad section.

Rental units were expensive, but house prices had gone down since our departure two years earlier. With the sale of our home in Courtenay, a sizable down payment could provide very low mortgage payments on a three-bedroom semi-detached home. Rent doesn't earn much equity. After considering the costs, it seemed more practical to buy.

Our new home was smaller, but only six years old. That meant no renovations. The much smaller yard was fenced all around. Cutting the grass would take less than fifteen minutes every two weeks or so. It would be a welcomed change from the almost daily routine of yard work during the previous two years.

Returning to Courtenay, we discovered the newspaper had printed the article about our situation. A number of calls from local people offered moral support. One of the calls came from Mary Everson, a local native woman, who was interested in having Amy explain the situation before the Royal Commission at Victoria. It was a big step for Amy, but she agreed.

In the meantime, the editor of the newspaper informed Amy that military authorities were angry with her story. They had not been asked about the matter before the article was published and they felt this was inappropriate.

Amy didn't have much sympathy for military criticism. As she pointed out, "Military authorities have tried to cover up this situation for years and now they're upset because it's coming out."

She went on, "Maybe they should think about investigating the problem rather than trying to cover it up."

I was proud of her assertive approach. Military authorities used their influence to prevent further articles from being published. However, the matter would resurface after Amy's return from the Royal Commission hearings. This time, military authorities had no comment. I wonder why? It had been made quite clear to Base Comox public affairs officer, Captain Reid Johnson, that Amy was not a military member and that it might be wise not to interfere with her right to free speech.

Ken's grandparents, Margaret and Smitty, travelled from Merritt with his aunt Rita for his graduation. They had brought him a number of graduation presents. When Ken began to open the large boxes, he was delighted to discover a complete computer system. Ken hadn't been this happy in a long time. Later that evening, there was no hiding the pride that glowed on their faces as they watched Ken walk up to centre stage to receive his graduation certificate. Once again, the video camera captured the event in moving colour. It also marked our last few days in Courtenay.

Ken's Graduation from Vanier High School in Comox 1993
L-R Ken's Grandpa Smitty, Grandma Margaret, Ken, Amy and Paul

Walking through the empty house, I felt sad. This had been our first house. So much work had gone into it that every wall told an unwritten story of painstaking effort in renovation. The mobile home had been different. Leaving this house behind was like saying goodbye to a lifetime of memories. Call me sentimental, but I had to choke back a few tears as I was walking out. Amy didn't say much. I think she sensed my emotions were close to the surface. Dropping the cat off at the kennel, we spent our last night in a Courtenay motel. Bear would follow in late July.

Promotion to Sergeant at Comox in 1993

THE NEW BOYS'
NETWORK IN ACTION

The first day of our trip took us across the Canada-U.S. border at Vancouver. This nine day trip held a schedule of planned stops at various points of interest across the States.

While visiting Yellowstone Park, we found ourselves driving through a foot of snow. Who ever heard of snow that far south on July 3rd? It was like mid-December in Ontario. Line-ups of visitors crowded the roadside rest stops. We managed to get through the park before the roads closed.

At Cody, Wyoming, all hotels were booked. The roads to the South were closed due to mudslides. The northern routes were opened to Powell. Arriving at Powell late in the evening we ate at the only restaurant that was open and went to bed.

Heading east over Bald Mountain the following morning, snow covered the popular Medicine Wheel site. Our trip took us through Mount Rushmore and Crazy Horse Monument before taking in the sites at Badlands National Park. Mississippi flooding forced us to take a northern route from Albert Lea. Having seen the sites we wanted to visit, the rest of the trip involved few stops.

I felt my chest tighten as we approached North Bay on that hot and humid Friday afternoon. Familiar sites brought back old feelings that I had hoped would never plague reality. Ken was excited about moving back to this city of misery. He looked forward to contacting his friends as soon as we reached the motel.

Amy smiled at my apparent mood swing. "Look at the positive side", she said. "It's not like we're going to be here forever."

With my release in the plans for April the following year, the next ten months might slip by without much notice.

We couldn't move into our house until the end of July. So a motel would serve as home until then. Although allowances covered meals and hotels, it wasn't like being at home. The novelty of eating in restaurants soon wore off. The summer heat and humidity kept us confined to our air-conditioned room during the day. Late evening walks didn't give us much relief from the heat and meant a compulsory craving for junk food on the way. Amy's headaches were becoming more frequent and intense but she never complained.

Reporting to work in the hole brought back vivid memories of arguments with abusive authorities. I kept telling myself it was different now. Years had gone by and those people would be gone to other places. Crossing through the security entrance at the north portal, one of the commissionaires recognized me.

"Back again," he laughed.

"Haven't they had enough of you down there?" he jokingly remarked.

"Obviously not," I replied with a smile.

The 2-kilometre ride down the tunnel seemed longer than I remembered. Perhaps it was anxiety. As the bus stopped in front of the familiar heavy blast door, I felt a deep dark mood sweep over me. I had to think positive. After all, this was my first day at work and I wanted to start off on the right foot. So I put on my shallow smile and walked down the corridor in search of the 21 Squadron Chief Warrant Officer's office.

Meeting Chief Warrant Officer (CWO) Gordon Aucoin, he introduced me to the office staff and explained I would be on training as a Surveillance Supervisor with 'A' Flight. The training was expected to take between three and four months.

By the end of July, we were tired of the motel lifestyle. Moving into our new home kept us busy for a few weeks. Carpet was laid in the basement. It was the only room large enough to accommodate

Ken's water bed and computer equipment. It also gave him the privacy to watch his television without disturbing my sleep. Shift work would once again play a role in our daily schedule of activities. Amy and Ken would soon be attending school and I would have more time to continue writing during the day.

An offer of Special Indefinite Period of Service (IPS) had been received during out-clearances at CFB Comox in late June. I couldn't accept it at that time because there wasn't enough time to research the reason why it had been addressed as a "Special" IPS. My request, to have the offer held in abeyance until the appeal tribunal could render a decision on my 1988 complaint, had been approved. Unfortunately, I had not been informed of the approval or new deadline.

Two days before the August 20th deadline, CWO Aucoin called me into his office and explained my decision was required right away. He had known about the new deadline since early July, but failed to let me know. I was expected to make a quick decision and sign the document. Not likely!

The review tribunal was scheduled to hear the appeal later in November of that year (1993). Consequently, it wasn't possible to provide a response until then. After all, what did the term "Special IPS" mean? And why was I informed at the last minute again? If the Special IPS couldn't be held until the appeal decision, then rushing a signature could present a problem later. The document went back once again with my request to hold the offer. Word came back a few days later that the offer was withdrawn because I didn't sign it. My scheduled release would take effect, as planned, in April 1994. I felt a sort of relief now.

With three months before the appeal, I began preparing the argument. I was on my own with this presentation. Not wanting to impose on the Human Rights Commission, I chose to guide my document in accordance with previous arguments on file. Eddie Taylor lent me the Commission's copy of tribunal transcripts. When comparing the decision to transcript evidence, the pattern of Lynch-Staunton's bias was apparent.

During the day, I trained for my new position while at night I reviewed documents. It felt like I was working on a university assignment again.

BULLIES IN POWER

Less than four weeks of training and I was prepared for the required evaluation to qualify me as Surveillance Supervisor Technician (SST). Although the usual allocation for training is 120 days, I managed to get qualified within thirty days. One might have expected less motivation from someone so close to retirement. For some unknown reason, I felt compelled to maintain integrity in my performance. I may not have attained the career goals that I worked for, but it didn't mean principles have to suffer the bitterness of unfair decisions from authorities.

A three-member Human Rights Appeal panel heard arguments on November 18 and 19, 1993. Donald Rennie's objection to the appeal, because of timing, would be heard first. Then, if the panel agreed that my application was on time, my argument would follow. I expected to submit a 37-page document supporting my argument.

Arriving at Ottawa a day early, I had met Eddie Taylor for the first time. Joining Rene Duval, the expected course of events was discussed. Questions appeared to be more of an exploration into my knowledge and feelings than a review of facts. I got the impression that what I knew posed a threat. Rene repeatedly assured me the Commission accepted responsibility for arguing the matter of timing.

Why so much concern with controlling that part of the hearing? During initial submissions, the following morning, it became clear that Rene didn't want me to point out why I had waited to submit my application for appeal. If the panel heard that my application was delayed, because I was misinformed about my right to appeal, it was likely to embarrass the Commission. I felt some strange sense of loyalty to Rene for his efforts. So I kept quiet and let him proceed with his argument.

After two days of debate between Rene Duval and Donald Rennie, the panel decided they could not render a decision on timing until Canada Post could outline whether or not a registered letter could be sent from Courtenay on Saturdays. It appears, if I had been able to send a registered letter on Saturday, May 8th, then my notice of appeal was late. It didn't matter that the relevant offices were closed on weekends.

Donald Rennie argued he would have accepted a registered letter being sent on the Saturday. What's the difference? He received the notice of appeal sooner by fax on Monday morning than if he had waited for a registered letter. Obviously, Donald Rennie applied technical details to delay the proceedings. If a registered letter had been sent and received a week later, then the argument would most likely have been that it was received late. I was angry that Rene Duval and Eddie Taylor had not allowed me to file the notice of appeal earlier. This delay was expected to take another month on the issue of timing.

When I returned to North Bay, it was obvious the appeal could be held up by legal arguments for another few years. A few months later, the tribunal dismissed my appeal because of the timing objection. Determined not to give up I decided that the matter would go before the Federal Court Trial Division.

Retirement, scheduled for April 29, 1994, was just a few short months away. It was time to begin plans for the projected move to our Intended Place of Retirement (IPR): Kamloops, British Columbia.

At the Base orderly room I received shocking news. Under the terms of Intermediate Engagement, costs of real estate and legal fees were not included as relocation expenses upon retirement. We had purchased a home because Married Quarters were conspicuously unavailable at North Bay and I didn't want to be accused of having a "confrontational" attitude. My efforts to "get along" with authorities left me with a heavy price.

The motives behind Chief Warrant Officer Poulin's decision to move us to North Bay suddenly became crystal clear. Why else would he move us across the country with less than ten months of service remaining on my contract? There were a number of places where I could have been assigned to work at CFB Comox. Instead, he chose to waste tax dollars to relocate us. It's obvious he didn't care about the cost to taxpayers if it meant we would incur financial costs upon returning to British Columbia.

Having inquired into the issue of retirement benefits and the matter of relocating to Kamloops at the end of my service, staff at CFB Comox had assured me all relocation expenses would be covered. Now it was explained that clerks had simply made a mistake.

BULLIES IN POWER

Seems like a convenient mistake! Suddenly we were stuck in North Bay, a place Chief Poulin knew we didn't want to remain. Facing a serious loss, to relocate at the end of my term of service, I searched for a solution. Regardless of the outcome, Kamloops is where we were going to be within a year.

Addressing the costly transfer to North Bay meant processing a Redress of Grievance. After considering the evidence, Lieutenant Colonel T.J. Hochban agreed that an injustice had taken place.

In his submission, he questions the logic for the Indefinite Period of Service (IPS) offer.

"Sgt Lagace was posted to North Bay for no compelling reason. The offer of an IPS was wasted on him since his situation was very familiar to NDHQ DPCAOR staff and they knew he did not want the offer. I also question if he met the requirements for receiving an IPS offer. CFAO 6-2 para 8d states that in order to receive an offer, a member should be motivated towards service life."

Up the chain, Lieutenant Colonel I.R. McConnell adds; "It is inconceivable that with only 10 months service remaining, and the fact that the career manager was intimately aware of Sgt Lagace's retirement aspirations, that a posting to North Bay was entertained."

So why was the transfer allowed? He couldn't offer a solution to the issue so the grievance was forwarded to the Base Commander.

Colonel E.R. Cornick further emphasizes; "It is my assessment that Sgt Lagace has presented sound arguments, and the additional points raised by his commanding officer are also valid".

Without recourse at that level, the grievance then went to the next level of command with support from Base authorities.

It would proceed to National Defence Headquarters where a web of deceit and lies could be woven. It began with Captain D.L. Fouts who was assigned to process the cover-up of facts and discredit the efforts of those who had dared to support the grievance.

Fouts outlines what he calls a summary of the grievance with a series of inaccuracies and concludes on a personal note.

He states:

"Sgt Lagace has a long history of tilting against the system. In the past year alone he has initiated one Human Rights complaint, two

MINQUIRIES, and this grievance. Prior to that, he has instituted a series of Human Rights complaints including, but not limited to: common law status, his wife's status as a native, his slow promotion progress, and his failure to be accepted as an officer. He had a prior grievance concerning the common law status of his wife, which he won. Apparently, he now believes that the system, in the person of the career managers, is persecuting him because of his record of dissatisfaction with it."

It's clear his intent was to launch a personal attack without concern for facts. As the reader may have noticed, nothing in Fout's statement relates to the issue of the grievance. Additionally, most of the statement represents outright lies.

In fact, only four complaints were ever filed. All four complaints related to the non-recognition of common-law relationships. This was because military authorities refused to apply the Federal Court Decision of December 1988 to any other issue than housing. Therefore, separate complaints were needed to address medical/dental coverage and the provision of moving allowances for common-law couples. The fourth complaint was filed after Dunsdon refused to process an Officer Cadet Training Plan (OCTP) application, as outlined in regulations, because he didn't agree with our common-law relationship. As for the internal Redress of Grievance process, there were three grievances which had to parallel the complaints because of Human Rights rules demanding that internal channels were exhausted prior to processing a complaint.

Fouts submitted his summary which was accepted by the chain of command without question. How a Captain can refute the evidence presented by two Lieutenant Colonels and a Colonel is beyond me. When the inaccuracies were brought to the attention of the Minister of Defence, David Collenette, the issue was ignored. Justice was later denied by the Minister of National Defence in late 1995. The costs involved over $35,000 to taxpayers and about $15,600 for us.

In attempting to resolve the issue of retaliation, a complaint had been requested through the Human Rights Commission. But, as luck would have it, military authorities had once again escaped investigation because of time limits on processing a complaint. It appears that any retaliatory actions must be reported and a complaint filed within six months of the event taking place. Since the damages associated to the transfer were not discovered until seven months after the fact, a complaint would not be processed by the Human Rights Commission.

It's the only criminal offence, that I'm aware of, where the accused can escape responsibility because of a six-month time limit in processing charges. I wonder if police officers would refrain from investigating bank robberies if the robber refused to discuss the matter or otherwise escaped for over six months.

When matters of transfer costs and previous harassment issues were brought to the attention of the Minister of Defence, David Collenette simply argued in favour of the move and perpetuated the lies of previous officials as though they were true. Documents indicate he was either seriously misinformed or he lied purposely. In either case, his performance was incompetent.

Chief Warrant Officer Rick Poulin, Captain Cote, and Major Michael MacCormack must have been happy with their accomplishment. Their financial vengeance was fully supported by military and political channels through bureaucratic manipulation.

Captain D.L. Fouts never spoke to either of the three who were involved in that final transfer. Obviously his task was to cover up the facts, and he was well supported in accomplishing that task. In order to ensure that officials were aware of the deception by Fouts and his superiors, I wrote to the Chief of Defence Staff and Minister of National Defence. After all but telling them that a network was working against them, the message was ignored.

Little did they know the pattern of cover-up would be exposed as the new boys' network was gathering evidence against authorities involved in the Somalia incident and maintained a low profile in Bosnia. Every possible incident of embarrassing potential had to be gathered and prepared for release to media sources. Those involved in this new network blended well with the spirit of discord that permeated the upper echelon of the military's senior ranks. The Minister of National Defence, David Collenette, was repeatedly advised of problems within senior ranks. He chose to disregard any attempt to call attention to corruption and collusion. Instead, he played political hide and seek.

My retirement took effect in late April, 1994, as planned. After selling our home in North Bay in late May we began our relocation to Kamloops, British Columbia also as planned. Ken had already been in Courtney for a few months to complete a high school course so the trip would be one for Amy and me to enjoy. This time there were no time limits and we would take as much time as we wanted.

We stopped at many of the places visited during previous trips. Perhaps the most memorable is just outside Thunder Bay, Ontario. Kakabeka Falls is a small community about twenty minutes west of Thunder Bay. We stayed at a motel and visited the campsite where we had stayed on that memorable trip in 1985. It was good to remind ourselves of that journey.

A few days later we showed up at David and Marg Williams' place outside of Calgary. I remember David asking, "What are you going to do? Have you got a place to move to? Got any leads for a job?" When I said it was all up in the air and we would deal with those things upon arriving in Kamloops, he laughed and said, "You're nuts."

The trip to Kamloops from David's was relaxed, even though we had no idea where we would live or where to start looking for work. We enjoyed the scenery at Lake Louise once again and Amy felt welcomed by the mountains of British Columbia once again. We reminisced about the days when we promised ourselves to return to British Columbia at the end of my twenty-year term with the military.

Within a few days after our arrival, I was getting nervous about having to find work. At the suggestion of a few old friends, I visited the Phoenix Centre and spoke to the Director about work as a counsellor. Marg Marshall explained that a position was about to open in the Corrections Program. It would involve working at the Regional Correctional Facility as an addictions counsellor. What a lucky break! Working in a correctional environment presented similar risks to those of military bureaucracy. However, I would be working for a community organization and authorities in corrections had no direct impact on my work. Starting work the following week meant the bank could approve a mortgage for the house we had chosen to buy.

House in Kamloops in 1994

I'd like to say that the transition to civilian life was easy. It wasn't! Getting rid of the attitudes that accompany life under someone else's direction is not as easy as expected. One might compare the sudden release from direction to the feeling that an inmate experiences upon release from prison. It's a very temporary feeling of exhilaration, followed by a sense of being alone and different from everyone else. Amy was very familiar with the feeling. Her quiet nature and loving support were so reassuring as she smiled with a glow of confidence that everything would be alright.

Dealing with the review tribunal became less important as Amy's physical condition grew worse. She had been experiencing severe migraine headaches since early 1985. A tumour had been forming around her pituitary gland. It was being treated with medication in hope of avoiding surgical procedures.

Shortly after settling in Kamloops, the tumour began to grow. Migraines were occurring every two or three weeks. I felt really helpless as the pain would cause her to vomit until she was so dehydrated that she required hospitalization. We kept blankets over all the windows in order to keep the house dark as light triggered such pain that she often found it difficult to open her eyes.

While at work one day in August, 1994, I had occasion to speak to a Native Elder at the Friendship Centre. Although I had heard of Sweatlodge ceremonies, I had never attended. During our conversation he asked, "Would you like to attend a sweat?" I recalled how Amy spoke about such invitations being an honour. I agreed and the following Sunday I attended my first sweat.

I learned that Sweatlodge is a traditional ceremony to attain a balance between physical, mental, emotional, and spiritual directions in life. "We only come here for two reasons" the elder would say, "that is cleanse and offer prayer". My childhood teachings in Catholic beliefs were not challenged as one might expect. Instead, I was taught that prayers are personal between me and Creator (God as learned in school). Each time I attended Sweatlodge, I learned a little more about spirituality. I shared with elders about Amy's condition. She could not attend Sweatlodge because of her illness and the medication she was taking. She would come with me in support. "Pray hard" the elders would say as the darkness closed in and the heat seemed unbearable. "We suffer only a short time here but those we pray for out there suffer all day every day," he would say. I prayed for guidance from Creator.

In early 1995, specialists argued that surgical removal of the tumour around Amy's pituitary gland was necessary. Throughout the years of battling military authorities I had never really felt powerless. I couldn't fight Amy's condition. Her quiet acceptance of the pain and vomiting she was now experiencing almost daily remained a mystery to me.

The words of an elder rang in my ears. "Support her - don't protect her," she had said.

On October 12, 1995, Amy underwent the most serious operation of her life. A tumour about the size of a golf ball was removed along with her pituitary gland. Recovery was expected to take about six days. After four days, Amy was still unconscious and hadn't shown any signs of waking up. Along with feeling helpless, I was angry at military authorities for denying medical coverage that might have helped detect and treat the illness before the tumour started.

Amy in a silent mood the day before surgery in Vancouver 1995

On the fourth morning I sat in the chair at the end of her bed and thought about prayers in the Sweatlodge. I fell asleep and a dream (or vision as elders would later clarify) came to me. In this dream I was helplessly observing as Amy was floating on a tube down a deep stream of fast water. The tube kept getting smaller and soon she sank. As much as I wanted to, I was unable to run to her and she went down for a third time. I woke up with a jump in the chair just as a nurse was about to administer an injection to Amy. I asked what the injection was and he said it was morphine for pain. I can't explain why but I felt a strange sense that Amy couldn't wake up because of the medication. I asked him not to do that yet. He agreed to give her a couple of hours to see if she would wake. Her breathing had become so shallow and difficult.

Nursing staff agreed to stop the morphine that was being administered. This would help to bring her out of unconsciousness so that her lungs could clear. It worked! Two days later, Amy was walking around. Once discharged from the hospital, we went home. My prayers at Sweatlodge from that day on were of gratitude as I had received guidance. It was stressful to wait for results of the tumour analysis. Although the tumour was benign, there was a threat that it would return, as the cause could not be defined.

With the migraines gone, Amy returned to part time work and began feeling good. Follow-up tests confirmed the tumour was coming back after only a few months. Amy was frustrated and I felt so helpless. Her condition continued to baffle specialists.

"A very rare case", explained Doctors Wilkins and Griesdale.

In late April, 1996, a second tumour was removed from the same area. This time recovery was much better. After only four days, Amy was on her way home. Once again, specialists could not confirm the cause or source of the tumour it again went to a waiting game.

Meanwhile, the Federal Court of Appeal ruled in favour of allowing a review tribunal to hear my appeal. David Collenette's office sarcastically argued that I could present my case at that time. It was well known that the review tribunal could not hear any new evidence and certainly not such a distant issue as the transfer of 1993.

Scheduled for July 22nd to the 25th, I was ready to represent myself. After preparing the documentation, the only barrier would be addressing objections from Donald Rennie. He would represent the Canadian Armed Forces and Justice Department in the proceedings. My intent to introduce new evidence in the form of affidavits would draw objections. I expected it and prepared for the challenge.

Eddie Taylor would attend to represent the Canadian Human Rights Commission as a formality. Donald Rennie didn't approve but there wasn't much he could do about it. Eddie informed me of the process and explained that he was not allowed to openly support my efforts. He also confirmed my suspicions about Rene Duval. It appears the relationship between Rene Duval and Donald Rennie was too close for Duval to objectively represent the issue. That's why the 1992 tribunal was such a disaster. Eddie felt I had been duped by Rene Duval and assured me that he would make every effort to help. For some unknown reason, I felt Eddie could be trusted. He seemed to understand the plight of being the underdog.

Amy was accompanied by a volunteer from the Victims Assistance Program. She wanted to hear the arguments. I was happy to have her there and it was a relief to have someone else supporting her. Although I expected to take about an hour to make my presentation, it took the entire first day.

At the end of the day, Eddie was impressed and so was Amy. Donald Rennie, on the other hand, was furious that Eddie had provided advice during one of the breaks. That may be why Rennie

BULLIES IN POWER

decided to use the media to launch vengeance and try to upset the process. This hypocrite had criticized me for telling the truth to the media in 1986, but now he took the opportunity to vent his frustration with lies.

The article printed in the next morning's paper was insulting to say the least. A focus on education costs placed a spin on the issue and left me looking like a leech after public moneys to cover my university. Nothing could have been further from the truth. When confronted with the matter, Rennie thought it was funny that he could lie to the media and they wouldn't even check. The Kamloops Daily News had shown its true colours. The truth wasn't as important as who was making the statements. Daily News editor, Mike Cornell researched the information and later wrote the truth about the hearings and how the public had been duped by Rennie's lies.

On the second day of hearings, Eddie Taylor made a brief presentation and was followed by Donald Rennie who presented a short repetition of his arguments of the 1992 tribunal. With final rebuttal left up to me, I made my points clear and concise.

First, the military policy of 1988 was of non-recognition of our relationship. That fact could not be denied. Second, the Officer Cadet Training Plan (OCTP) application did not require any experience or post-secondary education. Therefore, Rennie's argument that I was "unqualified" for the program shouldn't stand. In short, the evidence weighed in our favour. However, the tribunal members left no hint of which direction the matter could go. Eddie, on the other hand, confided I had convinced the tribunal and he felt no doubt that I had proven my case.

Eddie praised my presentation; "I've seen lawyers with 20 years of experience who couldn't do what you did before this tribunal". He went on, "If you ever decide to become a lawyer, I'll write you a reference anytime." For me, all that was left was the waiting.

On October 18, 1996, the Review Tribunal rendered its decision and agreed that Major Ray Dunsdon had engaged in retaliation and discrimination by refusing to process the 1987 OCTP application. However, Review Tribunal members argued Dunsdon's actions were because I had filed a redress of grievance and human rights complaint and not because of the non-recognition of common-law relationships.

According to military authorities, supported by Dunsdon's actions, I had no right to complain about abusive practices and discrimination. The tribunal attributed responsibility to Dunsdon.

Although Dunsdon engaged in retaliation and discrimination, the ruling did not attribute any career damages. They also did not agree with my apprehension of bias argument and supported Alfred Lynch-Staunton's decision. Consequently, the ruling expressed a limited view of the situation and assigned all the weight of evidence to the Department of Justice presentation. Guilty, but how could responsibility be assigned to the military as an institution? The political influence of such a decision would have shaken the traditional approach to dealing with aboriginal issues. It's crystal clear the unwritten policy, to prevent Native Peoples from accessing rights under the Charter, remains very active.

Therefore, for Dunsdon's retaliation, an award of $3500.00 fell far short of holding Dunsdon and his peers responsible for the damage of their conspiracy. There is no way to compensate for the bigotry, slander, insults, harassment, and destroyed career resulting from military authorities' intentions to punish anyone who dared to complain. However, this hollow victory remains a victory and a small step forward.

The Justice Department had argued, in 1988, that there was no evidence to show that Dunsdon's actions were discriminatory. The review tribunal ruling of October 18, 1996, proved the case against Dunsdon. However, he escaped prosecution through a loop hole in the form of "time limits" to initiate prosecution. RCMP headquarters in Ottawa confirmed Dunsdon had escaped prosecution even though the review tribunal decision attributed guilt. The Justice Department had refused to prosecute Dunsdon in 1988 because that Department was defending the military's discriminatory policy which Dunsdon supported.

Why was the pursuit of this case so important? Most of us only stand when we have no choice. If someone else is being abused, we tend to look away. We need to change our way of accepting abuse and neglect from political representatives. They are paid by us and need to be accountable. Challenging public officials has been made difficult by those who abuse their position. A brief look at our history confirms that only radical moves can motivate change and that we Canadians are far too tolerant of government controls. Our greatest leader, Louis Riel, secured Canada's western provinces and received the death penalty for his challenge of political abuse. It took over 100 years for history to be adjusted to the truth about the efforts of Métis Peoples.

As far as Amy and I were concerned the matter was now completed. We had lived up to our commitment to see the conflict of 1982 resolved to its end.

Amy's condition was being monitored after her surgery of April, 1996. Every six months she would undergo a Magnetic Resonance Image (MRI) of her brain to ensure the tumour was not returning. Doctors Todd Collier of Kamloops and Jeff Beckman of Vancouver remained baffled by Amy's condition.

On December 6, 1998, I was following my usual morning routine of making coffee and toast for Amy and me before going to work. Sensing Amy behind me, I turned to give her my usual good morning greeting but saw that she was unable to speak and her right arm was hanging at her side. As she stumbled forward it was apparent something was really wrong. By the time the ambulance arrived, she was able to speak very softly but her words were difficult to understand. It was as though she had something in her mouth.

At the hospital she began to regain her ability to move her arm and to speak with less restriction. It was concluded that she had suffered a mild stroke but tests would need to be done to find the cause and possible damage. Doctors Collier and Beckman administered a number of tests but could not determine the origin of the brain lesions. After six months it was found that Amy suffered from some rare condition involving inflammation causing the lesions. She would be treated with a very high dosage of Prednisone. This harsh medication would result in Amy's body retaining water and cause serious weight gain. She was devastated.

For years we had always discussed the possibility of taking a vacation to an exotic place. Amy had talked about visiting Hawaii some day. While at Doctor Collier's office in early November, 1999, I asked him if Amy could travel. He didn't see any reason why not and even suggested it would be good for Amy to enjoy a vacation away for a few days. Amy looked at me with that familiar little smile. I looked at her and asked her how she would feel about visiting Hawaii. Her smile really broadened but then she looked sad and said, "We can't afford it." Looking at Doctor Collier I asked if air travel to Hawaii would be a risk to her health. He responded that risks were everywhere and we should go and enjoy the trip.

I had been working for the AIDS Society of Kamloops since late December 1998, after a disagreement with the Correctional Branch convinced me to find a more ethical environment to work as a counsellor. When I approached the Executive Director about taking a vacation, I expected some resistance. However, Marianne and the Board of Directors were in full support. What a change from the military and Phoenix centre where approval was always in question.

A few days after our encounter in Doctor Collier's office we were on the beach in Maui. We had gone to British Columbia Automobile Association (BCAA) travel and booked a two-week stay at the Kaanapali resort hotel. For two weeks Amy and I had the most enjoyable visit of Maui's attractions. My fear of heights didn't stop us from going on Amy's first helicopter ride over the island. Talking to one of the locals, he suggested we visit the Seven Sacred Pools of Hanna. The hike would involve about two miles in the most beautiful tropical forest leading to the falls. The local had mentioned the water from the falls was very refreshing and it was believed to hold healing powers. Amy seldom spoke

Amy and Paul having a romantic moment in Mauii

of her beliefs in natural medicines but her determination to reach the falls was inspiring. She found the hike very difficult as she had gained so much weight. When we reached the falls she wasted no time in getting the feel of that water on her head. On our walk back down the winding trail it was getting dark but the beauty of the sunset was awesome.

We celebrated twenty years together at the Royal Lahaina Luau the night before returning home.

Amy's first helicopter ride in Mauii

Upon our arrival home it was time to begin preparation for Christmas. As usual we planned a big dinner at our house and invited all the relations to attend. We shared stories and recounted our experience. After dinner Amy enjoyed a few games of scrabble with her sisters and cousins. For months after that we would recall details of our visit to Maui.

A few months later it was determined that Amy's condition was stable but she could not return to work. She wanted to contribute to the household's financial support. It took months for her to accept that she would be unable to work until doctors found out what was causing the lesions in her brain. Her hand and leg had remained numb as she continued to suffer from the results of the stroke almost two years earlier. An elder had suggested a traditional medicine involving pine needle baths that I would prepare. After a few weeks it seemed to have a positive effect as Amy was less depressed and said she felt better.

In the summer of 2001, we picked soap berries. It was a traditional medicine that Amy had enjoyed since she was a little girl. We would also pack a picnic lunch when we went to pick bitter root. It wasn't important how much we picked, only that we did it together. We did these things together because we enjoyed sharing our experiences.

During a visit with Doctor Jeff Beckman on March 14, 2002, he was very positive and advised, "Amy your condition is very stable. In fact, we don't need to see you again for a year instead of every six months." We drove home with a renewed hope as Amy had thoughts of returning to work.

We arrived home in time for Amy to prepare supper while I did my usual sorting of the mail and review the bills. After supper Amy called her sister Grace to come and play a game of scrabble so she could share the good news with her. Scrabble was never my game so I decided to go to the gym.

I had barely started my workout when Grace called the gym. "Amy is very ill. She's collapsed in the hallway. I've called the ambulance because she can't move." I rushed home to find Amy still on the floor in the hallway in terrible pain. She couldn't get up and whenever she tried to move the pain would cause her to scream. I wanted to take her pain away. The ambulance arrived and she was taken to the hospital in Kamloops.

I followed the ambulance and stayed with her in the emergency room. It took doctors an hour or so to take Amy in for a scan. By then she had become unconscious. Shortly after the scan, the neurologist came in and said she had suffered an aneurysm and would be transported to Vancouver General Hospital by air ambulance as she would require surgery that couldn't be done in Kamloops.

Ken and I drove to Vancouver to be there when she came out of surgery. We stayed by Amy's side waiting for the expected moment of her awakening. The emotional turmoil of those sleepless days and nights remains too painful to describe. Those who have experienced such a loss understand.

Amy would not regain consciousness. Ten days later, on March 25, 2002, Amy's spirit began her journey to the Spirit World. A large part of my soul went with her that day. Although Ken has never spoken about it, I suspect he experienced the sudden emptiness too.

Ken offers his respect to his mother at her funeral March 28, 2002

Amy's funeral at Cook's Ferry Band Burial Grounds

Ken was quiet. I felt numb throughout the funeral. Reality would overcome my disbelief as I began to realize Amy would not be home for morning toast and coffee anymore. I found quiet places and cried.

Ken spoke very little and I didn't know what to say. What do you say to a son when his mother is gone? What do we talk about? He withdrew into work and so did I. For the next few months we would gradually face the fact that Amy wasn't coming back. There were times when I missed her so much that an emotional lump would move up into my chest and I couldn't breathe or swallow. I felt like I might not survive the next minute. At those times I would wonder, is this the time when I will finally join her? I knew Ken felt the same but we just never talked.

Time would offer healing and I continued to attend Sweatlodge. Elders shared how important it was to let her spirit go. "She earned her right to cross over to the Spirit World"... "You need to respect the will of Creator and let her go," he would say.

There are times when it seems so long ago that Amy and I first met. Yet when I look at her picture I feel like it was only yesterday and I miss her again. Sometimes I just want her back but I hear the elder's voice... "Let her go she earned her right to cross over."

Today, it's been over three years and I find it very difficult to write about our time together without feeling a deep sense of loss. I have found the support of relations at Sweatlodge has been a life force for me to continue with the work I do. As I look back, I can see that my prayers for guidance were answered by Creator through my work. The people I work with at the AIDS Society are unique in that they all possess a sense of empathy for the pain that death brings to the hearts of those left behind.

I learned about the seven sacred values practiced with Sweatlodge. They are: respect, wisdom, generosity, honesty, humility, courage and fortitude. Throughout the difficult years when I would get angry at authorities, Amy lived those values. I have come to understand and feel Amy's spirit in every gentle breeze and each petal of a rose.

Up to this point the writing was for my healing. It's my belief the healing will go on for some time. However, the lessons of our experience have been presented as an appendix in this book and are for the reader to consider.

Margaret Amy-Louise Walkem July 14, 1951 - March 25, 2002
Cherished Soul Mate to Paul and Loving Mother to Ken
We Will Miss You

Amy Walkem - Sam

Never in all my dreams could I imagine the gift of a soulmate like you. You taught us the meaning of friendship and love, as well as the many different ways of spelling it at scrabble. We now look to your gentle spirit for guidance and strength to move ahead with the brightness your life has left with us.

We Will Always Love and Remember You

Special thanks to Chief Arthur Dick of the Shulus Indian Band and Chief David Walkem of the Cook's Ferry Indian Band as well as all the members and relations from both bands for honouring Amy's life and final journey.

Kenneth and Paul

CONCLUSION

How should I conclude writing descriptions of life? Perhaps the most obvious effort in my presentation has been to speak the truth without passing judgement. It has not been an easy task. It's in our nature to pass judgement. However, there have been many historical facts contributing to the persistent arrogance of public servants exercising their authority with abusive practices. At the risk of accusations that I am simply venting, I want to share facts that have come to light in the process of my efforts.

Throughout our short military history, Canadians have earned the respect and support of most nations around the world. However, recent discoveries indicate that the Canadian Armed Forces have been plagued with deception of the public in the interest of saving face for corrupt military and political figures.

A number of examples seem to stand out in history. Of note is the travesty that many veterans endured as they returned from the battlefields of Europe only to be deprived of their right to return to the jobs they had left at the start of World War Two. Over 14,000 veterans who had fought bravely during the war were deemed never to have served by a government Order in Council that many Canadians have forgotten or simply don't care about.

One must keep in mind that social conditions of that era were not supportive of social assistance. Today, people assume social assistance is a right. In 1945, social assistance was stigmatized.

Consequently, those veterans needed to return to work. They had served their country. Order in Council PC 3264, dated 16 August 1946, had taken less than six months to implement. All veterans who had not waited, until the bureaucratic foot-dragging provided them approval to go to work were labelled "deserters."

It's sad to discover that bureaucrats, who had remained at their desks during the war, sat in judgement of the men who fought courageously and honourably in conditions that can only be described by those fortunate enough to return. The pride and integrity of those men did not allow them to challenge this bureaucratic injustice. They had done their duty and expected nothing more than to return to work in support of their families.

Soldiers like Gordon Broad, who was wounded in battle and went on to volunteer from Europe for duty in the Pacific, were denied all veterans' benefits by bureaucratic vengeance. It took less time for the Canadian government to pass the Order in Council than it had taken to provide demobilization papers to returning veterans after the war.

Bureaucrats and politicians argue that nothing can be done to change the injustice. It's as though the order in council was an act of God. I choose to call it bureaucratic bullying. The bottom line, for those ungrateful bureaucratic morons, is the dollars they saved in denying benefits to those veterans and their families.

However, Jacob Luitjens receives Canada Pension Plan benefits while in jail in the Netherlands. Convicted of collaborating with the Nazis during World War II, he fled to Canada in 1961 and hid his past until the late 1980s. He was stripped of Canadian citizenship for lying about his wartime activities, but he still receives a pension from Canada.

How could politicians like Eric Neilson and Mary Collins argue that veterans like Gordon Broad deserve to be punished for going to work? The war was over!! Where's the logic with Order in Council PC 3264? It doesn't seem to matter how much good you do. Bureaucrats who have never faced hardship will defend stupidity through the existence of stupid rules.

Questions to Defence Minister David Collenette about impostors from other countries collecting war veterans' benefits because they allege they have helped Canada during World War Two have gone without response. It became obvious a few years ago that some were simply too young to have been involved, but the benefits apparently kept going.

The systemic failure to face the truth is further reflected in the network that protects male senior officers and acts as a mechanism of locating scapegoats within the non-commissioned ranks. In early 1992, public attention to sexual harassment allegations by female military members at CFB Comox led to charges being brought against a young Master Corporal. Although he was convicted, there seems to have been an effort by Base authorities to focus on the individual's junior rank status.

Meanwhile at Canadian Forces Base Comox, another young woman who had been subjected to sexual harassment by a Master Warrant Officer and her Commanding Officer for some five months was treated with disbelief and released for attempting to bring charges against the two accused. It seems odd that reported "bad behaviours" have been limited to lower ranked individuals? You seldom hear about higher ranks being charged with such offences because they are protected. Exceptions are those expendable tokens. For them, the punishment seldom meets equal measures as exacted against lower ranks.

"Zero tolerance" is a catchy term that is aimed at appeasing the public. It means very little to the many victims who suffer discrimination and harassment under an imposed silence while authorities publicly preach such actions would never be condoned. Not only does this policy dilute the credibility of victims, it also discourages victims from coming forward thus presenting an impression that the policy is effective. It's obvious that military authorities are not mature enough to address harassment through internal procedures. Too many barriers are firmly established in traditional beliefs that only lower ranks can be guilty of deviant behaviours such as sexual harassment.

Just because officials say harassment won't be tolerated does not mean harassment has been vanquished. It simply means officials have found a new cloak to cover it. So don't be intimidated by fancy terminology. Stand firm and don't allow officials to hide behind bureaucratic smoke screens.

Another abusive military tradition is found in the MESS. This traditional military institution segregates members in accordance with the rank structure. It also acts as a social wedge between the soldier and his or her family. In some cases, the husband and wife are not allowed to socialize together because of differences in rank. Alistair McKenzie was promoted to Sergeant in 1993. His wife Moira, also a military member, was not permitted to attend social functions at his mess and he was also precluded from attending her mess. It's sad to see that husband and wife can be socially divided by archaic values belonging to a long past era.

But that's not the only disparity in social activities. While lower ranks pay their own way and are compelled to attend, senior officers and their spouses are given the choice and never need to worry about expenses in social activities. Taxpayers foot the bills for everything from beauty salon tabs for spouses as well as catering and golfing expenses of senior officers. All these fringe benefits come with the rank and high incomes of military senior staff. It's clear those who can most afford to pay their own way are also given the green light to spend in the name of "privilege".

Conflict of interest is often ignored along with financial abuse of public funds. I'm reminded of Major Ray Dunsdon's 1986 and 1988 electoral campaigns in Kamloops, British Columbia. Was it not convenient that his campaign manager happened to be the radar site Construction Engineering Officer? Campaign signs reflected a call to elect Major Ray Dunsdon in bright Air Force blue background. I suppose there could have been a sale on Air Force blue paint and plywood at that time.

I'm of the opinion that while serving as municipal councillor in Kamloops, Dunsdon's duties included negotiations for the use of the radar site after closure. Military authorities looked the other way as Dunsdon played the dual role of municipal councillor and radar site Commanding Officer. It's interesting to note that at the time he was also deeply involved in the local branch of the Royal Canadian Air Force Association in Kamloops. The lease for the Rossmore Lake military training area appeared to have suddenly been transferred to the RCAF Association in 1988. I wonder why? I suspect the transfer's reversal some time later may have been the result of inquiries into Dunsdon's activities.

My opinion extends to the irony that Dunsdon, who argued I lacked officer-like qualities, ordered military heavy equipment and personnel from CFB Chilliwack to upgrade the Rossmore Lake area into a resort-like development. His use of military equipment might have been intended as training for the personnel who worked at Rossmore Lake. It may only be coincidental that such training would take place during the final year of Dunsdon's service and at a time when RCAF Association members represented electoral votes.

An optimistic assessment of Dunsdon's role might suggest his position as Station Commander was in slight conflict with his elected position at the municipal level. On the pessimistic side of the argument, one might say Dunsdon used his military authority and elected status to promote his personal goals within the community as he prepared for retirement from the military. Perhaps the transfer of funds intended for public utilities to the non-public fund accounts also represented a retirement benefit? There wasn't much accountability for Dunsdon's actions and even less concern among those who knew they could cover up anything arising out of his tenure as Station Commanding Officer.

However, the most difficult situation for the military to cover up was the 1993 Somalia incident. Perhaps this was because of the way senior officials sought to escape responsibility by passing off the blame to those who were ordered to act aggressively against the stealing taking place in the Canadian compound. I still recall my duties at Ismailia, Egypt in 1976.

It is my opinion that officers gave orders to the four soldiers assigned to guard the prisoner. To discourage civilians from attempting to sneak and steal from the Canadian camp, orders were given to beat the Somali teen and make him scream "Canada" as proof of who was in control. Sadly, the teen died. Those who knew about the orders tried to hide the facts. They were partially successful but not very efficient. Additionally, are we expected to believe that other soldiers, including officers in command, did not hear the Somali youth screaming?

In a discussion I had with a Member of Parliament, a few days after Master Corporal Clayton Machee's so-called "attempted suicide", my suggestion on the possible sequence of events leading to the death of the Somali youth may have triggered curiosity among political channels. Then Defence Minister, Kim Campbell, was more interested in political fallout than allowing the truth to survive. As a result we may never know the truth.

Military officials first pointed the bureaucratic finger to white supremacists within the airborne unit. That cover-up route was quickly closed when it was discovered two of the accused soldiers were of First Nations origin. Certainly shot down the white supremacist theory.

So how else could it be covered? Well, in typical bureaucratic fashion, military authorities began to lie and change reports in order to hide facts. That route was made difficult by some in the new boys' network. Anyone who served on peace-keeping missions is familiar with unwritten orders to control civilians, particularly potential thieves.

The new boys' network involves a loosely formed group of lower and middle ranks whose aim is to embarrass senior officials by using cover-up attempts to expose corruption. It's a very effective mechanism and remains in place. The possible outcome could very likely lead to the demobilization and/or restructuring of the entire senior rank structure within the Canadian Forces. Power hungry incompetents have played a control game for too long. It's time to have them removed through their own game.

Although political channels were advised of corruption within the senior ranks of the military, ministers of defence ignored the warnings. The Somalia Inquiry saw General Jean Boyle pretend he knew nothing about the cover-up of facts related to events during the Somalia deployment.

Boyle accused his subordinates of lacking integrity. So what's new? We already knew that. The question is, how did they manage to avoid detection for so long? The answer is clear. General Boyle simply continued the tradition of his predecessors in heading a team of corrupt officers. Attempting to avoid responsibility for wrongdoing is evidence of his lack of credibility and integrity.

216

General Boyle was compelled to retire with an undisclosed golden handshake. On the other hand a Review Tribunal agrees that 14 years of discrimination and retaliation against our family situation does not even warrant an apology or acknowledgement by military authorities that an injustice ever took place.

What's most frustrating about corruption within government departments is that the media often takes a special interest in supporting whatever government officials expect. For example, the crisis in Oka, Quebec, was represented in the media as some sort of terrorist uprising.

Media focus on the activities of natives served to minimize the actions of Quebec police and the mayor of Oka who actually provoked the conflict in the first place.

After his return to the United States, Terry Waite pointed out that terrorism occurs when all legitimate channels of democracy are denied to individuals or minority groups. First Nations Peoples at Oka were denied protection under the law and saw no alternatives but civil disobedience. Violence erupted after the Quebec "Gestapo-like" police decided to use force where legal avenues were sought by natives. My question is simple: How many Human Rights complaints were processed on behalf of native citizens following the Oka conflict?

Media information is not always accurate. In fact, one might argue that information is often manipulated to sensationalise the news. That can lead to frustration for those victimized by false or unfair media reports. I can certainly confirm that the media is more concerned with who makes the statements than whether or not those statements are true.

What you have read in this book is the truth Through painstaking effort, the events described have been researched with meticulous attention to detail. Therefore, if authorities feel there is misrepresentation I would be happy to review documents related to events in question.

Receiving a promotion to Sergeant, ten months prior to my release, is like attending a banquet only to be fed crumbs at the end. Of course, I was expected to grovel in humble gratitude for having received an invitation. The many commissioning programs, for which I had been encouraged to apply, were served to others like rewarding plates kept out of my reach in punishment for some perceived immorality. In retrospect, not eating the fruits from their table prevented the fatal poisoning of my honesty, dignity and integrity.

Obviously, winning the battles meant losing the war. Reviewing personal experiences over the last fourteen years, I can see where errors were made during the course of addressing abusive attitudes at various levels of authority. Three important lessons need mention.

First, never delay addressing harassment. It won't go away on its own. Second, if you sense the true nature of a problem is rooted in racism, then focus on that aspect of the issue. Don't allow authorities, including the Human Rights Commission, to persuade you to limit corrective measures. Go after the disease not just the symptoms. Finally, get a sense of humour. You'll need it if you want to enjoy the battle. Although my career has served as prey for bureaucratic vultures, the process of writing about the loss provides relief from frustrations of dealing with double standards and unfair practices.

When setting out to write this book in late 1991, the aim was to produce a guidance map for people in search of freedom from the dependency that develops over years of institutional bondage. Instead, I may have unleashed a barrage of questions about the professionalism of senior military officers and elected public officials.

What were the costs, in public funds, for changing the policy regarding common-law relationships in the military? The fact that only a Federal Court ruling would motivate that change calls attention to the unreasonable nature of senior officials mandated to review the issue. You might be tempted to argue that I didn't have to challenge the discriminatory practices against common-law relationships. Some might argue that discrimination is acceptable when the cost of prevention becomes too high. While legal costs may have been high, the hidden costs are far greater. Those hidden costs are unveiled with questions about the after-effects of discrimination.

Discriminatory practices have left taxpayers to bear the cost of educating and training someone else to perform the duties for which I became qualified at my own expense. Unlike most of our officers,

I accomplished a Bachelor of Arts Degree on my own time, with my own money, while supporting a family that military authorities refused to recognize.

Challenging the military's policy of non recognition of common-law relationships was legally justified. However, the price was the loss of a career. Authorities responsible have not been held accountable. So perhaps a few revelations are in order.

I have identified a number of people in this book who have contributed to bigotry. They may not like what they read about themselves, but that's the unfortunate result of being arrogant enough to expect that bureaucratic bullying would be accepted without challenge. Some may feel my assessment of the situation is unfair in itself. To those people, I suggest they become familiar with the system they support. Authorities must be held accountable when they mistake their privileges for rights: in particularly when such privileges become the platform leading to abuse of authority.

There are a number of issues which were not discussed in this reflection of military problems. Abuse of power may be practised at any level of the rank structure. Fear of senior military staff has often served to redefine the truth. How can anyone expect young officers to stand by their men when courage and honesty are sources of punishment during officer's training? It is unthinkable that a lower rank soldier might suggest that an officer could make a mistake.

Calling attention to injustice within the military chain of command led to very harsh consequences. Although one would be hard-pressed to prove the existence of an "Old Boys' Network", its effects are most obvious. Experience at Canadian Force Base (CFB) North Bay in 1982 was followed by years of inadequacies with administrative procedures. This presents serious question about the selective process of officers in the Canadian Forces. There are too many dishonest facades among bullies in power. One might ask how many senior officers are known to be native. How many junior officers? But there is no lack of "French-Canadian" officers from Quebec playing the language game with Ottawa.

Today, my life in the military is but a mosaic of memories tainted by the reality that power corrupts. Since leaving the military, I have been honoured with invitations to participate in many First Nations cultural events. I have also seen how experiences in the residential schools have forged very painful memories in the lives of Native Peoples.

You, the reader, have a responsibility to stand against abuse of authority. It doesn't matter how insignificant the issue seems to you at the time. If a bureaucrat denies your rights, argue the facts. Otherwise, the bureaucrat's grasp on power strengthens with each victory over his or her victims. The results of inaction are becoming increasingly prevalent as voters seem to feel their only avenue of challenge is through elections. There are a number of ways to voice your opinion between elections. Do it! It's your right! It's never too late to challenge unfair practices. It starts with one determined voice. Yours!!!

Although you may have picked up on a small detail of history that has not been shared, let me present it clearly. My distant Aboriginal ancestry marks the Métis spirit that has guided the passion of my efforts to stand against authorities who bully those less fortunate. There are many things that can be said about being Métis. I'm proud to say that this Métis has been honest in addressing injustice. That can never be turned into a loss. After twenty-three years with Amy, the passion of being in love continued to bond our spirits as one to the end. The bonds of true love can never be broken.

All we really wanted was an acknowledgment of responsibility and an apology from Canadian officials who were found guilty of discrimination. All four Human Rights Complaints were supported in legal proceedings. To date, Canadian officials continue to act as though there was nothing wrong with their actions.

Section 67 of the Canadian Human Rights Act remains in force and deprives all Canadians from being considered equal.

Photo by Sergeant Guy Pelletier of the Canadian Forces Base North Bay Photo Section in February 1994.

I am Red Bear and I have spoken. All My Relations

Appendix I: Steps to Challenging Bureaucratic Injustice

When faced with the challenge of bureaucratic injustice, it's important to understand how to remain focussed on principles so that the process doesn't get bogged down in personality issues. To be well prepared, the system needs to be briefly described. The steps outlined are not limited to challenging the military. These steps will work with any administrative system. This is affirmed with post-military experience in counselling and advocacy.

It's important to understand the meaning of the term "bureaucrat". Although bureaucrats function at all levels of the system, it's been my experience to note that friendship and bureaucracy cannot co-exist. If you keep that in mind when addressing an administrative issue, it will reduce the degree of emotional turmoil you're likely to experience. Avoid falling into the trap of friendly chit chat with a bureaucrat in the course of addressing an important matter. It is a very common approach for bureaucrats to befriend you and undermine your self-worth with imposed guilt.

In learning about the system, one also discovers ways to address fears of that previously unknown world of secrets that authorities selfishly claim as their own. There's a universal rule which applies to all who choose to challenge a bureaucratic system: Never forego your convictions to satisfy the bureaucrat.

A bureaucrat will always perceive gained ground in an argument as a licence to humiliate you. In other words, when you think you're being cooperative, the bureaucrat assumes he or she has weakened your position. The result of cooperation is never positive, unless the bureaucrat can get the credit for "helping you out". That means you owe him or her. They'll never let you forget.

If I had followed the principle "never give an inch", I might not have lost a mile. There was a time when I felt it was simply bad luck to have encountered so many egocentric morons among military officers and political channels. Reality taught me an important lesson about the misguided belief that a bureaucrat can never be wrong. It's also an unwritten code among bureaucrats that only they can be

223

honest. Others, including you and me, are assumed to be dishonest in the course of a disagreement.

Bureaucrats possess an important character flaw. They lack the freedom to make their own decisions. They rely on the system to support decisions. Just ask a politician or government official about the plight of World War Two veterans. It's a fact that 14,000 Canadian veterans who were "deemed never to have served" because they went to work after the war.

Bureaucrats refused to provide demobilization papers to these men when they returned from the European front. While awaiting assignment to duty in the Pacific, the war ended. Many of these men were left to wait for months with nothing to do. Bureaucrats indicated demobilization papers would not be granted until all troops had returned from Europe. Now here were thousands of men who had priority in returning to Canada because they had volunteered to go to the Pacific. There was no respect shown to these loyal soldiers and bureaucrats withheld demobilization documents as though the end of the war marked the start of a race. This sombre fact of Canadian military history is but one of our officially hidden secrets.

There are many reasons why authorities behave in bureaucratic ways. Benefits and rewards are not always as obvious as a pay cheque. Examples of bureaucratic palm-greasing and patronage rewards might call attention to the 1992 appointment of retiring Chief of Defence Staff, General John DeChastelain, to the position of Ambassador to the United States. How many senior officers retire from the military and walk into civilian appointments with companies holding military contracts?

Consider retired Chief of Defence Staff, General Paul Manson, in a management position with the company awarded helicopter contracts by the Mulroney government. The only good that came of that smelly deal was when Prime Minister Jean Chretien flushed the contract down the cesspool of government patronage. I'm not going to say senior officers can't do the jobs. But if you believe they earned their new jobs in competition, you're as naive as a first-elected politician who thinks he or she can change existing corruption!

Bringing back General John DeChastelain, to the position of Chief of Defence Staff, was a sign of difficult times ahead for the military bureaucracy. There's nothing worse than a bureaucrat who feels he's been demoted. General DeChastelain could afford to selfishly seek out political power. He, like other officers at the rank of Colonel and above, will certainly never have to worry about financial cuts to the fringe benefits they pick up on their way out. It's not surprising that those who need more upon retirement actually get less. Hell, senior officers get more in retirement benefits than most people get in wages. The "golden handshakes" are too diversified to detail here. For now, I want to outline features of bureaucracy which make it so difficult to change.

The System

The term "system" represents an impersonal bastion of society from which authorities draw justification for resisting unwanted change. Any organization can be defined in terms of a combination of material and people. We know that material things can be shaped according to human expectations. Therefore, the only feature of any organization which may resist change is its people. Accordingly, the idea that one can't buck or change the "system" is misguided. Authorities draw support, for their control over people, from the faceless system they suggest is somehow inflexible.

So you can't fight city hall. Why? Because authorities who are in comfortable control say so! If you expect to change the way authorities treat you, then expect resistance from people rather than machines. In resisting change, authorities will assume a defensive stance and argue that they don't make the rules, they simply follow them. Who makes the rules, if not authorities at some level? It doesn't really matter where you go there are system-oriented people who expect you to fall in line behind them in support of the almighty "system". The key words are: "behind them".

The Rules

There are two sets of rules in a bureaucracy. The "visible" rules apply to those who often become victims of bureaucratic channels, usually the lower ranks. The "invisible" rules are the manipulative tools belonging to authorities. Invisible rules are often pulled out in order to justify a lack of common sense. Authorities always resort to those invisible rules to prevent the challenge of stupid visible rules.

So I asked, "Why are common-law relationships impossible to accept in the military?"

The visible rule is that the policy hadn't been changed yet. The invisible rule is that military authorities were not going to change the visible rule until a member of the senior brass could claim credit for doing it. So the real reason is not that the policy couldn't be modernized. It's simply that a corporal would not be allowed to suggest the change. More importantly, a corporal who sought to protect his native spouse from discrimination was clearly going against the will of bureaucrats searching for ways to establish control over family units. A native person's rights were not within their control. In the military, commanding officers expect individuals to give up any semblance of rights. Many commanding officers carry that expectation to family members. Not so long ago, if a military member's spouse became involved in controversial community issues, military members were often called in and told to control their family members. Talk about a dysfunctional group of egomaniacs in positions of authority.

The Structure

In the military, a rank structure defines levels of authority. It's also a mechanism which serves the dual purpose of control over subordinates as well as a shield from responsibility. The rank structure creates an impersonal atmosphere by calling on individual members to behave according to rank-appropriate guidelines. Along with guidelines, a set of benefits motivates the emphasis on rank. An invisible benefit is control. While some may assume control over their responsibilities, others assume control over subordinates. You may be tempted to argue there is no difference. When officers can't establish control over responsibilities, subordinates become available victims of "blame". Does Somalia ring any bells here!

It's important to note that "control", like "rank", is rooted in the individual's ability to deal with his or her environment. Although some people can take control of a situation, others expect to have control given to them. The leader who expects control to be given will draw on rank as a justification to impose his will. Without the rank, that leader is weak. On the other hand, the leader who can motivate others to trust will display accepted natural abilities of leadership.

The weak leader will display an exaggerated support for the rank structure in order to gain the favour of superiors. Once in authority, the weak leader will rely on the invisible "system" in attempt to maintain order. This is when "natural selection" fails to filter out the weak. Once a weak leader infiltrates the chain, he or she becomes the infamous "weak link" in search of protection from being discovered.

The issue of control is important to survival, as the strong feed on the weaker; the weak feed on the weakest so that the weakest die. Darwin's theory of evolution, through the process of natural selection, seems to be the overt argument for the merit system within most institutions. However, covert practices indicate informal channels have allowed a weakening of the structure, as the influence of weaker individuals has infested higher positions of authority, where only the strong are professed to survive.

Consequently, the weak link begins to establish its own pattern of self-preservation within the chain. Naturally, it will exclude any potentially strong links from participating in the process for fear of competition. The weak link that is promoted to a position that it cannot handle will make efforts to surround itself with weaker links in order to assure control. The results are most apparent in today's military structure, as we find an increasing number of less qualified individuals reaching positions of authority without the tools to deal with the consequences of their actions or inaction as the case may be.

There are some who believe the military requires complete obedience from its members. This extreme conviction, in the immaculate nature of military superiors, leads to expectations that only subordinates can be wrong. Therefore, a superior is often given free reign over subordinates through blind obedience of middle ranks in search of improved conditions for themselves. Thus the tools of oppression develop under the control of authorities.

The military structure is also based on a unique hierarchy of authority. It is unique because all members are expected to conform to regulations that remove individual rights. It's expected that because members volunteer, they also give up the right to make decisions on important issues affecting them.

The Canadian Armed Forces was once a well respected military organization. Recent changes have seen the inflation of our upper ranks, while equipment cuts have left our lower ranks in a state of imposed incompetence.

The officer corps is occupied by a new wave of "yes men" who can't change their underwear without three permission slips signed by superiors. Non-commissioned personnel traditionally relied on support from their commanding officers. Today, the selfish wants of those who profess to know the needs of the military have focussed on a political agenda in order to accomplish their own goals. You might think my assessment is pessimistic and somewhat antagonistic. Perhaps a closer look at the internal mechanisms of our military will confirm the accuracy of my statements.

Conflict

The military provides status through a rank structure that carries with it the authority and control over subordinates. The only right an individual appears to be allowed is that of religious belief. Support for religious denominations is represented through the provision of chaplain services. Recent evidence indicates that chaplains are more likely to serve the needs of authorities rather than the rights of a member's religious obligations. In other words, chaplains are bound by military regulations first and foremost. The strong criticism of our common-law relationship was initiated by a Roman Catholic padre who was able to exercise powers of control through his rank, not his religious affiliations. As an officer and padre, his powers are doubled because of his role in meeting moral expectations of military authorities. In our case, Major Dabrowski exercised authority of rank in order to dictate morality by the terms of his own bigotry.

There's nothing like conflict with a bureaucratic system to encourage the development of one's ability to separate facts from emotions. While most of my peers agreed that injustice was taking place, there was no means of lending support without risking serious reprisals. As in most large organizations, military officials maintain control of personnel through the threat of consequences. Superiors sought any opportunity to create difficult situations for us, including the denial of family medical and dental coverage. Imagine your employer expects you to relocate as a part of your job. An official of the company comes to your house to divide your family possessions into what they will move as your personal effects and what they consider effects of your common-law spouse and son. They agree to move only your effects not your spouse's or your son's. I don't know of any other military family that suffered such arrogance.

The imposition of compulsory social functions is another means of excluding the member's spouse from social contact. Mess dinners are not open to the wives or family members of Junior Non-Commissioned personnel. That privilege is reserved for officers. An incident in 1988 marks the degree of abuse that is made possible through the application of regulations on attendance to mess dinners.

While we faced a sensitive and urgent family matter, Master Warrant Officer Ed Skretka explained that only a medical excuse would warrant not attending a scheduled mess dinner. Knowing the circumstances, Doctor J.L. Mabee didn't hesitate to provide the appropriate document. Major Dunsdon refused to accept it and ordered my attendance anyway. As the matter at home required immediate attention, I didn't attend the dinner. Somehow, Doctor Mabee was convinced to reverse his decision some two weeks later. By then, it was too late to change history. I had not attended the mess dinner. Obviously he was influenced to corroborate Dunsdon's exercise in abuse of authority. I was charged a $100.00 fine and given a severe reprimand. It didn't seem to matter that I had attended three such social functions during the previous year, all of which proved to be nothing more than subsidized drunken parties.

Institutions are an important part of any social structure. They foster a cohesive relationship among members. However, when the cohesive bonds are maintained through abuse of authority, an individual may find it difficult to make decisions without the approval of institutional authorities. Decisions become dependent on approval. One of the more extreme incidents reflecting abuse of authority took place in Somalia, as four Canadian soldiers beat a

Somali civilian to death while Canadian authorities looked the other way. That incident marks the extent of the treachery that has become so common between authorities and subordinates.

Institutionalization settles into the member's coping mechanisms. Although free to make his or her own decisions, the institutionalized individual is not psychologically prepared to make independent choices on issues of importance. The military's control over various aspects of a member's life may lead to feelings of insecurity resulting in limited capabilities for independent life skills. The first signs of institutionalization become visible when the member argues his or her situation is too unique to be addressed through channels of authority. This leads to an acceptance of defeat or a sense of powerlessness in dealing with problems often generated by the bureaucracy.

Steps To Challenging Abuse of Authority

First Step: Address powerlessness and regain your integrity. Personalize your problem and recognize your right to address it through the channels. To become the master of your life, prepare for resistance from authorities. Therefore, learn what to expect by defining your goal and that of authorities. This step involves forming a psychological mindset in which you break the chains of dependency. Don't expect cooperation; you won't get it!

At first, be prepared for an antagonistic attack on your individuality. If intimidation fails, authorities will then try to persuade you to give up your principles. Perhaps the most common persuasive approach is to try and gain your trust through the use of comparisons that often don't even apply to your situation. It's the oldest trick in the bureaucratic book.

Authorities will argue; "Look at all these other people who don't rock the boat. They have it made and they know it. Why do you want to be different?"

The question is: What do others have to do with the issue? Additionally, consider the facts? Whose interests are being served in agreeing with the bureaucrat? Yours? Not likely! So don't take the comparison-to-others excuse. Be prepared to present your side of the argument and listen to the other side. Listening doesn't mean accepting. If the answer is not acceptable, then don't accept it!

I remember the first time I decided to address the issue of common-law relationships in the military. My supervisor, suck-hole extraordinaire, simply refused to bring the matter to the commanding officer. Consequently, the only solution left was to take it up in writing. He went as far as refusing to process the initial written request. The second submission was handed to him with the threat that I would take it myself the next time. So, to avoid being discovered as neglectful, he reluctantly processed the second request. But, in doing that task, he communicated his own perception of how the commanding officer should deal with the matter.

The influence had begun its negative cycle. Of course, had the commanding officer been a true leader, he would have addressed the matter with common sense. Instead, he chose to hide behind an unwritten policy in pretence that nothing could be done. It was as though one individual's problem wasn't worth taking the time to consider. After all, who was this corporal to ask that an injustice be corrected?

Step Two: That initial confrontation provided a very important learning experience. If you want to motivate action, PUT IT IN WRITING! Don't forget to keep copies. It's not important what their response will be. If you make a written request, expect a written response. Don't accept anything less. Not only will you develop your skills at addressing documentation, but you also have written confirmation of events.

It's too easy for verbal discussions to change in context when an officer explains the matter to superiors. A typical example of selective memory loss is reflected in Lieutenant Francois Jodoin's testimony during Tribunal hearings in November, 1992. Oddly enough, he stated that he "did not remember a discussion in early January of 1988". However, under cross examination he was confident about what was and wasn't said during that discussion.

Step Three: Assuring your own objectivity is most important in maintaining a focus on facts without the influence of emotions. Studying the facts means developing the ability to read the documentation with your eyes, not your heart. Divorcing your emotions will not always be possible, but it's most important you keep from reacting under stress. Reactions are exactly what authorities (bureaucrats) expect. In fact, provoking you to react is their goal. It's the only realm in which they can establish control over a victim. If you allow yourself to be sucked into the trap of reactionary defence, you'll most certainly become bureaucratic prey. When the heat is on, turn off the emotions and focus squarely on the facts. Consider your problem as though it were someone else's for a few moments and define the advice you might give him or her in dealing with it. Remember that life revolves around emotions. Be brief and concise with your written submission. Don't explain why you feel a certain way. Just state the facts clearly and exclude your feelings from the discussion.

Step Four: Preparing an acceptable solution to your problem is an important part of your strategic plan. Simply requesting the recognition of common-law relationships, without legislative support, might have been an illusive goal. Consequently, the law library provided a valuable source of information in presenting a legislated solution to their problem. Authorities refused to accept the solution, but at least it served as a spring board to support legal action. Provincial laws and most Federal Statutes recognized common-law relationships. But in the course of research, an obscure statute within the Superannuation Act defined the terms of common-law relationships as applied to military members.

The Canadian Human Rights Act and the Superannuation Act played an instrumental role in gaining support at the Federal Court level. Exposing the archaic values in non recognition of common-law relationships revealed the depth of resistance to change among authorities. Nevertheless, a solution had been prepared in order to ensure that common sense prevailed.

Step Five: Organize your documentation in a sequence. It's surprising how a pattern of events becomes apparent as documents accumulate. Keep in mind that bureaucratic authorities don't investigate; they cover up. Fourteen years of calling attention to inconsistencies within the military redress procedures confirms the theory that military officials and politicians are more interested in covering up than correcting.

Military officials and politicians chose to ignore incidents of abuse by authorities. Some, like Harvie André and Captain Fouts to name two, would resort to lies in response to inquiries from other officials. To make matters worse, politicians accepted lies without considering the facts. But, if you follow the written method of addressing questions, you'll have the written support to challenge those authorities. Assertive determination will most likely set you apart from peers and superiors. It may cause an uncomfortable feeling initially, but you'll gain the much needed self-respect that will change your outlook about being powerless in the face of abusive authorities.

It's obvious that passive dependence is a necessary component to getting your proverbial carrot. Some of us are eccentric in nature and often find ourselves challenging the unrealistic demands of those who would have us perform cartwheels in quicksand. It's difficult to appear inconspicuous when you're the only bear travelling with a herd of sheep.

My relationship with Amy and Ken was targeted by the hypocritical attitudes of a few influential officers within the administration of the Base at North Bay. But the cloak of authority soon veiled the Roman Catholic Padre's racism. Other officers were more interested in protecting one of their own from criticism than assuring the survival of honesty within their ranks. Organization of documents confirmed the patterns of abuse.

Step Six: Plan alternatives! This is a difficult step calling for objective assessment of possible success in your chosen path. The question addressed in step six is: What happens if this method fails? Are you prepared to take a different course of action? If you consider alternative avenues, you stand a better chance of success. Not only do you expand your field of vision, you also become more flexible with questions and responses.

In 1987, the Human Rights Tribunal Chairperson, John R.A. Douglas, ruled that military authorities could discriminate against common-law relationships. Anticipating that turn of events, the emotional impact was reduced by reviewing alternatives. One alternative was to appeal his decision. The appeal was successful. On December 20, 1988, the Federal Court decision overturned the tribunal decision.

Had the appeal failed, the alternative would have been to call provincial statutes, which recognized our responsibilities, to question. Common sense told me that a Federal Court decision against the recognition of common-law relationships would have created turmoil for the Ontario Family Law Reform which outlined the financial responsibilities of common-law partners. It doesn't really matter what your problem may be, there's usually always at least one alternative approach to addressing it.

Step Seven: Remain determined in accomplishing your goals. The fantasy of becoming an officer seemed more evasive with each attained goal. The completion of my first year of university appeared of little value to the Selection Officer who reviewed my application for a military university training plan. In his view, I possessed serious intellectual deficiencies which would not allow me to complete a university course, much less a degree. Additionally, he felt my successful completion of first year courses lacked credibility. Determination, along with Amy's words of support, helped me skip over that hurdle.

A second application, the following year, received even less favourable review as it was obvious the real reason for the denial of career advancement was rooted in my relationship. His report defined our family situation "BELOW AVERAGE". Captain Madill's release from the military, the following year, left my third application to be considered by Captain Gilman of the Personnel Selection office at Petawawa. Although his report indicated I had been under-rated on previous applications, the family circumstances remained at a rating of "BELOW AVERAGE".

A Selection Board conveniently returned the application with an "UNSUITABLE" rating for University Training Plan for Men (UTPM). Of course, the Officer Cadet Training Plan (OCTP) application never made it past Major Dunsdon in 1988. Time had slipped by with only negative input being inserted on record. Accomplishments were ignored or downplayed.

Reality rang clear after my fifth application was turned down in early 1991. I had just received the Governor General's Silver Medal Award as top graduating student at university. References from various community service organizations marked 12 years of serious effort at improving those sought after "officer-like qualities". I guess my understanding of qualities lacked some of the more realistic ingredients necessary to be a "good officer".

It appears a good officer needs a willingness to lie, cheat, deceive and abuse his position in support of superiors. Honesty and integrity no longer play the role they once did in determining one's ability to lead others. Earning respect also falls prey to self-glorification, as young officers are taught that rank is a useful tool of protection from responsibility. Poor decisions can easily be covered with one's rank. Keep in mind that the higher the rank, the larger the cloak.

Step Eight: Bureaucrats possess one serious weakness. Yes, that's right! It's time to reveal the ultimate weapon in bureaucratic warfare. Thanks to the guidance of the late Major James Lucas, frustrating bureaucrats has become second nature to me. This step calls for the exploitation of bureaucratic inconsistencies. At this point, we know that documented information is the only language bureaucrats understand. Interpretations are always limited to their own narrow-minded perceptions. Present an alternative view of written documents and observe the results. Even more effective, draw on documents they don't know exist. That really gets tempers flaring.

Imagine for a moment that you think you know everything about a particular topic and someone asks a question you can't answer. Wrapped up in self-importance, they are not able to contain the sudden challenge. During a narrow-minded rush to discredit common-law relationships authorities failed to consider that the root of disapproval for our particular relationship was firmly planted in the matter of native rights. Consequently, the message which identified Amy as my common-law spouse, in 1982, was overlooked when my files were expunged of incriminating evidence. A small note at the bottom of that message indicated that our common-law relationship was acceptable until it was discovered that Amy and Ken were native.

That seemingly insignificant document confirms that military authorities maintained a critical perception of anyone who is not entirely "dependent". Native rights continue to be a controversial issue within military ranks. How many senior officers are of native origin? Sound critical? You bet! The Canadian Forces has held a facade of equality while an underlying plague of bigotry rages on. They use catchy terms to disguise intentional lack of concern and the wilful cover-up of discrimination.

One of many examples of catchy terminology is the recent "ZERO TOLERANCE" harassment policy. What the hell does "zero tolerance" have to do with investigating harassment? It's quite simple. If the term "zero tolerance" is accepted, then we should expect that harassment will not be condoned or covered up. Right? Wrong!!!!

Think about it. If the public can be convinced that officials adhere to a strict policy against harassment, then the credibility of victims becomes diluted. If a case of harassment is brought forward and authorities don't want to act on it, then the flashing of "zero tolerance" suddenly becomes the focus of attention. The policy requires more than proof. It requires acceptance by officials, before the "zero tolerance" policy will be applied. Acceptance needs to meet certain criteria. The threat of public attention will send authorities scrambling in search of means to minimize the situation. Therefore, if authorities don't accept the proof, you don't have a case and the policy remains intact. So what does "zero tolerance" have to do with investigating and acting on harassment complaints? The rank and gender of the accused will define the actions of authorities.

The "Old Boys' Network" is well insulated against any official policy that threatens to address their abuse of authority. It's ironic that Brigadier General William F. Buckham put out the Air Command policy for "zero tolerance" of harassment. According to Major Karen Forster, this sensitive General found her aggressive management style "autocratic" and offensive enough to relieve her of her duties. So how is it that so many male senior officers have managed to get away with imposing abusive measures against our common-law relationship and the related redress of grievance? Maybe there's a great deal of substance to Major Forster's allegations that abuse of authority is acceptable when offenders are male senior officers.

Do The Steps Work You Ask?

It's rewarding to report that experiences acquired throughout the difficult years provided a wealth of resources in doing advocacy for people in need. Since becoming Client Services Coordinator with the AIDS Society of Kamloops, I have provided advocacy before some 63 appeal tribunals from 1999 – 2002 with only two tribunal decisions against the appellant. There is no doubt that the steps of my experience can result in successful challenge of bureaucratic injustice. If you take nothing else from this story, please take the steps outlined. They work. They're free to learn

Loyalty and Authorities

Having been told on many occasions that my challenge of a discriminatory policy was perceived as disloyal, it seems appropriate to define the meaning of loyalty. Webster's New World Dictionary (1979) defines loyalty as: "Faithfulness or faithful adherence to a person, government, cause, duty, etc." The sequence of expected loyalty flows from person to government. Note that "duty" falls in fourth place for a very good reason. Duties may be regarded as those matters which take us outside the family unit.

The family is the basic unit of any social structure. Without it, society cannot exist. Therefore, loyalty must begin at home. When military officials fail to recognize and respect the need for loyalty within a family unit, they undermine the very fabric that forms social supports for their existence. Loyalty to one's spouse and family members must take priority.

Most military authorities will be tempted to argue that my contentions are evidence of disloyalty. After all, I enrolled voluntarily. I didn't have to stay in the military. Although the Canadian Armed Forces is formed of volunteer personnel, too many members in recent years have chosen to leave rather than challenge abusive authorities. It's the kind of apathetic approach that contributes to a growing momentum of incompetence presently occupying the senior ranks. Without challenge, authorities are no longer held accountable. If you think I'm being disloyal, just look around you and observe how authorities behave. Don't forget to take the bureaucratic blinders off before you open your eyes.

Obviously, the weak-minded, egocentric, pompous bags of wind, who profess to be loyal leaders, have also appointed themselves as authorities worthy of respect and loyalty. They fail to understand the reciprocal nature of loyalty. Instead they hide behind the term without knowing its true meaning. This new wave of yes-men refuses to accept that "no" is also an answer.

Refusing to "leave my Indian wife" as ordered prompted severe criticism from authorities. How could I be so disloyal toward the expectations of Major Dabrowski? There was no concern for the matter of human rights. Attempting to redress the injustice only reinforced arguments that my actions were somehow disloyal. So let them hide behind a facade of pomp and pageantry. If you address bureaucratic issues with the detached emotional approach presented in previous pages, you're likely to earn self-respect if not absolute success.

There are many examples of poor leadership within the Canadian Armed Forces, but the time to focus on the excessive thirst for power among our senior ranks is long overdue. Military members of all ranks are taxpayers too. Civilians know very little about the "privileges" of senior military staff. Instead of covering up the facts, to protect senior officials from embarrassment, perhaps it's time to define loyalty in terms of honesty. Every military member must now ask the question: What am I willing to give up in order to move up?

Appendix II: In Recognition of Those to Commend

There are a number of people who deserve my most sincere appreciation for offering encouragement and positive insight at those moments when all seemed hopeless.

The Right Honourable Raymon John Hnatyshyn, Governor General of Canada.

Ian Mugridge	Principal, Open University of BC, 1990.
Iris Rich-McQuay	Open Learning Agency Advisor, 1981.
Nelson Riis	Member Of Parliament NDP House Leader, 1982-93
Rose Simone	North Bay Nugget Reporter, 1985.
Kathleen Ruff	Ed., Canadian Human Rights Advocate, 1988.
Cathy Levins	Civilian Clerk at CFS Kamloops, 1988.
Gus Paris	Retired Physical Fitness Instructor, 1988.
Irene Anderson	Civilian Clerk at CFB North Bay, 1989.

Military Members

Colonel E.R. Cornick	Wing Commander, North Bay, 1994.
LCol T.J.Hochban	Commanding Officer, North Bay, 1994.
Major D.J. Kelleher	Flight Commander, North Bay, 1982.
Major J.C. Comeau	Air Operations Officer, N. Bay, 1982.
Major A.S. Archer	Branch Commanding Officer, N. Bay, 1989.
Captain John Broughton	Branch Commander, CFS Kamloops, 1979-82.

Captain Jene Kleinschroth	Section Commander, CFB North Bay, 1990.
Captain Wendy Barlow	Admin Officer, CFB North Bay, 1989.
Chief WO N.P. Henderson	Career Manager, NDHQ, 1986.
Master WO Gary Carlisle	Section Supervisor, 1986.
Sergeant R. Lessieur	Supervisor, 1985.
Sergeant Mike Christie	Section Supervisor, 1989-91.
L/Seaman Andre Bigras	Co-worker and friend at Kamloops, 1988.

Canadian Human Rights Commission Directors and Staff

Michelle Falardeau-Ramsey,	Deputy Chief Commissioner, 1991.
S. Patrick Hunter, DND	Human Rights Coordinator, 1986.
Charles A. Lafreniere,	National Capital Region Director, 1984.
Paul M. Leroux,	Western Region Director, 1988.
Anne M. Rooke,	A/Chief National Investigation Policies, 1991.
Penny Goldrick,	A/Director Western Region, 1989.
Russell Juriansz,	Legal Counsel, 1986.
James Hendry,	Legal Counsel, 1987.
Eddie Taylor,	Assistant to Senior Legal Counsel, 1992.
Christine Gignac,	Legal Branch Staff Member, 1992.
Brian K. Stewart,	Conciliator, 1991.
Lorisa Stein,	Investigator, 1984.
Theodora Preito,	Investigator, 1984.
Michelle Crete,	Investigator, 1985.
Joan Ablett,	Investigator, 1986.
Marianne Hoyd,	Investigator, 1987.

Barbara Westerman,   Investigator, 1988.

Diane Stewart,   Staff Member National Region, 1988.

Lucie Veillette,   Staff Member National Region, 1992.

Canadian Human Rights Tribunal Staff

M.P. Glynn,   Registrar.

Sidney N. Lederman,   Human Rights Tribunal Panel President.

Gwen Zappa,   Tribunal Officer.

Bernard Fournier,   Tribunal Officer.

Stanley Sadinski,   Tribunal Chairman, 1996.

Linda Marie Dionne,   Tribunal Member, 1996

Miroslav Folta,   Tribunal Member, 1996

I also want to express my appreciation to those military members who provided covert moral and bureaucratic support. Your voices rang loud and clear over recent years as more of you began to ask about mechanisms of challenge. This book confirms that we are not different and you can challenge the system if you feel unjustly treated. Determination will earn you self-respect and victory.

Appendix III: In Recognition of Those to Blame

In my opinion, the Redress of Grievance initiated in December, 1983, followed some eighteen months of discrimination against our common-law relationship because Amy was Native. What began as a Roman Catholic Major's act of racial bigotry gained support from all levels of the military chain of command. To suggest that all Canadian Armed Forces authorities are bigots would be unfair to a majority of good service people. Consequently, I've sought to attribute responsibility to those who supported bigotry and harassment, openly or under the cloak of their authority.

***All Military Members are presented with the Rank at the time of their actions.

Generals

Gen. G.C.E. Theriault	Chief of Defence Staff, 1986.
Gen. A.J.G.D. de Chastelain	Chief of Defence Staff, 1994.
Gen. J.D. Boyle	Chief of Defence Staff, 1996.
LGen. P.D. Manson	Administration Personnel NDHQ, 1986.
LGen. J.E. Vance	Assistant Deputy Minister, NDHQ, 1985.
LGen. G.S. Clements	Commander Air Command, 1994.
LGen. D.N. Kinsman	Assistant Deputy Minister, NDHQ, 1997.
MGen. D.M. McNaughton	Assistant Air Command Commander, 1985.
MGen. J.R. Chisholm	Air Command Commander, 1988.
VAdm W.B. Hotsenpiller	Administration Personnel NDHQ, 1989.

Cmdre B.J. Berryman	Director General Career Boards, 1985.
BGen. A.J. Waldrum	Base Commander North Bay, 1990.
BGen D.E. Munro	Director General, CREW, 1989.

Colonels

Col. P.A. Hamilton	Base Commander North Bay, 1984.
Col. L.G. Jenks	Commanding Officer, 1986.
Col. P.A. Riis	Radar Control Wing Commander, 1988.
Col. J.A. Mitchell	Chief of Staff FGHQ, 1985.
Col. R.L. Martin	Dir. Pers. Legal Services, NDHQ, 1985.
Col. L.T. Doshen	Deputy Chief of Staff, FGHQ, 1985.
Col. L.C. Friesen	Air Command HQ, 1986.
Col. P.R. Partner	Dir. Pers. Legal Services, NDHQ, 1986.
Capt(N) R.G. May	Director Personnel Careers, NDHQ, 1988.
Col. G. Logan	D Charter, NDHQ, 1989.
Capt(N) P.R. Partner	Dir. Pers. Legal Services, NDHQ, 1989.
Col. R.C. Hersey	Director Personnel, NDHQ, 1990.
Col. E.J. Jackson	Base Commander North Bay, 1991.
Capt(N) J.C. Bain	Director Personnel Careers, NDHQ, 1992.
Col. J.H. Desrochers	Director Personnel Careers, NDHQ, 1993.
Col. M.P. Aruja	Deputy Chief of Staff, NDHQ, 1994.
Col. S.H. Forster	Dir. Pers. Legal Services, NDHQ, 1994.
Col. A.M. Brown	Director Personnel Careers, NDHQ, 1994.

LCol.	R.	Greaves	Commanding Officer, North Bay, 1983.
LCol.	J.E.	Baldwin	Fighter Group HQ, North Bay, 1984.
LCol.	M.I.	Chesser	Acting Base Commander, North Bay, 1984.
LCol.	J.B.	Riordan	Acting Base Commander, North Bay, 1984.
LCol.	G.T.M.	Findley	Aid to ADM Personnel, NDHQ, 1984.
LCol.	G.J.	Akamoto	Minister of Defence Office, 1984.
LCol.	M.A.	Pigeon	Minister of Defence Office, 1985.
LCol.	A.M.	Brown	Aid to ADM Personnel, NDHQ, 1986.
LCol.	R.F.	Barnes	Dir. Pers. Legal Services, NDHQ, 1986.
LCol.		Hunt	Dir. Pers. Legal Services, NDHQ, 1987.
LCol.		MacDonald	Judge Advocate General Office, NDHQ, 1987.
LCol.	W.D.	Reimer	Commanding Officer, 21 AC&W Squadron, 1988.
LCol.	R.R.	Reid	Acting Base Commander, North Bay, 1989.
LCol.	S.H.	Forster	Dir. Pers. Legal Services, NDHQ, 1989.
LCol.	W.A.	Weatherston	Dir. Pers. Legal Services, NDHQ, 1990.
LCol.	M.R.	Spooner	Commissioning Selection Board, NDHQ, 1991.
LCol.	G.S.	King	Technical Service Officer, Comox, 1993.
Cdr.		Price	Judge Advocate Office, Victoria, 1993.
LCol.	W.W.	Quigley	Senior Staff Officer Personnel, NDHQ, 1994.
LCol.	F.K.	Brownlee	Dir. Pers. Legal Services, NDHQ, 1994.

Majors

Maj. J.T. Dabrowski	RC Padre, CFB North Bay, 1982.
Maj. R.A. Nickerson	Branch Commanding Officer, N. Bay, 1984.
Maj. J.R.P. Beaudry	Minister of Defence Office, N. Bay, 1984.
Maj. Pendergast	Dir. Pers. Legal Services, NDHQ, 1984.
Maj. Buchanan	Computer Maint. Officer, N. Bay, 1985.
Maj. R.J. Parent	Branch Commanding Officer, N. Bay, 1986.
Maj. Priddle	Assistant Judge Advocate, N. Bay, 1985.
Maj. A.J.P. Pellicano	Dir. Pers. Legal Services, NDHQ, 1985.
LCdr D. Baltes	SO2/Chief Defence Staff, NDHQ, 1986.
Maj. M. Lehmann	SO2/Chief Defence Staff, NDHQ, 1986.
Maj. N.G. Girard	Assistant Judge Advocate, Victoria, 1988.
Maj. Ray Dunsdon	Commanding Officer, CFS Kamloops, 1988.
Maj. Robin Alford	Public Affairs, North Bay, 1986.
Maj. Michel Prud'homme	Branch Commanding Officer, N. Bay, 1991.
Maj. B.J. Cockerline	Commissioning Selection Board, NDHQ, 1991.
LCdr G.J. Droszio	Commissioning Selection Board, NDHQ, 1991.
LCdr B. Irvine	Staff Officer, MND, NDHQ, 1993.

| Maj. M.D. McCormack | Personnel Careers Other Ranks, NDHQ, 1993. |
| Maj. E.B. Thuen | Staff Officer, Military Grievance, NDHQ, 1994 |

Captains

Capt. K.W. Madill	Personnel Selection Officer, N. Bay, 1982.
Capt. F.G. DeJong	Area Social Worker, 1983.
Capt. D.A. Brontmeyer	Section Commanding Officer, N. Bay, 1983.
Capt. R.E. Lavigne	Section Commanding Officer, N. Bay, 1985.
Capt. C.R. Gilman	Personnel Selection Officer, N. Bay, 1985.
Capt. T.R. Milne	Dir. Pers. Legal Services, NDHQ, 1985.
Capt. R.J. Woroschuk	Administration Officer, North Bay 1986.
Capt. A.H. Kaulback	Administration Officer, North Bay 1986.
Capt. P. Verville	Dir. Pers. Legal Services, NDHQ, 1986.
Capt. S.A. Gillespie	Station Ops Officer, Kamloops, 1988.
Capt. W.C. Hussey	CFS Kamloops Accounts Officer, 1988.
Capt. B.E. Belec	Personnel Selection Officer, 1988
Capt. H.K. Richards	Admin. Officer, CFS Kamloops, 1988.
Capt. Natalie Leblanc	Supervising Officer, North Bay, 1988.
Capt. R. Smith	Dept. Legal Services, NDHQ, 1989.
Capt. D.H. Wong	Personnel Selection Officer, 1990.
Capt. B. Cathcart	Dir. Pers. Legal Services, NDHQ, 1992.

Capt. J.R. Godin	Detachment Holberg Commander, 1993.
Capt. R.A. Cumming	Personnel Careers Other Ranks, NDHQ, 1994
Capt. D.L. Fouts	Dir. Pers. Admin. Other Ranks, NDHQ, 1994
Lt. J.M.F. Jodoin	Acting Ops Officer, CFS Kamloops, 1988.

** Lt. Jodoin was promoted to Captain shortly after his transfer from CFS Kamloops in 1989. During his testimony at the 1992 Tribunal hearings he suffered <u>selective</u> memory loss related to any discussions he might have had with then Master Corporal P.M. Lagace.**

Non Commissioned Members

CWO Richard Poulin	Career Manager, NDHQ, 1993.
MWO Guy Baker	21 Sqn Chief, North Bay, 1988.
MWO Ed Skretka	Station Chief, Kamloops, 1988.
WO J.G. Aucoin	Assistant Career Manager, 1986.
Sgt Guy Cote	Base Orderly Room, North Bay, 1982.
Sgt Fred Wyman	Supervising Sgt, North Bay, 1984.
Sgt G.J. Chiasson	Clerk Orderly Room, North Bay, 1989.
Sgt Paul K. Livingston	Station Med. Assistant, Kamloops, 1988.
MCpl Gordon Boddy	Supervising MCpl, North Bay, 1984.

Civilian Employees

| R.J. 'Rolly' Orieux | Housing Officer, CFB North Bay, 1982. |
| Brian Saunders | Dept. of Justice Counsel for DND, 1987. |

Roger Levesque	Housing Officer, CFB North Bay, 1988.
Dr. J.L. Mabee	CFS Kamloops Medical Officer, 1988.
Corporal D.L. Ayers	Kamloops RCMP Office, 1988.
Inspector G. Timko	Federal Enforcement Branch RCMP, 1988.

Public officials whose mandate is to address injustice within the administration of government departments have also sought to cover up rather than correct the result of discrimination. To do nothing about bigotry and harassment is as damaging as taking an active role in it.

J.J. Blais	Minister of Defence, 1984.
Richard B. Logan	Executive Assistant MND, 1984.
Robert Coates	Minister of Defence, 1985.
Derek Blackburn	NDP Defence Critic, 1985.
Leonard Hopkins	Liberal Defence Critic, 1985.
Eric Neilson	Minister of Defence, 1986.
Moe Mantha	Member of Parliament, North Bay, 1986.
Harvie Andre	Associate Minister of Defence, 1986.
Linda M. Johnson	Special Assistant to Harvie Andre, 1986.
Paul Dick	Associate Minister of Defence, 1988.
Bill McKnight	Minister of Defence, 1986.
Bob Wood	Member of Parliament, North Bay, 1989.
Mary Collins	Associate Minister of Defence, 1991.
John Brewin	Liberal Defence Critic, 1993.
Fred Mifflin	Assistant to John Brewin, 1993.(R Admiral Ret.)

Kim	Campbell	Minister of Defence, 1993.
Tom	Siddon	Minister of Defence, 1993.
David	Collenette	Minister of Defence, 1994.
Doug	Young	Minister of Defence, 1996.
Jean-Marc Jacob		Defence Critic, Bloc Quebecois

Human Rights Tribunal Chairmen Who Showed Bias

John R.A. Douglas	Human Rights Tribunal Chairman, 1987.
Alfred Lynch-Staunton	Human Rights Tribunal Chairman, 1992.
Rene Duval	Senior Legal Counsel, Canadian Human Rights Commission, 1992.

References

Jamieson, Kathleen. Indian Women and the Law in Canada: Citizens Minus. Ottawa: Advisory Council on the Status of Women, Minister of Supply and Services Canada, April 1978.

Ruff, Kathleen. Editor of Human Rights Advocate, published comment in the Ottawa Citizen, April 11, 1988.

Webster's New World Dictionary, David B. Guralnik, Editor in Chief. Cleveland: William Collins Publishers, Inc., 1979.

ABOUT THE AUTHOR

Born in St George, New Brunswick on a very cold and snowy January 31, 1954, Paul Morel Lagace is the second of twelve children. Yvon and Jeannine Lagace relocated to the neighboring parish of Drummond in the summer of 1955. Paul's education began in a two-room school in 1959. Life experiences would include joining the Canadian Armed Forces in 1974 where life in the Armored Corps meant duties in Germany and the Middle East before a transfer to Air Defense led to duties at radar sites across Canada. In 1979, while stationed at Canadian Forces Station Mount Lolo in Kamloops, British Columbia, Paul met and fell deeply in love with Amy.

In 1980 and 1981 Paul attended Addictions Studies summer programs at the University of Sherbrooke which led him to embark on a Bachelor of Arts Program through the Open University of British Columbia. Along with his Bachelor's Degree, Paul was awarded the Governor General's Silver Medal for Academic Excellence at the convocation in 1990.

Retired from the Canadian Armed Forces in 1994 and relocated to Kamloops where he began working as an Addictions Counselor with the Phoenix Centre Corrections Program. Leaving the Phoenix Centre in 1998 he became the Client Services Coordinator with the AIDS Society of Kamloops where he continues to provide services to people living with or affected by HIV/AIDS.

Paul's experience with applying word to paper flowed from a brief essay that earned him an A at the University of Sherbrooke in 1980. Writing with a common sense approach in a convincing way would later contribute to Paul's successful challenge of the Canadian National Defense Act and Canadian Income Tax Act in written submissions before the Canadian Federal Supreme Court Trial Division.

Printed in the United States
33463LVS00003B/115-213